David McKittrick, who was born in Belfast in 1949 and educated in the city, has been Ireland correspondent for the *Independent* since the paper's launch in October 1986. He has reported on Northern Ireland and Anglo-Irish relations since 1973, principally for the *Irish Times*, acting as the paper's northern editor between 1976 and 1981 and London editor from 1981 to 1985. He has at various times been Northern Ireland correspondent for *The Economist*, *Le Monde*, the *Observer*, the *Sunday Times* and the *Sunday Tribune*. He has also contributed to many other Irish, British and American publications, including the *New Nation*, *Fortnight*, *Hibernia* and the *Listener*.

In 1989 he was co-recipient, with Mary Holland, of the Christopher Ewart-Biggs Memorial Prize; in 1987 he won the Irish Media Award for outstanding work in reporting on Ireland for a publication abroad, and was also runner-up as Reporter of the Year in the British Press Awards. He broadcasts regularly on BBC, ITV, and RTE television and radio.

DESPATCHES
from
BELFAST

DAVID McKITTRICK

THE
BLACKSTAFF
PRESS

BELFAST

First published in 1989 by
The Blackstaff Press Limited
3 Galway Park, Dundonald, Belfast BT16 0AN, Northern Ireland

Printed in England by
Billings and Sons Limited

British Library Cataloguing in Publication Data
McKittrick, David, 1949–
Despatches from Belfast.
1. Northern Ireland. Political events, history
1. Title
941.6

ISBN 0-85640-427-6

CONTENTS

INTRODUCTION

The years 1985 to 1989 were highly significant, politically hectic and often violent in Northern Ireland, including as they did a large-scale political initiative, widespread street protests and disturbances, and several separate campaigns of paramilitary violence.

This book represents a selection of journalism from Belfast, and occasionally Dublin, during this eventful period. The majority of the articles appeared in the *Independent* between the paper's launch in October 1986 and early 1989. The stories included here are drawn from almost five hundred written for the paper: they reflect the fact that from the start the *Independent* identified Ireland as a major issue and covered it in greater depth than any other British newspaper.

A number of the pieces appeared in other publications, including the *Listener*, the *Irish Times*, and *Fortnight*, the Belfast political periodical. My thanks are due to their editors for permission to reproduce them here.

Most of the stories are completely unchanged, though one exception is the profile of Enoch Powell, which first appeared in 1983 and which I have brought up to date. The pieces are not quite in chronological order: I thought it preferable to create a certain amount of thematic unity by grouping together, for example, most of the stories on the IRA and most of those on the loyalist paramilitary organisations.

The period can be divided fairly neatly into phases. The signing of the Anglo-Irish agreement in November 1985 was followed by intense loyalist protests and political activity. By the end of 1987, however, much of this had died away and the news was dominated by the escalation of IRA violence. In 1988 there was more violence, and in addition a series of major Anglo-Irish rows over extradition, the Stalker affair and other points of disagreement between the two governments.

Much thanks is due to the political, security and paramilitary sources who have regularly helped me but who would prefer not to be named here: the politicians might be embarrassed; the security people might get the sack; the paramilitants might get shot. So all had best remain anonymous.

Many journalists were of great help, in different ways, over the years and I would like to thank in particular James Downey, Jonathan Fenby, Sean Flynn, Deric Henderson, Ed Moloney, Eamonn Mallie, Fionnuala O Connor, Brian Rowan and John Ware. Deric, Ed, Eamonn, Fionnuala and Brian, who are based in Belfast, have all demonstrated that it is possible to produce accurate and objective journalism even in such a divided city. Ed made valuable comments on the structure of the book. Any errors in the text are all my own work.

For permission to reproduce their pictures, I also wish to thank Belfast's Pacemaker Press, those unsung heroes of the photographic front line, and Crispin Rodwell, the Northern Ireland-based photographer whose fine pictures have appeared in the *Independent* and many other publications. I am also grateful to cartoonist David Smith for permission to reproduce his caricatures.

A particular word of thanks is due to the *Independent*'s home editor, John Price, for his unflagging imagination and encouragement. Editors are generally supposed to be restraining influences on their reporters: Price regularly pushed me into places I had hesitated to venture and was the driving force behind many of these pieces.

Finally I want to thank my wife Pat for enduring it all without complaint; and the kids, Kerry and Julie, who serve as constant reminders why attempts to understand and improve this intractable situation must go on, whatever the odds.

David McKittrick
Belfast, July, 1989

In November 1985, after much patient diplomacy by the Irish Republic, Margaret Thatcher and Garret FitzGerald signed the Anglo-Irish agreement. This gave the south an unprecedented say in the affairs of the north. It was endorsed by an overwhelming majority in the House of Commons, but was regarded by Unionists as an outrage and a diminution of their British citizenship.

Unionists see only a sinister cloud with no silver linings

Some of the loyalist protesters who pushed and jostled police outside Hillsborough Castle in Co Down last week, as Margaret Thatcher and Garret FitzGerald signed their far-reaching accord on Northern Ireland, were actually the same people who objected to the last Anglo-Irish agreement more than a decade ago. It's worth remembering that the destruction of the last agreement – the Sunningdale powersharing initiative – took them a little under five months to accomplish. This time the loyalists will attempt to break that record.

The Sunningdale initiative was revolutionary in its own way, setting up as it did a mixed powersharing executive of Catholic and Protestant politicians, together with an advisory Council of Ireland. This time there is no executive, simply because there are no Unionists who are prepared to share power with Catholic representatives. Instead, the role of the Republic is greatly expanded to give the southern government a significant role in the running of Northern Ireland.

At the heart of the arrangement is a new "intergovernmental conference", to be chaired jointly by Tom King, the Northern Ireland Secretary, and Peter Barry, the Republic's Minister for Foreign Affairs. This will be serviced by a small secretariat of civil servants, both British and Irish, who will be based in Belfast. Within the conference, the Irish government will be able to put forward views and proposals on almost every topic, including political development and security. The Republic will have no executive power, but the agreement commits the two governments to making determined efforts to resolve their differences within the conference.

Nothing like this has been seen in Ireland before. From now on, the Republic will have permanent representatives in Northern Ireland working in close consultation with the British administration in the most sensitive areas of government. Both supporters and opponents of the agreement say it's probably the most significant political development since the state of Northern Ireland was created in 1921.

And what continues to puzzle many – supporters and opponents alike – is just why Margaret Thatcher should be the politician to take such a radical step. She has a reputation as one of the few British politicians who retain any personal commitment to the Union between Britain and Northern Ireland. Her record in defence of British sovereignty needs no restating. So why, Unionists in particular ask plaintively, is she giving the Republic a foothold in a part of the United Kingdom?

Clearly, the Prime Minister accepted at least some of the arguments advanced by Dr FitzGerald. His brief was provided by the report of the New Ireland Forum, a gathering of the major non-violent nationalist parties from both north and south. Its thesis, in sum, is this: nationalists are alienated from the Northern Ireland state. This is partly because they see themselves as Irish rather than British, and partly because they believe the institutions of the state – the administration, the courts and the security forces – to be biased against them. This alienation has led to general political dissatisfaction, seen most sharply in the rise of Provisional Sinn Féin. This party, which makes no bones about its support for the violence of its military wing, the Provisional IRA, has secured more than 43 per cent of the nationalist vote. FitzGerald sees Sinn Féin as a malignant dry rot in the body politic in Northern Ireland. What's more, he fears its next move will be an attempt to establish a similar political base in the south, where the problems of high unemployment, inner-city decay and drugs could help it attract the protest votes of the disaffected.

FitzGerald – taking a sizeable political risk for an Irish Taoiseach – said openly that the cherished ideal of Irish unity must take second place to providing a more stable society. In his analysis, northern nationalists have to be weaned away from Sinn Féin and the IRA by a demonstration that results can be achieved through constitutional, non-violent political action.

The calculation is that this can be achieved only by having nationalist hands

November 1985: Margaret Thatcher and Garret FitzGerald sign the Anglo-Irish agreement, together with Northern Ireland Secretary of State Tom King and Foreign Secretary Sir Geoffrey Howe.

on the levers of power. The Sunningdale agreement was an attempt to achieve this by placing on those levers the hands of the SDLP, the party of non-violent nationalists in Northern Ireland. That attempt was possible because there existed, in 1973–4, moderate Unionists who were prepared to share power with the SDLP. No such Unionists can be found today. In their absence, the nationalist hands have to be those of Dublin: hence the intergovernmental conference.

In taking this approach, FitzGerald and his government have left themselves open to the criticisms of the nationalist purists. They argue that the beginning and the end of the problem in Ireland is the British presence; that there will be no peace until the British depart; and that FitzGerald's line will have the effect of encouraging the British to stay. Charles Haughey, leader of the opposition Fianna Fáil party, argues that the agreement has struck the concept of Irish unity "a very major blow". The first indications are, however, that the deal is being widely welcomed in the Republic, and that Haughey may have overstated the purist case. The fact is that southern nationalists, while hoping one day for Irish unity, see that day as being a long way off; in the meantime, their short-term aspirations are in general easily enough satisfied. The thought of actually being given sole responsibility for governing the loyalists of the Shankill, not to mention the republicans of Crossmaglen, tends to give Dubliners the shivers.

All the violence of the past 16 years has diluted aspirations towards unity; but in addition, a quiet redefinition of unity has been under way for many years now, and actually predates the Troubles. The key men involved are three friends – FitzGerald himself, SDLP leader John Hume, and Sean Donlon, permanent secretary at the Republic's Department of Foreign Affairs. Between them – FitzGerald and Hume in public, Donlon in private – they have shifted the focus away from the idea of the territorial unity of Ireland and towards the idea of reconciling its differing traditions. Their brand of nationalism accepts, as traditional nationalism never did, that unity can come only with the consent of a majority in Northern Ireland. Their definition of consent is, however, wide enough to include the idea that such consent can be worked for through a mixture of pressure and persuasion from the British and Irish governments.

All this is, of course, anathema to the IRA and Sinn Féin, who say, more or less openly, that the way to solve the problem is first to fight the Brits and then to deal with the Prods. They are scared stiff of the agreement. They believe it offers help to the SDLP in its campaign to show that progress can be made without recourse to the gun. They also fear it will offer new scope for a joint north–south security initiative which could do serious damage to the IRA. The IRA has proved itself infuriatingly resilient over the years – its kill-rate has remained constant for the past eight years – but it is not the organisation it was in its heyday, the mid-1970s. It has not the capacity to mount a sustained campaign to bring down the new agreement. Instead its leaders will sit back and hope the loyalists can do the job for them.

Certainly, Unionist politicians will pull out all the stops to see to it that the Hillsborough accord meets the same fate as the Sunningdale agreement. The two main loyalist parties, James Molyneaux's Ulster Unionist Party and the Rev Ian Paisley's Democratic Unionists, have formed a pact to oppose the initiative. Even before the results of the summit were announced, they declared a boycott of British ministers. Molyneaux, who is one of Northern Ireland's most civil and mild-mannered politicians, spoke bitterly of "the stench of hypocrisy, deceit and treachery in London" and said Hillsborough Castle would have to be fumigated after Mrs Thatcher and Dr FitzGerald left.

The two parties have called on their members to resign from all government-appointed committees. They intend to test the agreement's validity in the High Court, and their MPs will resign to force a string of by-elections.

4

All this, they've made clear, represents only phase one of their opposition. Afterwards, there is talk of a withdrawal of consent to be governed, of civil disobedience. And in the underworld, the loyalist paramilitary groups, who over the years have killed several hundred Catholics, are stirring restlessly again after a long period of comparative inaction. They are smaller now – say 7,000 men, compared to the 40,000 they could mobilise in 1972 – they are older, they are flabby and rusty. But their structure is still there, and the Hillsborough pact has re-excited their interest and may well stimulate recruitment. Already the Ulster Defence Association, the largest outfit, has bluntly warned that "members of the proposed secretariat and anyone who collaborates with them will be classified by us as legitimate targets for assassination". The threat is being taken seriously.

At the moment, these two aspects of Unionist opposition, political and paramilitary, are being kept strictly separate (at least for public consumption – in private there is some surreptitious contact between them). But the experience of the 1974 anti-Sunningdale campaign is that the two elements can be forced together, even against their own wills. In 1974 they linked up on a committee to direct the two-week general strike which forced moderate Unionists to quit the powersharing executive.

This time there is as yet no sign of planning for such a strike. There is, for a start, no local Northern Ireland component on which pressure can be brought to bear (assuming the southern civil servants are safely protected against assassination). This time, to win, the loyalists must defeat Mrs Thatcher. To have any chance of doing so, they must first form a united front of Protestants in general.

The fact is that the agreement, in the eyes of most Unionists, is a sinister cloud with no real silver linings for them. Its assurances of a new-found respect for the Unionist tradition are, they say, just words; so too is the affirmation that Northern Ireland's status within the UK will not be changed without their consent. That status has, they argue, already been changed by the new role granted to the Republic.

The strategy of the loyalist politicians will be to build up resistance gradually. In that way, they hope to enlist the more moderate Protestant elements to their protests. There is at least a chance that they will manage to do that; much will depend on the Government's handling of their agitation. A united Protestant front would be a formidable bloc of opinion – one which would test to the full Mrs Thatcher's commitment to the new agreement. Unionism, when united and set on all-out confrontation, has never been defeated, down through all the years. But then, neither has Margaret Thatcher.

The Anglo-Irish agreement came about
through Irish nationalists persuading the
British government that a radical new move
was needed to break the political deadlock. The
concept of the accord came from the leader of
the Social Democratic and Labour Party,
John Hume.

PROFILE

DAVID SMITH

John Hume, a practical nationalist

John Hume and his family pay a high price for living in the republican Bogside district of Londonderry. Twice in recent years their cars have been set alight outside the door; there have been various attacks and bomb hoaxes; the word "traitor" has been daubed on the wall. Those who carry out the attacks believe Hume has sold out on the old certainties, the old purities, of traditional nationalism and republicanism. They think he has abandoned the old dream: and they are right.

The leader of the Social Democratic and Labour Party has played a pivotal role in changing the face of Irish nationalism, jettisoning the ancient and cherished beliefs that the answer lies in defeating the British and subduing the Protestants, and that doing away with the border would solve the Northern Ireland problem.

Instead, his rhetoric is that of searching for agreement, of seeking unity in diversity. The new dream is of uniting people, not territory. That can sound nebulous, but Hume's powers of formulation, exposition and political strategy are so formidable that they have made him the most internationally respected of all Irish politicians.

He is capable of addressing a roomful of powerful men, not necessarily favourable to his point of view, and almost mesmerising them with the forcefulness of his analysis and argument. And the further he gets from home, the greater is his influence: he is much-respected in the Irish Republic and within the institutions of the EC, but he has real clout in Washington.

Generations of Irish political leaders have tried, with little success, to harness the enormous inherent power of the Irish in America – 40 million US citizens, after all, describe themselves as Irish-American. The thought of even a fraction of the Irish diaspora's potential lobbying power being mobilised is enough to make Foreign Office palms damp with perspiration. Hume has an apparently unerring gift for impressing the powerful – one meeting is often enough – and has enlisted the active support of almost all the big Irish-American political barons.

Several years ago Tip O'Neill, the former Speaker of the House of Representatives, was visited by the present Irish Foreign Minister, Brian Lenihan, who was then asking him not to support the Anglo-Irish agreement. O'Neill cut him short: "I go by what John Hume says," he growled. O'Neill made sure, at his own farewell dinner, to place Hume beside his successor, Jim Wright, and Hume has continuing access there.

He has exerted his influence to engineer American pressure on British policy, but has used it even more against the IRA and Sinn Féin. Many Irish-American politicians who once leant towards militant republicanism are now firmly in the Hume camp, and he has been a key figure in containing and reducing American sympathies – and thus finance – for the IRA.

Hume was born in Londonderry in 1937, one of a family of seven squashed into a two-bedroomed house. The name Hume comes from a Scots Presbyterian great-grandfather, but the rest of the family is Catholic. His father fought with the Royal Irish Rifles in France in the First World War, served in the Irish Free State Army, then worked as a clerk and a riveter before falling victim to the unemployment which has for decades been the scourge of Londonderry. Hume passed the 11-plus examination in its first year of existence and won a place at the local St Columb's grammar school before attending St Patrick's College, Maynooth, where for several years he trained as a priest. He was a teacher before becoming involved in self-help projects such as the Credit Union. He married a Londonderry woman, Pat, who today runs his office in the city, and they have five children.

Hume quickly came to public attention when the Catholic civil rights movement emerged in 1968, establishing himself as one of its leading theoreticians. In the splits which affected the movement right from the start, he was firmly on the reformist wing, opposing left-wingers and republicans who sought revolution and confrontation. His reputation for non-violence was established on the streets of Londonderry at this time.

When the SDLP was founded in 1970, he became deputy leader to Gerry Fitt, and later leader. He became a Member of the European Parliament in 1979 and was elected to Westminster, as MP for Foyle, four years later. The SDLP was the first properly organised nationalist party in Northern Ireland and through the storms of the past two decades has averaged around 20 per cent of the vote.

Hume's unique feature is his ability to combine theory with practical politics. As the chief intellectual force of constitutional nationalism, Hume articulated the feelings of the growing Catholic middle class and constructed a theory which has changed little over the years. This holds that the heart of the Irish question lies not with the British but with the Protestants, and that partition is not the cause of division but a symptom of it. The historic mission of nationalism, then, should be not to drive out the British but to convince Unionism that its concerns can be accommodated in a new Ireland. Traditional nationalism did not know what to do with Unionism, saying, in effect, that if only Britain could be driven out, the Protestants would be defeated politically (and, if necessary, militarily) and thus cease to be a problem.

Hume dismayed the old guard by conceding that Unionism had a veto on Irish unity, and that Protestants could not be forced into a new arrangement against their will. Their numbers, he argued, gave them a natural veto, preventing agreement without their consent. The recognition of the need for consent has not, however, precluded Hume from marshalling his various spheres of influence to put pressure on Unionism. His new formulation of nationalism may have made him the bitterest opponent of Sinn Féin and the IRA – he describes them as fascist – but it has won him few friends on the Unionist side.

"The general view of Hume," according to a senior Unionist politician, "is that the IRA provides the muscle and he milks it for all it's worth." The standard Protestant view is that he shares the aims, if not the methods, of the IRA and if anything is more dangerous because of his intellect and his powerful allies.

It is true that in the last European election 1,200 people voted under proportional representation for Paisley 1, Hume 2 – most of these were probably small farmers, appreciative of his efforts on their behalf in the EC. But in general the SDLP leader is regarded by Protestants as the man who helped start all the trouble, and whose objects are inimical to theirs.

Hume is one of nature's poker-players: his frustration has always been that Unionists have declined to sit down and join the game, regarding negotiation as a sign of weakness. So in the late Seventies he moved away from the idea of dealing direct with them, and instead set out to convince Dublin, London and America that the time had come to move.

In one sense he had a clear run, for Unionist politicians adopted a defensive posture of sitting tight rather than attempting to block his manoeuvres; they failed – and the failure may be a significant one – to envisage how his various areas of influence could be combined in a coherent whole.

The eventual outcome of this orchestration of pressures was the Anglo-Irish agreement of 1985, of which he is regarded as the principal architect. In his theoretical terms, this removed Unionism's other veto – the belief of Protestants that they could wreck any British initiative of which they did not approve. In practical terms, the agreement drove a wedge between Britain and Unionism. It also gave formal expression to Hume's constant assertion that the Northern Ireland problem has international dimensions.

Since then he has played down the recurring disputes which the agreement has run into, contending that it will weather any little local difficulties. The accord itself, to his mind, will always be worth preserving for its long-term effects. Major problems are posed for him here by Mrs Thatcher and the IRA, who persist in regarding the problem as a military rather than a political matter.

None the less, Hume regards the agreement as a historic step which will, sooner or later, succeed in its purpose of demonstrating that Britain has no long-term commitment to the Union and thus convince Unionists that they must come to terms with nationalists.

It is an article of faith with him that Unionism will one day agree to negotiate rather than sit tight, or threaten to fight. He has been waiting for a full two decades to do business; he will continue to wait, he says, for as long as it takes. He remains, in the meantime, a human illustration of the fact that political action can achieve more than the gun, and an important symbol of non-violence in a violent country.

Hume's concept was translated into the form of the agreement by Irish diplomats such as Sean Donlon, Michael Lillis and Noel Dorr. But the accord only became possible because of Mrs Thatcher's liking for, and trust in, the then Taoiseach, Dr Garret FitzGerald.

24 JANUARY 1987   THE INDEPENDENT

PROFILE

Garret FitzGerald, Irish charm without the blarney

David Owen once said that if a worldwide poll were held among heads of government and foreign ministers as to who was the most likeable politician, their overwhelming choice would be Garret FitzGerald.

The same is true within Ireland. Many of FitzGerald's severest critics preface their attacks with the admission that he is quite the nicest man in Irish politics. His sincerity, charm and lack of guile are legendary: they help to explain why his career has been such a striking mixture of outstanding success and conspicuous failure. Perhaps his greatest political flaw has been a failure to grasp that not everyone is as nice as himself. As a rationalist, he has found it difficult to come to terms with the fact that Ireland has more than its fair share of unreasonable people.

The consequence is that his greatest achievements have been outside the Republic, where he has excelled in his negotiations with other premiers and foreign ministers. In domestic terms his recent record has been less than glorious. The problems of the Irish economy, with its huge burden of foreign debt, simply overwhelmed his administration. Budget deficits and unemployment have risen steadily; emigration to England and elsewhere has started again; tax rates remain cripplingly high. Only inflation has been conquered.

The irony is that long before entering politics FitzGerald had established himself as Ireland's best-known economist. Although qualified as a barrister, he never practised law. Instead he joined Aer Lingus, Ireland's national airline. Rapidly promoted through the ranks, he made astonishing improvements to the airline's efficiency and profitability. The story goes that when he left he was replaced by four men and a computer. Ten years of economic lecturing, consultancy work and freelance journalism followed. The remarkable point here is that he had no background in economics: his first from University College Dublin was in French and history.

By the time he entered the Dáil in 1969 he was established as one of Ireland's brightest and best. He was one of a clutch of intellectuals who came into public life in the Republic at that time with a mission to modernise the economy and liberalise society. Those aims remain largely unfulfilled.

Some say that part at least of the celebrated FitzGerald drive comes from the example set by his father. Desmond FitzGerald, like his son, packed a great deal into life: he was by turns poet, revolutionary and cabinet minister. A friend of Yeats, Pound and T.S. Eliot, Desmond fought in the General Post Office in

Dublin during the 1916 rising against the British. He later served, like his son, as Ireland's Foreign Minister. FitzGerald's mother too was out of the ordinary. A Belfast Presbyterian, she renounced her Unionist background to become a suffragette, a socialist and an Irish nationalist. She too fought in the GPO.

FitzGerald's wife Joan is also a woman of note. They are, after 39 years of marriage, inseparable; so much so that associates complain that Joan, who is strong, intelligent and opinionated, takes up altogether too much of the Taoiseach's time. Blessed with a talent for informality and a complete lack of pretension, they live in a cosy basement flat in a tree-lined Dublin road. FitzGerald's devotion to Joan is well known. She suffers badly from arthritis and in 1986 a Munster weekly newspaper described as "unseemly" FitzGerald's unaffected habit of pushing her wheelchair in public. FitzGerald said nothing but took deep offence. Six months later the incident came to light when he cancelled an important press conference in Munster rather than meet the paper's representative.

When a Fine Gael–Labour coalition came to power in 1973 FitzGerald was the obvious choice as Finance Minister. But the then Taoiseach, Liam Cosgrave, was uneasy about his progressive views and so, unexpectedly, FitzGerald found himself Minister for Foreign Affairs. He was an enormous success. A confirmed Francophile, he was once asked by a French minister, in the middle of a complex technical exposition, to slow down – FitzGerald was speaking in French.

His international reputation and his range of powerful overseas contacts date from this time. He was one of the first to see that the European Community might be valuable not just for its own sake but as a means of diluting Britain's predominant economic influence over the Republic.

When Fine Gael was crushed by Fianna Fáil in the 1977 election, he was Cosgrave's natural successor as leader. In the years that followed he ripped the comfortable conservative party apart, cutting local barons down to size. His key hatchet-man was Peter Prendergast, a former marketing consultant. "He just let Prendergast go through the party like a bloody wolf," says one observer. As many of the old guard were booted aside, FitzGerald broadened the party's appeal, persuading younger and more liberal elements to join. The approach worked. In the 1981 election Fine Gael shot up from 43 seats to 70, and he became Taoiseach with the support of Labour and independents.

It was obvious that he was destined to hold that office; yet, when it came, his characteristic sureness of touch deserted him. The problem lay in the gap between his aims and their practical realisation. His objectives were clear enough: to do something about Northern Ireland, "desectarianise" (his word) southern society, achieve social reforms and eliminate poverty. The aims are laudable but most have not been achieved. "With Garret it's wishes, not action," one supporter complained. "It's like an intellectual pubcrawl from one idea to another." He has been a reforming Taoiseach, regularly outwitted by the forces of reaction or by Fianna Fáil's superior cunning.

An example came with his 1986 attempt to introduce divorce to Ireland. To do so meant holding a referendum to delete the anti-divorce article from the Republic's antiquated, Catholic-dominated constitution. FitzGerald originally decided such a vote could not be won and reluctantly shelved the idea. Then, on the strength of a single opinion poll showing a majority in favour of reform, he called a snap referendum.

But he had prepared no detailed campaign. In the weeks that followed, the various anti-divorce elements fought a brilliant campaign; the government's response was pitiful. The opinion poll results were reversed and FitzGerald suffered a crushing defeat. His time as Taoiseach has been littered with such episodes. Cartoonists who once pictured him as a whizz-kid now draw him as the absent-minded professor.

One northern nationalist summed him up: "When you make a deal with Garret, you know you can trust him, but you also know you mightn't be able to rely on him." He added that with FitzGerald's principal opponent, Charles Haughey, the problem is the opposite. FitzGerald and Haughey have represented the opposite poles of Irishness: one the essence of rectitude, the other his slightly racy counterpoint. They are the Gladstone and Disraeli of modern Irish politics.

Certainly in one respect FitzGerald has put himself alongside Gladstone in all future Irish history books. The Anglo-Irish agreement which he signed with Margaret Thatcher was, in Irish terms, a breathtaking achievement. A British Prime Minister has been induced to instal Irish civil servants in Belfast. She has committed Britain, in an international agreement, to make "determined efforts" to resolve differences with Dublin. Whether the agreement survives or falls, the relationship between Britain and Unionism has been changed utterly.

The agreement was not FitzGerald's achievement alone. But it would never have come about without his international reputation for integrity, his negotiating skills and his persistence. The fact of the agreement will serve as a monument in years to come, when his domestic shortcomings have been forgotten. He will be remembered as the Taoiseach who sought to modernise Ireland; most of all, he will be remembered as the most decent man in Irish public life.

The original hope of the agreement's architects was that Unionists would, after the initial shock, go to the conference table for negotiations. But instead they continued to oppose the accord with various forms of protest. Members of the extreme Ulster Defence Association staged firebomb attacks on the homes of police officers, while in January 1986 the fifteen Unionist MPs resigned their seats to stage a mini-referendum on the agreement.

9 JANUARY 1986   THE LISTENER

The Protestant backlash: Unionists could provoke a constitutional crisis

The current political scene in Northern Ireland is particularly rich in irony. Protestant extremists are demonstrating their willingness, indeed their enthusiasm, to attack the mainly Protestant Royal Ulster Constabulary. John Hume's SDLP, which once denounced Margaret Thatcher on a daily basis, now sees her as potentially the best British Prime Minister since Gladstone. The two main Unionist parties, who fought the last election with the slogan "smash Sinn Féin", are about to go to the polls with the same policy as Sinn Féin – that of wrecking the Anglo-Irish agreement.

The wheel finally turned full circle last week when a group of Unionists staged their protest march from Londonderry to Belfast. It was consciously modelled on the march by Catholic demonstrators along a similar route in January 1969. The Catholic demand was for civil rights, for equality in housing and jobs; the

Protestants of today say they want their due "constitutional rights", arguing that the agreement with Dublin diminished their status as full United Kingdom citizens. Like the Catholics of 17 years ago, Unionists today feel isolated, misunderstood and ignored by Parliament. Their mood was best described by, oddly enough, a Catholic bishop, Dr Cahal Daly, when he said: "Unionists have seen their cherished institutions dismantled, their control of Northern Ireland's affairs decapitated, their sense of security suddenly undermined. They feel they have been forced, against their will and without consultation, into a future of insecurity and powerlessness."

The agreement, which gives the Irish government a significant consultative role in the running of Northern Ireland, was signed in November, but the final Unionist response to the accord has yet to emerge. So far there has been one enormous, dignified rally in Belfast, followed by two marches which ended in ugly clashes between Protestant rioters and police. It is plain enough that few Protestants support the agreement; what is much less clear is the extent to which they will be prepared to press their opposition.

The political leaders of Unionism, however, are unanimous in declaring, without equivocation, that they can never live with the agreement. James Molyneaux's Ulster Unionists and the Rev Ian Paisley's Democratic Unionists have united on a steering committee which has as its sole objective the downfall of the accord. They have mapped out a two-phase approach: first, a series of by-elections designed to demonstrate the extent of Protestant feeling; and second – on the assumption that the by-elections will leave Mrs Thatcher unmoved – a general withdrawal of Protestant consent from the British administration.

This second phase, should it be reached, will obviously take us into deep waters. Protestants make up more than 60 per cent of the population, and if Mr Molyneaux and Mr Paisley do succeed in persuading a large proportion of them to engage in civil disobedience or even passive resistance, then the scene could be set for a constitutional crisis of perhaps historic significance.

But first, the elections. Fifteen Unionist MPs have resigned from Westminster, and all the by-elections will be held on 23 January. The most likely result is that all the sitting members will be re-elected, though the SDLP has an outside chance in two places, one of them Enoch Powell's South Down seat. The loss of a seat would be a blow to the Unionist campaign, though they will argue that the aggregate of anti-agreement votes cast is the more meaningful statistic. The electorate is almost exactly one million, and they hope to chalk up a total of 400,000 against the accord. This is entirely feasible, but there is one difficulty. It may well be that in some constituencies there will be no opposition candidates at all. In that event the Unionist parties will field "dummy candidates" who will ask people to vote against them.

Standing in at least four seats, on an anti-agreement ticket, will be Sinn Féin. It opposes the agreement, believing it will facilitate new joint initiatives, north and south of the border – political moves aimed against Sinn Féin, and security measures against the IRA. Already there is evidence that the two governments are thinking in exactly these terms. The Republic is in the process of expanding its army by 1,000 men, and has posted more police to border areas. The RUC recently arrested 18 Sinn Féin members. None the less, the IRA demonstrated its continuing capacity for violence by killing two policemen in Armagh city only a few minutes into the new year. It is a fact, however, that the IRA alone has not the strength to bring down the new agreement. Fewer people died from IRA violence last year, though it inflicted heavy casualties on the RUC. Recent IRA violence has been designed to needle and goad extreme loyalists into doing the job for them.

So how far will the Unionists go? The joint Ulster Unionist–Democratic Unionist manifesto, to be published next week, will ask voters to authorise their elected leaders to deny the Government the moral authority to implement the agreement. Beyond this carefully constructed form of words, the parties will not be specific about their tactics for the withdrawal of consent. There is an excellent reason for this – they have not yet decided how to go about it. The self-image of the Protestant is based on a respect for the law and authority. Devising disobedience tactics which fit in with this has proved immensely difficult.

Meanwhile, the centrepiece of the agreement, the intergovernmental conference, has been proceeding with its work in spite of the Unionist unhappiness and protests. There has been a series of small but significant developments: the much-criticised Ulster Defence Regiment is to have more training in Britain; the RUC is to have a new code of conduct, based on that of British forces; there are to be reforms of anti-terrorist legislation; another Catholic judge will shortly be appointed. In addition, Dublin has been consulted on the conduct of the controversial supergrass trials, and has registered its views on the handling of a hunger strike launched by a number of republicans in the Maze prison.

The Government maintains that not all of these developments resulted from the intergovernmental conference, but this contention is widely disbelieved. From now on, every single decision of government will be open to the interpretation that its impetus comes not from London but from Dublin. The Unionists will find continuing confirmation for their fear that they are being ruled jointly by Britain and the Republic. Their dissatisfaction with this situation is clear, but the grassroots is divided on whether a head-on confrontation with Mrs Thatcher can be won.

Already, elements in the Ulster Unionists are worried at the way their partnership with the Democratic Unionists is working out. Their leader, the reticent, soft-spoken James Molyneaux, is overshadowed by the Rev Ian Paisley. Mr Molyneaux's career is based on Westminster – he has been an MP for 15 years –

and has been founded on the contention that his lobbying skills are highly effective in the London corridors of power. But the Anglo-Irish agreement has made nonsense of his party's boast that he has a special relationship with the Prime Minister. Mr Molyneaux has already found it necessary to deny rumours that he might step down as leader; but at least two of his MPs feel that a more forceful personality should be placed in charge of the party now that extra-parliamentary activity may be the order of the day.

On the other side of the spectrum, there are a few – a very few – Unionists who are prepared to contemplate, instead of confrontation, some form of power-sharing with the SDLP. They are certainly not prepared to advance the idea publicly, for to do so would mean instant denunciation from Mr Paisley and most of the Ulster Unionists. But they are prepared to explore the idea of powersharing as a means of reducing the power of the intergovernmental conference. It will be some time, though, before such heads appear over the parapet; and they may never appear at all. In the meantime, Unionists must decide which course represents the greater danger to the Union with Britain: acceptance of the agreement or confrontation with Margaret Thatcher.

The January 1986 by-elections produced no appreciable effect on government policy, and one of the Unionist MPs lost his seat to the SDLP. With political protest against the agreement apparently ineffective, the focus, in mid-1986, shifted to the streets.

Northern Ireland braces itself for a long, hot marching season

Protestants proclaim their opposition to the Anglo-Irish accord.

CRISPIN RODWELL, *Independent*

It was the Rev Ian Paisley's own choice to be carried, head first, out of the defunct Northern Ireland Assembly by four puffing policemen last month. His enthusiasm for protest is renowned, and he hoped for a symbolic illustration of his argument that the Anglo-Irish agreement has abandoned democracy and forced Unionists on to the streets.

That was the theory, but it all went wrong. The man who is a Westminster MP, a European MP, leader of the second-largest political party in Northern Ireland and head of a substantial church scrambled to his feet and, in a rage, told the police: "Don't come crying to me the next time your houses are attacked. You'll reap what you sow." His fellow Assembly members applauded his words. The incident was extensively televised.

Now it's an indisputable fact that a large majority of Unionists are very much opposed to the agreement which Margaret Thatcher and Garret FitzGerald signed at Hillsborough last November. Yet they are no closer today than they ever were to finding a way of wrecking the accord – and Paisley, it's been commonly said recently, has gone too far.

Clearly, it's not politically healthy, in the longer term, to have such a lack of consent, but there is no lessening of determination evident on either the British or Irish side to press ahead with the agreement, whatever Unionists do to try and deflect them. However, the next few months will see the accord put to the test by pressure from other directions.

It has been a rough eight months since last November. Hardly a week has passed without an anti-agreement protest of some sort, and many aspects of political life have simply come to a standstill. Unionist MPs first refused to speak to any British minister except Mrs Thatcher, and now say they will not meet her either until she suspends the agreement.

Few Unionist MPs attend at Westminster, and they take no part in Northern Ireland business. Even before the Northern Ireland Assembly was wound up, its activities were confined to once-weekly anti-agreement debates. Most local councils have ceased to function. Rallies and parades, often occasions for fierce rhetoric, are regular events. Thousands of posters proclaim that "Ulster still says no". There are plans to field Unionist candidates in marginal English and Scottish seats, in the hope of dishing the Tories. (This particular ploy got off to an inauspicious start in the Fulham by-election when a pro-Unionist candidate polled fewer votes than the Monster Raving Looney Party.) A "Friends of the Union" support group has been established at Westminster, but has attracted little support outside the far right of the Conservative Party. There is talk of withholding rates, of refusing to pay TV licence fees. One Unionist, a former Assembly member, congratulated Argentina on beating England in the World Cup. Another advocated withholding dog licences because, he said, it's a dog's life under the Anglo-Irish agreement. Unionism today is immersed in the politics of protest.

Yet Unionists have a strong self-image of themselves as a respectable and law-abiding community, and one part of the Protestant mind is uneasy with all this. Besides, things can easily get out of hand. A one-day strike in March quickly degenerated into intimidation and violence. The homes of dozens of policemen and policewomen were firebombed by extreme Protestants some months ago – the attacks which Mr Paisley referred to that night at the Assembly.

To put it another way, there is widespread Protestant apprehension that the medicine (Mr Paisley's protests) is more dangerous than the disease (the agreement). If someone could think of a non-hazardous and essentially peaceful means of destroying the accord, then most Protestants would swing behind it; but no one can.

Protestant unhappiness about the agreement is not paralleled by Catholic satisfaction. The past eight months have produced none of the major reforms on security, the courts or other areas where big changes had been expected. Until recently, the Irish government and John Hume's Social Democratic and Labour Party accepted the British explanation that, with Protestant feelings running so high, major changes would have to wait. But Dublin is now complaining that discretion has become procrastination, and so it's been agreed that a reform package will be unveiled in the autumn.

The nationalists would like to see a new code of conduct for the RUC, three judges instead of one in terrorist-type trials, RUC accompaniment for the much-criticised Ulster Defence Regiment and a series of other changes designed to make the institutions of Northern Ireland more acceptable to the Catholic minority. London has in mind much more modest reforms, and a great deal of argument over the dimensions of the autumn package lies ahead.

In the meantime, the marching season is upon us. There are actually well over 1,000 Protestant marches and a couple of dozen Catholic ones every summer. Most pass off peacefully, but some traditionally lead to trouble – especially in the Co Armagh town of Portadown, where Protestants insist on parading through an entirely Catholic district. The town is braced for bother: Protestants say they must get through this year to demonstrate that Dublin isn't calling the shots. Catholics say that if the agreement's words about respecting their rights and identity mean anything, they must mean that unwelcome parades will be halted.

In the longer term, the prospects are unclear. The agreement is signed and sealed, but it is not yet delivered, in the sense that it has not been accepted by the Protestant majority; they simply refuse to recognise its validity, in the way the IRA used to refuse to recognise British courts. They hope they can stop it from taking root. But time is probably on the side of the two governments, and their hope – their only hope, really – is that as the months and the years pass, Unionists will, however reluctantly, come to terms with the fact that the agreement is here to stay.

In the event the marches passed off reasonably peacefully, with the RUC winning nationalist praise for dealing firmly with potential Protestant troublemakers. But the late summer of 1986 was none the less a time of apprehension and uncertainty.

Peter Robinson, deputy leader of the Rev Ian Paisley's Democratic Unionist Party, emerged as champion of hardline Protestant opinion and in August 1986 he was arrested in the Irish Republic when a large force of loyalists staged a nocturnal takeover of the Co Monaghan town of Clontibret.

The hazards of putting the fear of God into Unionists

Northern Ireland is at the moment a tense and dangerous place. Government ministers venture out of their heavily fortified bases only furtively and under heavy escort. Unionist politicians refuse all contact with them; some Unionist MPs now appear regularly at menacing midnight shows of strength along with masked men carrying cudgels. The IRA has recently scored significant successes. Protestant murder gangs have meanwhile claimed half a dozen lives. Normal political life has ground to a halt and the extremists are making all the running.

It all sounds pretty grim, yet in a sense events are proceeding largely, though not entirely, according to plan. The plan in question was conceived by the architects of the Anglo-Irish agreement which Margaret Thatcher and Garret FitzGerald signed in November last. Their analysis of the problem, and their remedy for it, went something like this. Nationalist alienation from the state of Northern Ireland was running dangerously high, providing support for the IRA and its political wing, Sinn Féin, to an extent which was threatening the stability not just of Northern Ireland but of the Republic as well. The central problem was the Unionists, because they doggedly refused to share power with their Catholic neighbours, something which the British and Irish governments and the main Catholic party, the SDLP, all wished to see. The IRA menace could be tackled in two ways. First, closer security co-operation between the British and Irish would help combat an IRA campaign which has in recent years come to be concentrated along the border. Second, pressure would be applied to the Unionists to persuade them to opt, however reluctantly, for powersharing. And giving Catholics a say in the running of the state – at first via the Irish government, later through the SDLP – would in time decrease the alienation on which the IRA feeds.

From the start, it was recognised that involving Dublin in the administration of Northern Ireland would send the loyalists up the wall. Extra troops were drafted in, contingency plans drawn up. In fact, London reckoned on a more violent backlash than we actually saw. A few months ago a government minister said privately: "I would say that we are at the lower end of the range for which we have prepared." The key point about this is that loyalists were *supposed* to be shocked by the Anglo-Irish agreement. A degree of political trauma was specifically prescribed in order to soften their attitudes. The idea was to provoke a political debate among Unionists, a rethink which would lead them to the inescapable conclusion that the agreement is here to stay. They would realise it could not be removed by force and see that their only option was negotiation.

So much for the theory. In human terms, it is uncomfortable and occasionally hazardous to live through such a transition period, whether it has all been foreseen or not. Besides, the plan is behind schedule and has taken a few hard knocks. In the springtime, optimists had forecast a summer marching season in which the authorities would teach the loyalists that the old days had gone for ever; to be followed, with luck, by serious negotiations in the autumn. Instead, what they got was a serious public disagreement between the two governments, and the rise to prominence of Peter Robinson.

Opponents of the Rev Ian Paisley – and they are legion – have over the years consoled themselves with the thought that once he retired – or ran out of steam – his politico-religious movement would probably disintegrate. The emergence of Mr Robinson has shattered that fanciful dream. His nocturnal excursion across the border into Co Monaghan, and the subsequent court appearance, demonstrated that he has inherited his leader's flair for dramatic publicity. Mr Paisley, it's widely said, has lost some of his energy. Mr Robinson, it's said, lacks the Big Man's charisma, oratory, humour and larger-than-life personality; but he's ahead in imagination, organisational ability and cool calculation. He also frightens more people – Protestants as well as Catholics – because he appears to lack Mr Paisley's talent for pulling back from the brink at the last moment.

The particular brink which Mr Robinson is suspected of heading towards is independence for Northern Ireland. He is, at 37, a child of the Troubles. In his two decades of political activity – he started early, as a passionate teenage advocate of capital punishment for IRA men – he has been a constant critic of Britain. The only way of restoring Protestant majority rule, *sans* powersharing, seems to be to chase the British. Independence would mean repartition, in order to give an independent Ulster a larger Protestant majority. It is inconceivable to think of this without violence on a level not yet seen, and without large-scale population movements. Mr Paisley always drew back from such a prospect. Mr Robinson might not.

But whether or not he would go that far, Mr Robinson (like Mr Paisley) declares that the political processes are at an end, and that the agreement can be defeated only by other means. Yet, although he is now the Paisley heir apparent and the darling of the extremists, Mr Robinson worries many Unionists. Many, in fact, are more afraid of him than they are of the Anglo-Irish accord. In their eyes, the agreement weakens the Union with Britain – but Mr Robinson might sunder it completely. He has come to personify the fear that there can be worse things than the agreement.

As Mr Robinson has dominated the headlines, James Molyneaux, leader of the less extreme Ulster Unionist Party, took the extraordinary step (for a politician) of formally severing contacts with the media. He suspended his party's weekly press conferences and will give no more interviews, saying the media were more interested in reporting violence and disruption than political activity. Mr Molyneaux has almost, though not quite, come to agree with the Paisley–Robinson line that political action does not work. It could, of course, be argued that this is because the Unionists have themselves opted out of politics: the major Unionist parties now virtually never attend Westminster, they have shut down all the local councils they control and they forced the closure of the Northern Ireland Assembly. Molyneaux's gesture is a symptom of the frustration felt by many of the more respectable Unionists. They feel they've tried everything to convey to the Government their sense of betrayal over the agreement, but nothing works.

The fact is that the agreement, conceived as it was to deal with nationalist alienation, has at a stroke alienated the entire Unionist community. The shock treatment has been successfully administered. This is, of course, in accordance with the plan of the agreement's architects; none the less, these are anxious times as we await the results of the treatment. Will they join Mr Robinson on the streets; will they fight; will they negotiate; will they opt out, like Mr Molyneaux, and wait it out, in the hope that changes of government in London and/or Dublin will alter things? The decision is not yet made.

Unionist attitudes to the agreement might conceivably soften if it could be demonstrated that the accord was bringing about a reduction in IRA violence. Unfortunately for the authorities, it has yet to do so. Statistically, IRA killings are running at exactly the same rate as last year. In addition, the threat to kill anyone who supplies materials of any sort to the security forces was a major coup for the IRA. At a stroke, it seriously disrupted the £200-million building programme designed to provide better bases for the RUC. It also demonstrated, to maximum propaganda effect, the sheer brute force at the IRA's command. It will take time to make a significant dent in its violent capability, even with the vastly increased north–south security co-operation which the agreement has brought.

In the meantime, however, important political differences have appeared between the two governments on how to operate the agreement, centring on the person of the Northern Ireland Secretary of State, Tom King. Last month the RUC, with Mr King's approval, allowed loyalists to parade through a Catholic area of the Co Armagh town of Portadown. The incident was seen as a vital test case for the agreement. The Irish government and the SDLP said the parade infringed the rights of Catholics and should not have been allowed. When it was permitted, Dublin was furious: Foreign Minister Peter Barry said it was a victory for the bully boys. Privately, the Irish accused Mr King of something close to treachery, claiming he had assured them the march would be stopped. It's further alleged that Mr King has, in public pronouncements on the agreement, been guilty of gross inaccuracies and distortions. The Irish have briefed journalists that they see Mr King as deceitful, incompetent and harbouring Unionist sympathies. In short, the agreement's honeymoon period is over: it will never be glad confident morning again.

Mr King is seen as being too soft on the Unionists, too concerned to soothe and reassure them: he has even suggested that changes might be made in the agreement itself to accommodate them. Further, the charge is that he is concerned at every point to minimise and play down reforms due under the accord. In the next few months a series of changes is due to be introduced: the removal of legislation which inhibits the display of the Irish tricolour flag in Northern Ireland; a higher standing for the Irish language; a more independent police complaints procedure, and so on. The most important measure for which Dublin has been pressing is the replacement of single judges in terrorist-type trials by a three-judge panel. But Mr King – as well as the Lord Chancellor, Lord Hailsham – has yet to concede the reform. What's more, any changes will not be announced as a single package, but are to be introduced piecemeal. The point for the Irish government is that this November marks the agreement's first anniversary. Of course, its very existence, in the face of such spirited Unionist opposition, is a victory in itself; but in addition Dublin needs at least a few meaningful reforms for which it can claim credit.

Both governments have a legitimate point here. Tom King is responsible for a country which at the moment contains one million quite seriously disaffected Protestants. Sensitivity will be needed to keep them out of the clutches of Peter Robinson. Yet according to the master plan, there should not be *too* much sensitivity. The idea, after all, is to deliver a short, sharp shock to put the fear of God into the Unionists. They should, when they finally appear at the negotiating table, be suitably chastened and ready to make a fresh start. It will be a delicate matter, surrounded by enormous risks, to judge just when they're worried enough to talk, but not worried enough to rebel.

Behind the scenes in late 1986 Mr Paisley and Mr Robinson were involved in the organisation of "Ulster Resistance", a new grouping of Protestants intended to oppose the Anglo-Irish agreement. Before it actually emerged, Mr Robinson laid the groundwork in a series of speeches at loyalist meetings.

Mobilising Unionist anger

The scene is a half-filled hall in Bangor, Co Down, a placid seaside town which is the Northern Ireland equivalent of Southend. More than half the audience of 200 are in their sixties and seventies. The speaker is Peter Robinson, deputy leader of the Democratic Unionist Party and Westminster MP for East Belfast. Standing behind a table draped with a Union flag, he denounces

Britain with a ferocity which the IRA and its supporters would find difficult not to admire.

Mrs Thatcher's signing of the Anglo-Irish agreement with Dublin was "an act of pitiful surrender to the IRA". The Mother of Parliaments is a sham. The agreement "is about getting the Union flag down and getting the tricolour up".

He lightens his speech with references to "Tomcat King" and "Curlytop FitzGerald", but most of his address is a sombre warning that Ulster is in peril. The key section concerns his views on the use of force. Mr Robinson argues that Ulster Protestants today have the right to use force to oppose the agreement. They should try argument and reason but "while we hope for the best we must prepare for the worst. Therefore I do not hold back in saying that it is essential that Ulster mobilises at this time.

Peter Robinson, wearing the red beret of Ulster Resistance

PACEMAKER PRESS INTERNATIONAL

"There are certain things throughout the history of the British people that we have been justified in using legitimate force to uphold. Does anyone deny the right of the soldiers in the First or Second World War to fight for liberty and freedom? I believe that people in Ulster are just as entitled to fight to preserve liberty and freedom and justice and truth and democracy in Northern Ireland today as our forefathers were. The battle is very much the same."

Mr Robinson's colleague, Nigel Dodds [later Lord Mayor of Belfast], repeats: "It's time for people to be mobilised, to be organised." They should be ready to respond "when the call comes and the orders are given".

The Democratic Unionists are warmly applauded, though meaningful "mobilisation" is clearly beyond the capacity of the largely elderly audience. But similar calls are being made at rallies and meetings all over Northern Ireland, and in many areas Mr Robinson's words do not fall on deaf ears and young men are taking his advice.

The same pattern was seen in the high tension of the early 1970s: Unionist politicians used violent rhetoric and teenagers joined paramilitary groups like the Ulster Defence Association and the Ulster Volunteer Force. Several hundred of them are still in prison serving life sentences for murder, attempted murder and possession of firearms. Mr Robinson, who is very much the coming man in loyalist politics, was then in his early twenties, and has said that he could easily have opted for a paramilitary rather than political career. In those days he listened to speeches calling for action; today he delivers them.

The signs are that some hundreds of men are putting their names down for "action". But the Protestant community as a whole has grave doubts about a resort to the use of force. The Ulster Unionist Party of James Molyneaux and Enoch Powell is just as opposed to the Anglo-Irish agreement, but emphasises that any action against it should be political and within the law. Mr Robinson speaks for most of Unionism when he denounces the Government as treacherous and the agreement as dangerous to Northern Ireland's position within the Union. But many Unionists see as many dangers in his approach: they fear that a direct and possibly violent confrontation with the Government could place the Union in even greater jeopardy.

He is on that wing of Unionism which regards the Union not as an end in itself, but rather as a means of staying out of a united Ireland. A majority in Unionism have grave doubts about the proposition that Unionists may have to fight Britain in order to stay British. But there are young men in Northern Ireland today who are preparing to do precisely that.

To begin to fathom the Protestant psyche it is necessary to delve back into Irish history, since the philosophy of Unionism has displayed an extraordinary consistency over a period of centuries. The willingness to resort to the threat of force springs from the ancient conviction that the Protestant cause faces an implacable and essentially unchanging foe – Irish nationalism and Catholicism – which on occasion had to be held at bay by physical rather than political means.

Nineteen eighty-eight marked the three-hundredth anniversary of a pivotal event in Protestant folk memory – the siege of Londonderry. The passage of three centuries has done little to alter the perception that Protestants are surrounded by enemies, that compromise is dangerous, and that politics is about resistance rather than consensus.

The enemy within: the siege of Londonderry

Ulster Protestants, when accused by the outside world of having a siege mentality, often respond to the charge not with resentment but with pride. There is, they say, nothing wrong with a siege mentality when you are actually under siege.

The fact is that the collective self-image of the Unionists of Northern Ireland is today not far removed from that of their ancestors when they arrived in Ireland three and a half centuries ago. They see themselves as a frontier community facing wily and violent enemies, and backed only by half-hearted friends. They are for the most part an inward-looking people, conservative, cautious and suspicious of change. In this they follow the model of their forebears who, transplanted from England and Scotland and given territory in a hostile land, adopted such slogans as "No surrender", "Not an inch", and "What we have we hold". Socially they can be warm-hearted and tremendously hospitable; politically they are eternally on the defensive.

The siege of Londonderry, when the Catholic Irish came within an ace of over-running the Protestant settlers, began in December 1688. In three centuries it has never lost its potency and immediacy as a symbol for Unionists, for they believe that the enemy is forever at the gate, waiting for the sentry to fall asleep.

The siege has been commemorated, so far as is known, in every year since 1688 — not so much as a pleasant piece of folklore, but as an event of continuing political significance. It is the great symbol used to pass on to each new generation the secret of Protestant survival in Ireland: to an extraordinary degree the men of 1688 still continue to provide the political role model for their descendants. An understanding of what happened at the siege of Londonderry — and of what Protestants *think* happened — is essential for a real understanding of the Unionist psyche.

The folk memory is clear enough and runs as follows. It was a battle between the rival kings of England, the Protestant William III and the Catholic James II. James's forces drove Protestants north until they stood with their backs to the sea at Londonderry. The defiant city was the only thing which prevented James from becoming lord of the whole island. The Catholics called on the city to surrender, and its traitorous governor, Lundy by name, almost delivered it into James's hands. But stronger counsels prevailed, and Londonderry, enduring tremendous hardships, heroically held out until help arrived from England.

The essential moral of the story, as recounted in this way, is that the very idea of negotiation with the foe is dangerous, and that resistance and defiance, not compromise and accommodation, are the tried and trusted methods for maintaining the Protestant heritage in Ireland.

Although this version is in one sense largely correct, its broad brush strokes conceal as much as they depict. Important points have been distorted or played down because they do not fit the straightforward image; yet they have not been entirely forgotten, and are often to be found lurking in the loyalist subconscious. It is sometimes these points which help throw full light on the beliefs that underlie the actions of today.

Protestants arrived in Ireland in large numbers from the beginning of the seventeenth century, as James I gave Englishmen and Scotsmen Irish land previously held by indigenous Catholics. The grand design was to stock the island with men loyal to London, whose presence would reduce the menace of the Irish linking up with England's Catholic enemies, France and Spain.

Catholic resentment was intense, boiling over into open rebellion in 1641. Both the rebellion and its suppression were a bloody business, and relations between the settlers and the dispossessed were, at best, strained. Then in 1688 Ireland became the focus of attention when William III pushed James II off the throne and James attempted, with French help, to strike back through Ireland. James had already alarmed Protestants by transforming the army in Ireland from a Protestant to a Catholic force and expanding its size. The occupants of Londonderry refused to admit a new Catholic garrison, 13 apprentices slamming the gates.

A large Catholic army now swept north, routing a Williamite force near Hillsborough. Many Protestants fled to Scotland while others flocked to two strongholds, Londonderry and Enniskillen. James's plan was to mop these up then ship his Irishmen to Scotland, join up with the clansmen and march on London.

Londonderry, a settlement which since the Middle Ages had been regularly looted and burnt by Vikings, Normans and unfriendly locals, seemed set to be sacked once more. It was commanded by a military governor, Robert Lundy, who ranks as one of history's great defeatists. He was indecisive and incompetent, unnecessarily abandoning useful ground and panicking in the face of the enemy. On one occasion, he raced back to the city and closed the gates on several thousands of his own men. When a relieving force of ships arrived from Liverpool, he told them that the situation was hopeless and advised them to return to England.

He attempted secretly to surrender the city to James, but his intention was discovered. He resigned and, reasonably lucky to escape with his life from the enraged defenders, was smuggled out of the city disguised as a soldier. For centuries historians have differed on whether he was a fool or a knave, a complete incompetent or an active Jacobite agent. The judgement of Unionism, however, allows of no doubt: to this day the word Lundy means traitor. Each year in Londonderry a "Lundy" figure is burnt in effigy.

Lord Macaulay [in *The History of England*] was correct in describing the siege as the most memorable in the annals of the British Isles, but seen in close-up it was a shambles. Neither the defenders nor the attackers had been involved in a siege before, and they did not know the basic rules. James's army was badly trained and badly led and, crucially, lacked the heavy artillery to penetrate the city's defences.

James himself suffered from the delusion that the garrison would capitulate if he were to present the royal personage at the city. He thus made the difficult journey from Dublin to Londonderry, but when he rode up to the gate, the response was not surrender but "a terrific discharge of cannon and musquetry" which killed an officer beside him and forced him to beat a hurried retreat.

The besiegers then settled down to starve the city out, but the Jacobites foolishly allowed 10,000 of the 30,000 inhabitants to leave, thus greatly easing the pressure on the garrison's food supplies. Disease struck, killing thousands of people both inside and outside.

Within the city, famine, fever and dysentery killed many more than the mortar bombs which the Irish lobbed over the walls. As the weeks passed, the food shortage became acute: a cat came to be worth 4s 6d, a mouse cost 6d and a dog's head sold for half a crown. Macaulay records with a shudder: "There was scarcely a cellar in which some corpse was not decaying. Such was the extremity of distress that the rats who came to feast in those hideous dens were eagerly hunted and greedily devoured."

Nor was the garrison a united body. One of the leaders struck another with a sword, and mistrust was such that different regiments were set to guard each other. One commander was court-martialled and a number of officers deserted.

One of the bitterest blows came when a relieving fleet of 30 ships appeared in Lough Foyle, within sight of the beleaguered city. The initial euphoria of the defenders vanished when it became clear that the English commander was unwilling to attempt to pierce the Irish blockade. For six weeks the fleet sat within sight of the city as its defenders continued to die.

Pleading for help, Governor George Walker sent a message saying: "Above 5,000 of our men are dead already from want of meat and those that survive are so weak that they can scarce creep to the walls, where many of them die every night at their post." It took a direct order from London to galvanise the fleet into action and, when it did, it proved a relatively easy task to break the boom and bring in food.

The siege came instantly to an end, with the Protestants of Enniskillen almost simultaneously inflicting a major defeat on the Jacobites. The momentum of James's challenge for the throne faltered; the siege marked a turning point, and in 1690 William scored a decisive victory at the Battle of the Boyne.

The centuries of the Protestant ascendancy in Ireland followed, but domination did not diminish the Protestant sense of insecurity. They have never forgotten that they are in a minority on the island, and as a community they have found it impossible to move away from the belief that Catholics represent danger. Unionist historian A.B. Cooke noted in a recent work on the siege: "The lack of magnanimity displayed by many Ulster Protestants emerges naturally and inevitably from their history – and, in particular, from the siege of Londonderry. The strongest emotions of the Ulster Protestant spring not from a sordid triumphalism but from a deep sense of vulnerability."

But the seventeenth-century experience did more than shape Protestant–Catholic relations into a mould which still persists today: it also helped to define the Protestant relationship with Britain. The six weeks that the fleet looked on as Londonderry starved left their mark on the Protestant subconscious and helped instil lingering suspicions about British intentions. Why, they wondered in 1689, did the fleet not come to the rescue earlier? Today Unionists constantly ask why Britain does not take sterner measures against the IRA, and they live in fear that the British will some day withdraw from Ireland, abandoning them to their ancient enemies.

In the meantime, the siege of Londonderry serves as an icon to demonstrate the immutable nature of the conflict. The Protestants draw from it the moral that Britain can be trusted only up to a point, that compromise is perilous, that Lundys must be guarded against and that endurance and resolution are in the end the only way to hold the fort. The siege, in the minds of many men, is still going on.

November 1986 brought the public unveiling of "Ulster Resistance", with a series of rallies addressed by Mr Paisley and Mr Robinson. They marched through the streets of Northern Ireland's towns behind uniformed flag parties, calling on able-bodied Protestants to join the new organisation. It was an attempt, in a minor key, to re-create the activities of the man who is Unionism's, and Mr Paisley's, greatest political hero – a man whose activities in the early years of the century did much to reinforce the Protestant faith in the efficacy of shows of strength.

Twin barrels of the loyalist shotgun

The second time as farce: Ian Paisley and Edward Carson

PACEMAKER PRESS INTERNATIONAL

As the Rev Ian Paisley stages almost-nightly recruiting rallies for "Ulster Resistance", the newest in a long line of private armies, he does so in conscious emulation of his greatest political hero, Edward Carson.

Lord Carson was a Conservative cabinet minister; a brilliant advocate whose piercing cross-examination led to the downfall of Oscar Wilde; and the man who instilled in Ulster Protestants the belief that they could, through the threat of force, overcome the will of British governments.

33

Seventy years on, Mr Paisley copies his tactics, his rhetoric – even, at times, his style of dress. He is engaged in an attempt to build a replica of Carson's Ulster Volunteer Force, a body of men formidable enough to force the British government to repudiate the Anglo-Irish agreement with Dublin. The tradition of unofficial citizens' armies in Ireland stretches back for centuries but the UVF which Carson led in 1921 was among the largest and best-organised ever seen. It was also, in the end, the most successful; and that success has had the most profound effect on the subsequent history of Ireland.

The Protestants adored the dour Dubliner who had served as Irish Attorney General. First, he became head of the Unionist MPs and then, as the political campaign against the Liberals' Home Rule Bill failed, leader of the UVF. This began as a series of local militias, which were then co-ordinated by the political leadership. They drilled and marched and staged a series of rallies, culminating in an impressive show of 100,000 men at the Balmoral Showgrounds in Belfast.

Carson repeatedly stressed the readiness of the UVF to go outside the law. The Unionist campaign had the support of important elements in the Conservative Party, the Army and the aristocracy: Tory Party leader Bonar Law took the salute at a UVF rally, and among those who subscribed to its fighting fund were Lord Rothschild, Waldorf Astor and Sir Edward Elgar. More than half a million men and women signed an "Ulster Covenant", pledging themselves to oppose home rule using "all means which may be found necessary". In 1913 Carson and other Unionist leaders designated a provisional government to take power "the morning home rule passes".

In the spring of 1914 the UVF smuggled 25,000 rifles and three million rounds of ammunition into Northern Ireland from Germany. Then, just as military confrontation between the British Army and the Protestant rebels seemed inevitable, the First World War broke out and crisis was averted.

After the war the home rule issue re-emerged. A measure of independence was granted to southern Ireland, but no attempt was made to force the north to accept it. Instead, the six northern counties were excluded from home rule and given their own parliament, subordinate to Westminster.

Carson was regarded as the founding father of Northern Ireland. Various factors were involved in the decision to exclude the north from home rule – not least the blood sacrifice of the UVF, for tens of thousands of them joined the British Army *en masse,* and were cut down at the Somme. But the Unionist folk memory is that Ulster was delivered from the menace of a united Ireland by Carson's defiance of parliament and the law.

As the decades passed, Unionist governments continued to honour Carson – he received an elaborate state funeral in 1935 – but the rebellious aspect of the formation of the state was played down. This left Mr Paisley free to claim the Carson mantle. As Ed Moloney and Andy Pollak relate in their fine biography

Paisley, he has for decades been imitating and invoking his hero's image. He used to sport a Carson-style homburg. He once brought Carson's son to Belfast. In an early publicity exercise he rescued the original UVF gunrunning ship, *Clydevalley,* from a Nova Scotia breaker's yard and brought it back to Northern Ireland. A portrait of Carson, his jaw set defiantly, hangs in Mr Paisley's well-appointed dining room. Last week he growled at a television interviewer pressing him on the morality of violence: "I am a Carson Unionist. I'm making no apology to you or any of your ilk for the actions of Lord Carson. I will do exactly as Lord Carson said."

The charge against Carson and the UVF is that they reintroduced the gun into Irish politics. In 1912 constitutional Irish nationalism was making progress towards home rule without resort to violence; the tradition of republican rebellion was largely discredited. As historian Michael Laffan points out: "Carson's methods were more important than his objectives. He abandoned the rules and conventions of democratic political conflict, took command of a private army, secured guns and ammunition from Britain's principal foreign rival and prepared to lead a rebellion against the Crown."

In 1916 a group of republicans and socialists were following in Carson's footsteps when they took over the GPO in Dublin and staged the Easter Rising, which began a chain of events leading to British withdrawal from the south of Ireland. He was one of the inspirations, it can be argued, not just for violent Unionism but for violent republicanism as well.

The success of Carson's methods has never been forgotten in Ireland, and it is a fundamental tenet of Unionism that British governments can ultimately be faced down. Exactly the same belief can be found in the IRA: the lesson they draw from the Carson era is that Britain can be shifted only by violence.

The lawyer who defied the law has cast a long shadow in Irish politics. His heirs include both Mr Paisley and the IRA, for his legacy has convinced them both that force, or the threat of force, is a legitimate and historically sanctioned political activity.

October 1988 brought the twentieth anniversary of the emergence of the civil rights movement, the point which most people regard as signifying the beginning of the Troubles. The *Independent* marked the occasion with a major supplement reviewing the sixty-eight-year history of the Northern Ireland state, and setting out to explain how it was that an attempt to bring stability had in the end achieved the opposite effect.

The making of the Protestant state: compromise that sowed seeds of violence

I n Northern Ireland the standard Unionist preoccupation has always been with achieving greater security. Nationalist demands have always been divided between calls for equality of treatment and for the abolition of the state and the establishment of a united Ireland.

None of these demands has ever been satisfied. The problem with the Unionist search for political and military security is that its community resists thinking of itself as Irish, yet finds itself geographically located in Ireland – forever stranded from what it thinks of as the mainland. Thus in logic no guarantees can ever be enough to reassure that community that Britain will never withdraw. The problem for the nationalists has been that both the Unionists and successive British governments have refused them Irish unity; and that for various reasons grievances of equality still persist. In the meantime, the three sides – Unionists, nationalists and Britain – have for the past 20 years found it impossible to achieve even peace, let alone a solution. A brief review of the state's history helps explain this.

In 1912 London was preparing to answer nationalist agitation for independence by granting a measure of self-government. This prospect filled the mainly Protestant north-east of the country with alarm. In addition to the important religious difference, the northern Unionists regarded themselves as British rather than Irish. The north's economy was different from that of the rest of the island: it was part of the British economic complex, having experienced the industrial revolution which largely missed the rest of Ireland.

Unionists would argue that the new border drawn across Ireland in 1921 was not, as nationalists claimed, an unnatural contrivance, but the recognition of existing differences. The Unionist tactic against imposition of home rule for Ireland was to threaten a revolt. In 1912 up to 100,000 men marched and drilled, and 25,000 rifles were smuggled in to arm the Ulster Volunteer Force (UVF), a private army fronted by Lord Carson and Sir James Craig. In the event of home rule, Lord Carson warned: "We will set up a government. I am told it will be illegal. Of course it will. The Volunteers are illegal, and the Government knows they are illegal, and the Government does not interfere with them. Don't be afraid of illegalities. I do not care tuppence if it is treason or not."

The coming of the First World War averted a confrontation between the Unionists and the British. When it was over, Britain opted for a compromise: home rule was granted to the twenty-six southern counties, but the six northern counties, which had a Protestant majority, were allowed to remain in the UK. Under the Government of Ireland Act 1920, these six, to be known as Ulster or Northern Ireland, were given their own parliament, which came to be known as Stormont, subordinate to Westminster.

This was a victory of sorts for Lord Carson, the Unionist Party and the UVF, but not the one they wanted. They, concerned with the integrity of the British Empire, had wanted home rule denied to the whole of Ireland. They also originally opposed the idea of having a devolved government in Belfast, being suspicious of its purpose. They were aware that many in London and Dublin saw Stormont as a device which would in time help ease the new six-county state out of the UK and into a united Ireland.

The importance of this episode lies in the moral which both sides in Northern Ireland drew from it. Nationalists said the new state was unnatural and illegitimate, having been established by the threat of force. Extreme republicans extended this argument, asserting that a state established by violence could legitimately be opposed by the same means.

The lesson taken by the Unionists, grassroots and leaders alike, was that they had been saved from a united Ireland only by their own strong right arms. And, crucially, it led them to conclude that the fledgling state had to be maintained by the same means. The settlement placed the fate of half a million Catholics in the hands of a million Protestants who regarded them with deep hostility and suspicion; and at this point Westminster withdrew from the scene.

The relationship between Britain and Unionism was left ill-defined: Westminster retained sovereignty but devolved power over most aspects of life, including security powers, to Protestant leaders who, a few years earlier, had declared themselves ready to fight Britain in order to stay British.

The six counties which made up Northern Ireland were chosen after a mathematical calculation, the object of which was to find the largest possible unit with a sufficient Protestant majority. Other counties such as Donegal and Monaghan had sizeable Protestant populations but were excluded because they included too many Catholics. Thus not merely the existence of the state, but its very shape and size, were determined by considerations of the religious balance.

From the start, the new Unionist administration treated the Catholic minority as the enemy within the gates. Unionists believed the best way of maintaining the Union was through the continuation of the existing sectarian differences, combined with the systematic exclusion of the minority from power.

On the face of it, Stormont resembled the Westminster system: it was called a parliament and had a Prime Minister, Speaker, Mace and so on. The first Prime Minister was Sir James Craig, later to become Lord Craigavon. But the system was designed so that the Unionists would remain in power permanently: the alternation of government, vital to the Westminster model, did not exist.

The exclusion system operated on many levels. The Westminster Act which set up Northern Ireland forbade religious discrimination, but successive Unionist Prime Ministers advised their followers not to employ Catholics. Beneath Stormont were 74 local councils and 30 quangos, manned by 1,400 councillors. The majority of these bodies were Unionist-controlled and exercised a great deal of power and patronage; in many places this was used to favour Protestants, especially in terms of jobs and housing.

Life in many parts of Northern Ireland was reasonably harmonious, but in a number of areas there were regular complaints of discrimination against Catholics. It is no coincidence that such areas – Armagh, Londonderry, Dungannon and Fermanagh – are among those where the 1968–9 clashes occurred, and are still affected by IRA violence today.

One striking feature of local government was that areas such as Londonderry and Fermanagh had distinct Catholic majorities, yet their councils were controlled by Unionists. Thus in 1938, for example, 32,000 Catholics elected seven councillors while 25,000 Protestants elected thirteen Unionists. A property qualification in council elections meant that a quarter of those who could vote in Westminster elections were disfranchised. This affected Catholics disproportionately.

38

Second, gerrymandering – the manipulation of boundaries – ensured that Catholics would elect a few councillors with huge majorities, while Protestant voters were spread so as to return more councillors. Since gerrymandering depended on carefully corralling voters into certain areas, it became crucially important to some councils not to disturb delicate balances by building too many houses for Catholics, thereby raising the number of Catholic voters. Some councils therefore built very few houses, or ensured that most of those built went to Protestants. The net result was that many Catholics were for decades badly housed because of the Unionist desire to obviate their voting power.

Lord Cameron, the Scottish judge appointed to report on the causes of the 1968 disorders after the first civil rights marches, noted drily: "The principal criterion in many cases was not actual need but maintenance of the current political preponderance in the local government area." Such housing practices probably caused more resentment than any other form of discrimination: to the families affected, they amounted to a daily reminder of unequal treatment for a political purpose.

Job discrimination was another cause of resentment. Prime Ministers and cabinet ministers publicly advocated giving employment to Protestants rather than to "disloyal" Catholics, and many employers followed suit. Lord Craigavon declared in 1934: "All I boast is that we are a Protestant Parliament and Protestant State." Lord Brookeborough, Prime Minister from 1943 to 1963, said: "I have not a Roman Catholic about my own place", and appealed to Unionists, wherever possible, to "employ good Protestant lads and lasses". Councils openly favoured Protestant applicants; so too did many private firms. Whole industries, such as shipbuilding and heavy engineering, employed Protestants almost exclusively. Catholic unemployment was more than twice as high as that of Protestants, and Catholics were over-represented in the less desirable semi-skilled and unskilled jobs.

Some of the patterns which developed under Stormont persist to the present day, defying official efforts at improvement. Today, Catholic male unemployment stands at 2.5 times the rate for Protestants. The Government is finalising new fair employment legislation but some elements in Northern Ireland are waging a rearguard action aimed at watering it down.

All this is not to say that everyday life for all Catholics was intolerable and oppressive. But there were everywhere reminders that the Unionist grip on power was complete. The Royal Ulster Constabulary, for example, was 90 per cent Protestant and the heavily armed official militia, the B Specials, founded in the 1920s, had no Catholic members. Almost all judges and magistrates were Protestant. Some judges, who had been Unionist MPs, had made anti-Catholic remarks during their political careers which did nothing to inspire Catholic confidence in judicial impartiality.

The system achieved an extraordinary continuity between 1921 and 1963, defeating occasional attempts to introduce class politics. Unionist unity was complete: all issues were settled within the party. Yet even when Unionist rule and the Union looked most secure, no thaw was ever attempted in the cold war between Catholic and Protestant.

Catholics reacted in a variety of ways. Their first instinct was that the new state would not survive, and they attempted to speed its demise through boycotts and abstentionism. Catholic political activity later reflected deep bitterness: they felt that they had been abandoned to their fate.

The foremost Catholic political organisation was the Nationalist Party, which had a few MPs elected to Stormont. Its representatives, mainly farmers, concentrated on appeals to "do away with the border", but avoided full participation in politics: the feeling was that doing so would tend to confer legitimacy on the Unionist system. This was also the attitude of successive Dublin governments. They took the view that Britain should simply pull out of Northern Ireland, thus achieving Irish unity. But Dublin offered no plan on how this might be done without sparking a general Unionist uprising; nor did it feel obliged at any stage to attempt to reassure Protestants that their religious rights would be safeguarded in a united Ireland.

Sinn Féin, the political wing of the IRA, was formed in 1907 and after 1916 it was the principal voice of militant republicanism. It attracted a sizeable vote at certain periods but made no sustained attempt at political activity.

The IRA staged several small-scale bursts of activity along the border, but was easily dealt with by the overwhelming weight of numbers of the RUC and B Specials, coupled with the use of internment without trial, which was first used in 1920 and repeated in every decade thereafter. At no time did the IRA pose a serious threat to the existence or even the stability of the state.

The general Catholic political attitude settled down into one of hopelessness. Neither political activity nor physical force appeared to offer a real prospect of effecting change to their situation; many therefore retreated into sullen resentment.

The Stormont system was based on keeping Protestants in control and excluding Catholics from power. With Dublin powerless and London uninterested, this was a closed world for four decades, almost hermetically sealed from outside influences. The question posed by the events of the 1960s was whether Northern Ireland could ever move away from the politics of permanent confrontation.

Troubled years from civil rights protests to Bloody Sunday and direct rule

On 5 October 1968 a few minutes of television ended Northern Ireland's political isolation from the rest of the world. They showed burly policemen using batons and water cannon to break up a civil rights march in Londonderry. Northern Ireland has rarely been out of the news since.

The attitude of various outsiders towards the situation was then, as now, one of reluctance to become involved unless there was absolutely no choice. The well-informed in both London and Dublin had been aware for some time that something was stirring in Belfast; but until 5 October they had followed their instincts and kept clear. It was the civil rights movement which succeeded in placing the issue on the national and international agenda. Yet, perhaps paradoxically, the first impetus for change had come earlier from the most unlikely of sources – within the Unionist monolith itself.

Captain Terence O'Neill, of Eton and the Brigade of Guards, made an unlikely Gorbachev. But on becoming Prime Minister in 1963 he embarked on a programme of political and economic reform as radical in Northern Ireland terms as perestroika in the USSR. He followed Lord Brookeborough who, as Prime Minister for a full two decades, had presided Brezhnev-like over a stagnant society and economy. Brookeborough, who had helped found the B Specials, was a prime example of the Unionist siege mentality and an embodiment of its slogans – "Not an inch" and "No surrender". Under O'Neill, the rhetoric changed quite suddenly: the new buzzwords were "community relations" and "bridge-building". Violating traditional taboos, he visited Catholic schools and convents and stressed the need for reform and modernisation.

O'Neill was from ancient Ulster stock, but had lived much of his life abroad and had a broader perspective than previous Unionist leaders. He had closer political and social links with Britain than they, and was more sensitive to outside influences. In 1965 he took the historic step of inviting Sean Lemass, the Taoiseach, from Dublin for talks at Stormont – the first-ever meeting of northern and southern premiers. It was an unmistakable sign that a new and less confrontational form of Unionism was in the making.

41

There were a number of reasons why O'Neill, apart from his strong personal commitment to reform, should have made change the theme of his premiership. For one thing, he had to deal with a Labour administration in London – the Wilson government came to power in 1964. The institutional links between the Unionist and Conservative parties thus ceased to be an advantage and became a liability. Labour appears to have exerted only mild pressure for reforms but, as a former Stormont finance minister, O'Neill was well aware of Northern Ireland's financial dependence on London: one third of the £300-million annual public expenditure total was provided by the British exchequer. Stormont, should it displease London, would be instantly vulnerable to financial pressure.

There were other pressing economic factors in favour of reform. Traditional industries such as shipbuilding and linen were in decline and shedding substantial numbers of jobs. New industries were needed, and O'Neill's strategy was to attract British, American and multinational companies. All efforts were bent to this purpose: generous incentives were offered and the face of large parts of the country altered as new roads, houses and advance factories were built to create a ready-made infrastructure. A completely new city, Craigavon, was mapped out to house new firms from abroad. The need was to project Northern Ireland as a modern state with prime investment potential.

In this context, the O'Neill–Lemass meeting made sense: both men were pragmatists more concerned with the economy than ideology. Both parts of Ireland had entered a phase of trying to attract foreign industry, an objective not served by any appearance of instability or hostility in the area. Writing in 1967, O'Neill alluded to this: "The whole basis of my political effort of the last four years has been to demonstrate that the historic divisions cannot be allowed forever to stand in the way of that community spirit without which we will never realise our full economic or social potential."

It was clear from the start – 1963, when he took office – that O'Neill's new approach had its opponents within various sections of Unionism. This included his cabinet, where its most able member, Brian Faulkner, was intent on displacing him. Faulkner was a pragmatist, who in later years appeared in a reforming guise, but during O'Neill's premiership presented himself as a hard-line right-winger.

Outside the party itself, the long and varied public career of the Rev Ian Paisley was beginning: his first hurrah came in 1964 when his speeches pushed the RUC into removing an Irish flag from the Falls Road, occasioning serious rioting. O'Neill regarded Paisley as an embarrassing dinosaur, but the latter's support seemed to grow as he denounced government policies as appeasement and launched an "O'Neill must go" campaign. Every year that followed saw a stream of marches and street demonstrations, some of which posed serious public order problems for the authorities. Paisley's activities helped unsettle the

Unionist monolith and put extremist pressure on the Unionist Party – in O'Neill's time and right up to the present day.

In 1966 a small group of extreme Protestants emerged as the "Ulster Volunteer Force". Fired in equal measure by misguided patriotism and a surfeit of alcohol, they killed two Catholics and a Protestant before being rounded up by the police. O'Neill had a great deal of enthusiastic support from moderate Protestants but from the start there were signs that he would face opposition – politically, on the streets and through the use of the gun.

On the Catholic side his policies were given a general welcome, though with important qualifications. The Lemass meeting won widespread Catholic approval, and the feeling was that a reforming Unionist leader was far preferable to what had gone before. At a deeper level, however, there was a Catholic sense that it was a very conditional advance – that what was on offer was simply an improved deal from a benevolent plantation owner. The suspicion was that O'Neill was the purveyor of a more intelligent Unionism, not somebody who was going to sponsor a genuine breakthrough on behalf of Catholics. This point was made in an early *Irish Times* report: "Hardliners see in Captain O'Neill's policies the danger that Northern Ireland could consolidate itself and create a prosperous, united and modern community which would make partition more permanent and a united Ireland more remote."

There was also a curious downside to the reforms themselves. Many apparently laudable modernisation moves proved, on closer examination, to benefit Protestants more than Catholics. Something went wrong between the rhetoric and the reality. Most of the new roads and factories, for example, were in the mainly Protestant east of Northern Ireland. Most of the towns zoned for industrial expansion had largely Protestant populations. In 1965 Stormont opted to site Northern Ireland's second university in Protestant Coleraine rather than Catholic Londonderry – a decision which seemed explicable only in sectarian terms. The mainly Catholic west complained of neglect. Thus the modernisation process, while ostensibly designed to benefit everyone, in fact appeared to be giving undue rewards to the supporters of Unionism. Catholic cynics saw the whole thing not as progress but as an ingenious new form of discrimination.

The civil rights movement which encountered RUC batons on the streets of Londonderry in October 1968 was the only political organisation – before or since – ever to represent the broad mass of Catholics under one umbrella with agreed aims. It was inspired by a mixture of influences, among them O'Neill's policies, which were reckoned to have promised much but delivered little; the return of a Labour government in Britain in 1964; and the American civil rights movement, from which was borrowed the tactic of peaceful marches. The coalition included students, enthused by the "Year of Revolutions" in Europe and emulating Tariq Ali or Danny the Red; a fast-growing middle class, the result of educational reforms; a Labour element, including Gerry Fitt, who had links with British Labour backbenchers; old nationalists and young radicals – and the IRA.

The 1968 IRA bore little resemblance to today's IRA. After its 1956–62 campaign fizzled out, the organisation contracted, swung to the left and became reformist rather than revolutionary; guns were put away and its statements dwelt on the need to unite Protestant and Catholic workers. The fact that the IRA had abandoned traditional methods and analysis was not, however, appreciated by Protestants, and the IRA presence within the civil rights structure was a major reason for Unionist hostility to the movement. IRA members played only a minor part in the campaign. Much more important were the articulate and ambitious John Hume and Austin Currie, who were later to lead the Social Democratic and Labour Party (SDLP) and left-wing students such as Bernadette Devlin and Michael Farrell, who mixed republicanism with revolutionary socialism.

Although militants wished to go further, a set of demands was agreed, concentrating on local government voting reforms, an end to discrimination in housing and jobs and the repeal of draconian anti-IRA legislation. The 5 October protest in Londonderry followed a successful march in Co Tyrone complaining about housing discrimination. Opinion was divided on whether to go ahead with the march but the situation was transformed, and unity assured, when Stormont imposed a ban.

The 2,000-strong march went ahead, and when it reached a police cordon, the physical clashes came: Lord Cameron's report into the disorders later concluded that police officers had used their weapons indiscriminately and without justification. Television pictures showing police enthusiastically batoning the crowd and marchers with blood pouring from head wounds ensured that the event was the greatest political catalyst ever seen in Northern Ireland. World attention was attracted; the embryo civil rights movement swelled and plans were laid for more marches; Harold Wilson summoned O'Neill to Downing Street for urgent talks on reform. For once the cliché was justified: nothing was ever quite the same again.

More marches quickly followed but a new element emerged. In many places, Paisleyite counter-demonstrations were held or threatened, leading to a steep increase in tension. Moderates in the movement wanted to suspend the marches but the militants favoured confrontation. Serious violence finally erupted at Burntollet Bridge in January 1969, when a student march from Belfast to Londonderry was ambushed by loyalist extremists with stones and cudgels. Rioting followed in Londonderry city.

By this stage, events were moving at a bewildering pace. Westminster had for years been relatively immune to the blandishments of Irish nationalism, but was

44

much more vulnerable to the civil rights arguments and now pushed hard for reform. For the first time in almost 50 years a wedge had been driven between Stormont and Westminster. The performance of the Unionist government, together with the televised activities of the RUC and the Rev Ian Paisley, left it with few sympathisers outside Northern Ireland. The Catholic minority's tactical shift from demanding Irish unity to asking for civil rights within Northern Ireland proved devastatingly difficult for Unionism. It was similar to letting the rope go a little in a tug of war; the Unionists could not cope.

On questions of discrimination, the old Unionist argument – that it was justified on the grounds that Catholics represented a danger to the state – was no longer respectable or usable. Stormont therefore fell back on the assertion that no inequalities existed, a case which it failed to make convincingly. Rarely has a propaganda battle been so decisively lost.

It was too much for O'Neill and he resigned in April 1969, criticising Faulkner's machinations. He was brought down by several factors, principally his inability to balance hardline Unionist demands with reform pressure from the civil rights movement and Westminster. This was probably beyond the capabilities of any man.

Support for O'Neill had ebbed away as rising tensions and physical clashes created a highly charged atmosphere. The Unionist monolith was split asunder. Some Protestants backed O'Neill; others preferred politicians such as Faulkner, who were less committed to reform; still others supported Paisley. In essence, O'Neill lost control of events and of his own party. He had not put the Unionist machine together and did not know what to do when it started coming apart.

His successor as Prime Minister, Major James Chichester-Clark, was a hapless aristocrat who had no more luck in bringing events under control. After sporadic disturbances, in August 1969 a riot during a loyalist march in Londonderry developed into a major confrontation between the RUC and Catholics in the Bogside district. The disturbances spread to Belfast, where protracted large-scale fighting developed, with the RUC, B Specials and Protestants clashing with Catholics in the north and west of the city. Suddenly the state itself seemed unstable, as two types of running battle ensued. In the Bogside, residents held off the RUC for days; in Belfast, the police failed to hold back Protestants attacking the Catholic Falls Road district.

Although neither Stormont nor Westminster wanted to call in British troops, it became clear that the RUC was an exhausted force desperately in need of reinforcement. In August 1969, when there was no other option, the soldiers were ordered in. Most observers assumed they would be withdrawn after a short operation to restore order: none guessed their stay would be measured not in weeks or months but in decades.

The deployment of the military was another historic moment since, constitutionally, the Northern Ireland government could not control British troops. This meant that Britain had, after almost 50 years on the sidelines, taken over direct responsibility for security from Stormont – a major diminution in the powers of Unionism.

When the smoke cleared, the cost of the August disturbances could be counted: seven people were dead and 750 injured. Millions of pounds of damage was caused to property and 1,800 families, 1,500 of them Catholic, had fled their homes. It was the worst outbreak of violence for a decade: again, none guessed that it was just the start of a trail of death which continues today.

For a moment after August 1969 everyone recoiled in horror at the re-emergence of primal passions assumed to be long dead; but the violence did not stop. The various factions crystallised: it was a formative period during which most of the patterns still evident today emerged. The demarcation lines were drawn for the next two decades of disturbance.

Unionism was divided. Within the old party various factions continued to struggle with each other, while outside Paisley won seats in both Stormont and Westminster and set up his own party. Large working-class loyalist paramilitary groups, such as the Ulster Defence Association, emerged holding menacing marches and carrying out sectarian assassinations.

On the Catholic side John Hume and other moderates formed the Social Democratic and Labour Party and broadened the complaints about discrimination in jobs and housing to direct demands for participation in government.

The IRA split into the Marxist Officials and the violent Provisionals: the latter began to bomb Belfast in mid-1970 and early the following year shot the first soldier to die in the Troubles. The Republic, which during August 1969 had moved troops to the border and trembled on the brink of intervention, abandoned such notions of adventurism and instead aligned itself, to a large extent, with the SDLP.

Stormont's last chance came with Chichester-Clark's resignation and a final attempt by his successor, Brian Faulkner, to restore order with a mixture of reforms and tough security measures. But internment without trial, introduced in August 1971, was followed not only by a veritable explosion of violence and scores of deaths, but by a widespread Catholic campaign of civil disobedience and withdrawal from public life.

The Army, whose arrival had been welcomed by Catholics, was now treated as a hostile force and attacked. Catholic estrangement became almost total when 13 people taking part in a march in Londonderry were shot dead by troops on what came to be called "Bloody Sunday". Edward Heath, the then Prime Minister, concluded that Unionism no longer had the capacity to preserve order in Northern Ireland, and in March 1972, with the stroke of a pen, he abolished Stormont, the system which had stood for half a century.

Lingering agony of an unloved orphan state

A generation which has never known peace has grown up in Northern Ireland in the past 20 years. Not a year has gone by without serious violence and disturbance. Thousands of people have been killed; many thousands injured or bereaved; thousands have been to jail. Thousands more are involved in paramilitary activity, or will become involved: they will kill and perhaps be killed.

In some parts of Belfast, Protestants and Catholics are separated by 20-foot-high steel walls. No one under the age of 26 can remember a society without regular bombings and shootings; without soldiers on the streets; without police with rifles and sub-machine-guns. Abnormality has become the norm.

The problem is, at root, one of nationality: of whether Northern Ireland is to be treated as British, or Irish, or a bit of both. It is currently part of the United Kingdom, though not an integral one. For 60 years Britain's position has been that it would become part of a united Ireland if a majority of the Northern Ireland people wished it. Disputes of nationality are notoriously difficult to resolve. Acceptable compromise is almost impossible, yet attempting to impose one nationality or the other is scarcely more satisfactory. It probably would not work; and if it did it would mean victory for one side and defeat for the other – a recipe for lasting bitterness. The two communities in Northern Ireland seek closer links with either Britain or the Irish Republic, both of which, under a thin veneer of rhetoric, wish to have less rather than more contact. After 20 years of hatred and violence Northern Ireland is an unloved orphan state.

While British policy has varied over the past two decades, the reluctance to become more involved than is absolutely necessary has been constant. The desire to keep British intervention to a minimum has been evident over the years. It was visible in the urge, immediately Stormont was abolished, to reassemble with all haste a devolved government in Belfast. The crucial difference in the scheme which Edward Heath, the then Prime Minister, and William Whitelaw, the first Secretary of State for Northern Ireland, envisaged as Stormont's replacement was that Protestant ascendancy would be replaced by Catholic participation.

It was this central principle which dominated policy in the early years of direct

47

rule. The theory was that Unionism had failed to preserve order through its insistence on excluding Catholics from power. John Hume's Social Democratic and Labour Party was pressing for the right to share power. Therefore, the theory ran, the way to stabilise the state was to reassemble Stormont with a Catholic component. It was thought that a coalition of the two religions would isolate the extremists on both sides and Catholics could be brought to identify with the state as they never had before. Looking much further ahead, Protestant–Catholic relations could improve to the point where Protestants might at some future time drop their objections to unification.

Against considerable odds, Heath and Whitelaw succeeded in putting together such a coalition in 1974, with Brian Faulkner and John Hume sitting together in a powersharing administration at Stormont, with links to Dublin. It lasted only five months, before being brought down by a loyalist general strike supported by a majority of Protestants. Within two weeks the stoppage brought Northern Ireland to a standstill and the executive collapsed.

Despite protests that the strike had succeeded largely because of a weak response by Merlyn Rees, the new and inexperienced Labour Secretary of State, the moral drawn from the stoppage was that Unionists had demonstrated their power to veto any arrangement of which they disapproved. That element of Unionism which had been prepared to share power virtually disappeared overnight. Thereafter, the principle that Catholics must be got into government was matched by the belief that Protestants would not have them. It was at this point that most London and Dublin politicians lost interest, concluding that nothing could be done.

In the years that followed, Britain continued to hold out the prospect of devolution on a partnership basis. But the main Unionist parties stuck rigidly to the principle that they would not share power with the SDLP. They offered to consider safeguards for Catholics, but were adamant that any new Stormont must be run on the old basis, majority rule. When one Unionist leader, William Craig, broke ranks in 1976 to advocate a form of powersharing, he was expelled from the Unionist umbrella group of the day, losing his support, his party, and his Westminster seat in quick succession.

Politicians gradually came to terms with the idea that direct rule, far from being a quick holding operation while a new devolved administration was constructed, was to be the means of running Northern Ireland for an indefinite period. A series of ministers and civil servants at the Northern Ireland Office watched constantly for signs of political movement, but in its absence became resigned to holding the fort.

The idea arose, when Roy Mason was Secretary of State in the late 1970s, that direct rule was not simply a regrettable necessity but a system which could itself have beneficial effects. The local parties were as far apart as ever, but the economy showed signs of picking up, and large amounts of public money were poured into the De Lorean car project in Belfast, which was to be the forerunner of a new wave of American investment. The aim was to demonstrate to Catholics that an end of terrorism could bring jobs and prosperity. At the same time, violence from both loyalist paramilitary groups and the IRA significantly decreased. An attempt at a second loyalist strike failed.

Internment had ended in 1975, but the IRA was hit hard by the security strategy which replaced it. This consisted of extracting confessions from IRA suspects in specially designed interrogation centres, principally at Castlereagh in Belfast. The confessions were usually enough to secure convictions, and a steady stream of IRA members was imprisoned. There were rumours that the IRA, which was undoubtedly much weakened, might be forced into a ceasefire. Roy Mason said: "My view is that their strength has waned to the point where they cannot sustain a campaign."

He was wrong. Within a few months the IRA staged a comeback, assassinating Lord Mountbatten and on the same day killing 18 soldiers at Warrenpoint. Allegations of ill-treatment of suspects at Castlereagh brought closer monitoring of interrogations and the confessions virtually stopped. The De Lorean project disintegrated, taking with it almost £80 million of taxpayers' money and any hopes of large-scale US investment. The episode marked the last time a government has believed the IRA could be defeated by military means alone, and the last time anyone believed direct rule might itself constitute a solution.

The Thatcher years have demonstrated that the Prime Minister has no particularly settled views on Northern Ireland, beyond a characteristic desire to stand up to terrorism. She sent one minister, Humphrey Atkins, to Northern Ireland as a reward and demoted two others, Jim Prior and Tom King, to what Prior described in a disgruntled moment as the dustbin of British politics. The attention she gives to the problem is intermittent, her policies changeable. Ireland has few pleasant connotations for her: her friend Airey Neave, a Conservative spokesman on Northern Ireland, died in a bombing and the IRA came close to killing her in Brighton in 1984.

Her relations with Dublin have at times been friendly and on other occasions frigid. She was thought to have Unionist sympathies, but in 1985 she signed the Anglo-Irish agreement which caused Protestants to burn her in effigy on the streets of Belfast. That act transformed her from a friend of Unionism into, in the words of Unionist MPs, a traitor and a Jezebel.

In February 1987 the Republic went to the polls. The result was a "hung" Dáil, no party securing an overall majority. But Fianna Fáil won most seats and Charles Haughey replaced Garret FitzGerald as Taoiseach, governing with the support of small parties and independent members.

His return to power represented an extraordinary revival in the fortunes of a politician who had more than once been written off. It was an important moment for the Anglo-Irish agreement: its nationalist supporters worried, and its Unionist opponents hoped, that the new Taoiseach would scrap it. It was an ironic moment for Unionists, in that they were hoping to be rescued by the politician they had always regarded as a bogey man. He had been extremely critical of the accord while in opposition, but in the event he swallowed his pride and learnt to live reasonably amicably with an agreement he had once denounced.

PROFILE

Charles Haughey, the rogue who returned from beyond the pale

C harles J. Haughey, known variously as Charlie, C.J. or simply The Boss, is the most controversial figure in modern Irish politics. He may be on the point of becoming Taoiseach for the third time in an extraordinary career. Yet many in Ireland question not his policies but his fitness for public office. Haughey excites both loathing and adulation. In a series of Irish cities, towns and villages he has been mobbed by adoring crowds. To them he offers hope; to others he personifies the darker side of the Irish political character.

51

While Garret FitzGerald, his archenemy of the past decade, has been the decent man unable to translate good intentions into practice, Haughey has deployed his formidable political skills in pursuit of a single goal – power. In the process he has managed to frustrate many of FitzGerald's attempts to create a secular and more liberal Republic.

Haughey has several times returned from the near-dead in a manner which his enemies – and he has many – compare unflatteringly with the career of Richard Nixon. His inner drive has seen him through many crises. Some of his enemies are literally frightened by the strength of his tenacity and what they view as a lust for power. His severest critic, Conor Cruise O'Brien, says he fears for the survival of democracy in the Republic, should Haughey win the election. Few go as far as Cruise O'Brien, but many have expressed concern about his approach to politics. A senior member of his own Fianna Fáil party once spoke pointedly of "low standards in high places". FitzGerald (in a speech he later regretted) spoke of Haughey's "flawed pedigree".

His critics find fault with almost every aspect of his career. He has a reputation for vindictiveness and a notorious taste for settling old scores. When he entered politics he was one of a new breed in Fianna Fáil. The old party, rural-based, solid and traditional, was transformed by a wave of entrepreneurs – brash, flamboyant, self-made men with their initials on their cufflinks. They were known as "the men in the mohair suits", and Haughey was foremost among them. He departed from the Irish political tradition of affected reticence, making no secret of his ambitions. Today he is as ostentatious as ever – he lives in a north Dublin mansion and owns his own west coast island – though his private life is less colourful. And he has grafted onto his sharp businessman's image the idea that he embodies the essence of Ireland itself. His collected speeches are entitled *The Spirit of the Nation*.

An accountant by profession, Haughey had got rich quick by the time he entered the Dáil in 1957. Critics want to know where so much money came from so quickly, but he will not discuss his personal finances. Within months he had been given minor office and four years later he was, at the age of 36, Minister for Justice. Here the charge is nepotism: the Taoiseach who promoted him was Sean Lemass, his father-in-law. That particular accusation will not stick. Haughey had quickly distinguished himself through his ability and intelligence. He proved to be an imaginative and energetic minister helping to accomplish, among other things, the defeat of the IRA campaign of 1956–62.

By the time of Lemass's retirement in 1966 Haughey headed a significant faction and was a contender for the leadership. But the prize eluded him: fearing a divisive contest between the old guard and the new men, the party united around a compromise candidate, Jack Lynch. Although Lynch went on to become, in Fianna Fáil terms, one of its great leaders, those two factions remained at war with each other for almost two decades. The battle ended only when Haughey finally expelled Des O'Malley, his remaining significant enemy, from the party in 1985.

Yet in 1970 Haughey's career looked to be in ruins. In that year he was dismissed by Lynch, arrested and charged with conspiring to import arms illegally. The guns, it was alleged, were for the defence of Catholics in Northern Ireland against marauding loyalist extremists. Haughey and another cabinet minister contradicted each other in court. FitzGerald's "flawed pedigree" remark relates to this episode, although Haughey was acquitted by a High Court jury. There followed long, bitter years in the wilderness as Lynch kept him off the front bench.

For seven years Haughey ate crow. He started at the bottom, working his way round the country to rebuild his credibility. It was a terrible ordeal but he refused to regard it as humiliation: rather, he used it to prove his loyalty to Fianna Fáil. Some of the critics say those seven years of grind deadened his soul: power can corrupt but so can the lack of it. His ambition and his determination sustained him until 1979, when Lynch went, and Haughey, triumphant at last, took his place. He brought with him to power some frankly awful cronies – men who had stood by him in the wilderness years. Prizing loyalty above ability, he has wound up with an unimpressive team. He thinks nothing of contradicting and correcting their public utterances. His press officer once described his style with the memorable quotation: *Uno Duce, una voce.*

The old guard have never accepted him, and his years as leader have been marked by a series of highly disruptive heaves aimed at removing him. His superior in-fighting skills eventually banished his rivals, but in the process it became clear that many traditional Fianna Fáil voters baulked at supporting him. As a result he has never won an overall majority in the Dáil. Furthermore, his banished rival, O'Malley, has successfully launched the Progressive Democrats, which might deny him his majority again.

In 1982 Haughey was the head of a minority Fianna Fáil administration, struggling desperately to hold on to power. His efforts made it one of the most extraordinary years in Irish politics. To secure the support of Tony Gregory, a young left-wing independent, Haughey visited him in his rundown office. According to Gregory: "He walked in, put the briefcase on the table and said, 'Right lads, you know what I want – tell me what you want.'" Gregory asked for, and received, a most remarkable deal. In a ceremony witnessed by a trade union leader, Haughey signed a 30-page document committing the government to spend about IR£100 million in Gregory's constituency. His own party gasped when he appointed a Fine Gael opponent as Ireland's European Commissioner, simply in order to cause a by-election.

He threw money at a succession of pressure groups, putting the country into catastrophic foreign debt. His Justice Minister tapped the phones of two respected political correspondents in the name of national security – the actual purpose was to collect material on his opponents within Fianna Fáil. A pro-Haughey cabinet minister bugged a meeting with an anti-Haughey minister, using equipment supplied by a senior Garda officer. There were other reports of improper political use of the police force.

Haughey's election agent was charged with voting twice. (The charge was dropped but he has been known ever since as Pat O'Connor, Pat O'Connor.) A double murderer on the run was apprehended in the home of the Attorney General. His administration collapsed in a welter of such scandals and mis-adventures. Haughey lost the support of many voters who had viewed him as a rogue but none the less an effective manager. He seemed dogged by poor judgement, incompetent and divided colleagues, and terrible luck.

Haughey's rhetoric has often, in traditional Fianna Fáil fashion, had a strong anti-British flavour. "Is there any manliness left," he once asked FitzGerald in the Dáil, "or is the government going to grovel for ever to these people?"

Both of his parents came from south Londonderry, a particularly hardline republican area, and both were involved with the IRA in the Twenties. As an undergraduate in 1945, he helped burn a Union Jack in Dublin on VE day. Yet in office he worked well enough with Britain: certainly the RUC had no complaints about the level of security co-operation. He cultivated a reasonable relationship with Margaret Thatcher, but it fell apart when she refused his advice to show more flexibility during the Maze prison hunger strikes. And she lost her temper completely when he withdrew support for Britain in the Falklands conflict after the sinking of the *Belgrano*.

He has criticised the Anglo-Irish agreement even though he could lay reason-able claim to be one of its architects. Where FitzGerald had hoped for Unionist–nationalist powersharing within Northern Ireland, Haughey correctly saw that a Dublin–London alignment held greater prospects for nationalist advance-ment. When the agreement came, however, he denounced it as a historic sell-out, claiming an Irish government had for the first time formally recognised the legitimacy of the British presence in the north. But the consensus in the Republic – and among most northern nationalists – was that Haughey's point was highly abstract and paled into insignificance in comparison with the practical gain of achieving a say in the running of Northern Ireland. He went down sharply in the opinion polls and was forced to soften his criticisms. The general feeling now is that the agreement is too popular for him to scrap, no matter how much he resents the fact that it bears FitzGerald's name.

The election is Haughey's last chance. He has three times failed to gain an overall majority, and the party will not forgive a fourth failure. Whatever the result, this extraordinary man has already left a deep mark on Irish politics.

Mr Haughey returned as head of a minority administration, and his behaviour in office shattered one Unionist dream – the hope that, having opposed the agreement while in opposition, he would proceed to dismantle it. Another such hope disappeared with the Westminster election of June 1987, as Mrs Thatcher swept back to power with an increased majority. This dashed the Unionist hope that their MPs might hold the balance of power in a "hung" parliament.

As usual, the contest in Northern Ireland had its own unique characteristics.

25 MAY 1987   THE INDEPENDENT

The early and often tradition lives on

In spite of elaborate precautions by the authorities, party apparatchiks in Northern Ireland are plotting ways of following the ancient Irish political precept – vote early and vote often. The traditional art of personation, vote-stealing, has been inhibited by a recent tightening of legislation, but no one considers it completely dead. A great deal of ingenuity is being put into the search for loopholes.

In Northern Ireland – and to a lesser extent in the south – personation is simply the stuff of normal politics. MPs who publicly condemn it will in private cheerfully admit their complicity in the practice, and swap stories about how it was in the old days. The folklore is full of stories of people who voted 10, 20 or 30 times. Gerry Fitt, who fought 23 elections in the sectarian cockpit of west Belfast before retiring to the House of Lords, recalls polling stations where the turnout bafflingly exceeded 100 per cent.

The crucial loophole in the law was that people suspected of casting someone else's vote could be challenged only by a "personation agent" appointed by one of the candidates. The police and polling clerks were statutorily forbidden to apprehend anyone attempting to vote – even a person who showed up 20 times.

A station discovered to be without a personation agent for the other side was known, Gerry Fitt recalls, as "an open box". Every effort would be made to "riddle the box" – pushing in as many personators as possible. Officials at the station would helplessly watch the illegal parade. One clerk said: "Sometimes I'd get fed up with it and try to embarrass them. I'd say, 'Long time no see' or 'Welcome back'. But usually it didn't faze them." Houses and halls were set aside as "dressing stations", where the personators would sometimes go for a change of clothes. Complicity in these activities went right to the top. One woman campaign volunteer recalls a former Unionist Prime Minister shaking her hand and urging her to "vote early and vote often".

Yet it was not anarchy: the system might have been corrupt, but it had carefully observed rules. Most contests were straight fights between a Unionist and a nationalist, and the strict understanding was, in the words of an MP now seeking re-election, that "You only did your own side." In other words, Unionist campaigners only personated Protestant votes; and nationalist candidates only "plugged" Catholic votes. It was a gentleman's agreement, aimed at maximising one's own vote. But the whole thing, of course, did little for the general image of politics. In some areas the convention was that no attempt was made to challenge the other side's personators. To do so, it was understood, was to invite retaliation which could escalate into all-out war. This cosy arrangement was put under strain in the early Seventies when the two-party system fell apart. A whole series of smaller parties emerged and great changes ensued, but personation persisted. A leading electoral expert says privately that he has yet to find a party which does not cheat.

The whole system got out of hand, however, when Sinn Féin burst on to the voting scene in the early 1980s. The effect was described, with disarming frankness, by the Unionist MP Harold McCusker in the Commons: "In the comparatively recent past there occurred benign personation, practised by both sides, operated by both sides and with unwritten rules. But that has now changed because Sinn Féin have broken the rules. They have engaged in vote-stealing on a massive scale."

What Sinn Féin did was to cast the old conventions aside, "plugging" as many votes as possible. Large teams of bogus voters were used. Personation reached a crescendo: in the 1983 Westminster election there were 149 arrests and at least 949 people arrived at the polls to find that their votes had already been cast. Unforgiveably, Sinn Féin stole Protestant votes as well as Catholic ones. The other parties howled in protest that the whole system had been brought into disrepute.

The result was a major tightening of the legislation: voters must now produce proof of identity. This has apparently reduced polling-day cheating, for in by-elections last year only one arrest was made. But experts say the new legislation has major flaws, and fear it may simply shift the focus of abuse. The rules on proxy voting and postal voting have been cast extremely wide. They are, in the ominous words of one party official, "a mechanism well worth exploiting".

The 1987 general election brought the defeat of Enoch Powell, who for thirteen years had represented South Down in the Commons. During that time he had been, as well as a nationally known figure, one of Unionism's chief theorists and strategists. Margaret Thatcher and many other Conservatives respected him, and within Unionism he had a close personal and political relationship with James Molyneaux, the Ulster Unionist Party leader. In this way his ideas played a key role, for more than a decade, in helping to shape Unionist policy.

[This examination of his role, written for the *Irish Times* in 1983, was updated in 1989.]

PROFILE

The integrationists: James Molyneaux and Enoch Powell   BOBBY HANVEY

The gospel of Enoch

E noch Powell succeeded in placing the idea of integrating Northern Ireland with Britain back on the Unionist agenda after an absence of 50 years. It had been Lord Carson's preferred option, but the existence of Stormont for half a century brought Unionism to believe its interests were best served by a system of devolution. Powell resurrected the integrationist theory and convinced Molyneaux of its correctness; this meant that the largest Unionist party, which was in the main devolutionist, had at its head an integrationist. Molyneaux did a great deal, often surreptitiously, to ensure that devolution did not become a reality; and always Powell stood behind him, supplying the theory which guided his leader's actions.

He always remained steadfast in his central belief, which was that the key to the problems of Northern Ireland could be summed up in a single word – certainty. His thesis was that the violence was caused by the uncertainty which surrounded the attitudes of successive British governments. "Nobody knows for sure – neither friend, foe, citizen or alien – where the British government stands," he complained in 1972. Eleven years later, he rose in the Commons to make the same point during a debate on the Falkland Islands.

His argument was that just as General Galtieri had been encouraged to invade the Falklands by the uncertainty surrounding Britain's desire to hold on to the islands, so too were enemies closer to home encouraged by ambiguous British attitudes towards Northern Ireland. If it were made perfectly clear to the IRA and its allies that they had absolutely no hope of separating Northern Ireland from Britain, the theory runs, they would then eventually realise there was no point in fighting on and throw in the towel. Time and again, Powell has made this point.

"It is hope in relation to which the mercury of violence rises and falls in the gauge," he said in January 1971. "It is that uncertainty which nourishes the hope and strengthens the hands of the enemy," he said the following year. "The violence feeds upon ambiguity. Ambiguity gives the green light to murder," he declared in 1974.

As is his wont, Powell has from the beginning pursued his theory to its logical conclusion. Thus, remarkably, he was an integrationist even while Stormont was still in existence, and if he never actually advocated its abolition, he made no secret of his belief that Unionists would be better off without it. In January 1971 he spoke disparagingly of "the quaint anomaly of a narrow-gauge parliament and government" and declared: "Stormont itself is a threat to the so-called link with Britain because it is an assertion of separateness." He made this speech to a Unionist audience, and it was well received – even though it struck at the heart of the orthodox Unionist belief that Stormont helped cement the Union. Perhaps his listeners did not grasp his meaning; or perhaps they were simply pleased at the rarity of an MP from England siding so openly with their cause.

Powell told me recently: "I would not have advocated, or wished to see, in the years before 1969, a disturbance of what was running." But after Westminster's intervention, necessitated by the deployment of the British Army in Northern Ireland, he clearly came to see any move to revive Stormont as one of the causes of the uncertainty.

In the early years of the 1970s Powell became increasingly identified with the Unionist cause, though not necessarily with that section which went on to become, after the split with Brian Faulkner, the Official Unionist Party. He supported the reform programme, his argument being (of course) that the reforms brought the Northern Ireland law and administration more closely into line with those of the rest of the UK.

It seems ironic that when Stormont fell in March 1972, Powell opposed direct rule. This was not because he wished to retain Stormont but, he explained, because the form of direct rule introduced served to mark "in a special and unique way, the separateness of the Six Counties from the rest of the United Kingdom and not their unity with it".

Thereafter, he opposed "all the fiddle-faddle about conferences and constitutions and fancy franchises" – in other words, the efforts of William Whitelaw which were to lead to the introduction of powersharing and an Irish dimension. Instead, he advocated "thorough-going total integration and unification of the Six Counties of Northern Ireland with the rest of the United Kingdom". Powersharing, he declared extravagantly, was "an outrage, an absurdity, a chimera, a monstrosity". He wept no tears when the Sunningdale agreement collapsed, though the methods by which the loyalists brought it down were not those which he would have chosen. "As a parliamentarian, the use of any action other than the ballot box to influence the behaviour of parliament and government is abhorrent to me," he told me. "You're entitled to say to me, here is action of which you disapprove and it produced a result of which you do approve. Yes, you're entitled to say that, but I'm entitled to say that that's life."

Late in 1973 it had been rumoured that Powell might join the Unionists but it was not until a year later that he fought, and won, South Down. It is often said that he was desperate for a parliamentary seat, and went to Northern Ireland out of necessity, but this is unfair. When Edward Heath called an election during the miners' strike of February 1974, Powell simply refused to stand, on the principled if rather eccentric grounds that he did not agree with the reason for having an election. He was thus out of Parliament by his own choice, and had it not been for Harold Wilson's action in calling another election eight months later, he would have been absent from the Commons for four or five years.

Membership of the Official Unionists brought problems for Powell. Chief among these was the fact that his new party was firmly committed to devolution; so too was the United Ulster Unionist Council, the uneasy coalition it formed with Ian Paisley's Democratic Unionist Party and William Craig's Vanguard party. Yet in public he managed to reconcile his beliefs with mainstream loyalism's attachment to devolution.

When I mentioned the word "integration" to Powell, he said: "Integration is, of course, a propaganda word used by the enemies of the Union." He had forgotten that he used to use the word himself. The reason he had forgotten was that since becoming a Unionist MP he had displayed an uncharacteristic circumspection on this vital point of policy. As Tory MP for Wolverhampton, he was free in calling openly and unequivocally for integration, but as a Unionist MP for South Down he has found it advisable to fudge. He has, in fact, deliberately contrived to produce that ambiguity of meaning of which he accuses successive British governments.

A senior Conservative, an admirer of Powell's, says that he has compromised on the issue of devolution and the Union in a way that he has never compromised on any other issue in his political career. Yet the compromise has been in the way he has expressed his beliefs, not the beliefs themselves. His commitment to integration has never wavered.

The two measures he has advocated for at least nine years – extra Northern Ireland seats in the Commons and a reform of local government structures in the north – are both clearly integrationist in character. The extra seats have been granted, due principally to Powell; and Northern Ireland returns 17 rather than 12 MPs to Westminster. The extra five seats, for which Powell fought so long, mean that Northern Ireland will henceforth be represented in the Commons on the same basis as the other parts of the UK, according to population. This, Powell argues, helps to guarantee the Union. It is an integrationist measure in a number of ways – it places the emphasis on Westminster and it will make more potential seats available to ambitious politicians and thus encourage them to focus on the Commons rather than a devolved assembly.

It will also have an obvious symbolic significance, though it has to be said that while the SDLP have been offended by the move, few Unionists and scarcely any MPs at Westminster view it as a gesture intended to strengthen the Union. Hardly anyone agrees with Powell's description of the extra seats as "the great achievement of Ulster Unionism in the last 10 years", or with his declaration: "The importance of the event cannot be overestimated – we must now make it the means of winning the war itself."

Powell is unperturbed by the fact that the extra seats came not as a gesture of solidarity with Northern Ireland, but as a reluctant concession to himself and James Molyneaux at a time when Jim Callaghan and Michael Foot were anxious to secure Unionist goodwill for the last (minority) Labour government. He told me: "That is how things happen – one maintains a position and, eventually, events reward you, they give you what you were wanting. You remain there with your hands open, or your mouth open, and the wind shakes the tree and the pear falls."

So far in this survey of Enoch Powell and the Irish question, it is difficult to withhold a certain respect for the consistency of his approach, the determination of his efforts and the measure of success he has achieved. But in 1979 a new and extraordinary element suddenly appeared in his analysis. He came to believe, and still believes, in a conspiracy theory more grandiose, more fantastic, more breathtaking than anything ever propagated by Ian Paisley.

"I was slow, I admit it, to understand the full devilry of the United Kingdom's policy towards Northern Ireland from 1920 onwards," he told me. In summary, Powell believes that for decades a conspiracy has existed to push Northern Ireland into an all-Ireland republic. Involved in this conspiracy are British government officials, British ministers, successive governments in the Republic, the American State Department and NATO. The key, he thinks, lies with NATO. He said: "We now know that since 1948 the Republic of Ireland has had a leverage directly and indirectly upon the United Kingdom, through the desire of the United States, the United Kingdom and NATO not to see what is called a gap in NATO." In other words, America, NATO and elements in UK governments favour uniting Ireland in the hope that a united Ireland would join NATO.

Powell continued: "People say, 'Ah yes, but the Irish Republic never would go into NATO, so this can't be true.' They forget that people cheat. The Irish Republic has used the desire of NATO to have Ireland in the western alliance as a lever – without necessarily either intending, or being able, to deliver if its terms were fulfilled. Its object is to get its terms fulfilled and then cheat, bilk the other party."

He says that for decades the strategy of the Republic, supported by various treacherous or foolish British elements, has been to achieve devolution for Northern Ireland. He cites John Bowman's book, *De Valera and the Ulster Question*, as "marvellously setting out" the Republic's approach. Thus, to his mind, devolution is shown to be inherently perilous.

He believes that in October 1979, not long after the assassination of Lord Mountbatten and the killing of 18 British soldiers at Warrenpoint, British and Irish officials entered into a secret agreement, "in return for an undeliverable and unspecified promise of co-operation against the IRA". He has said: "Britain undertook to institute a process which would lead, through a series of planned stages, to the absorption of Ulster into an all-Ireland state." At the Thatcher–Haughey summit of December 1980 the Prime Minister misguidedly authorised a plan "which officials of the two countries had prepared behind her back".

By 1982 Powell had come to the conclusion that the grand conspiracy included the IRA. He said in a speech: "What then was the object of [successive] British governments? A united Ireland. Who were their allies? The [American] State Department, with its eyes upon Ireland as a strategic position, and the Irish Republic, with its eyes upon the proclaimed aspiration of that country. What was their instrument? The IRA and international terrorism. What were the methods? Outrage, murder and assassination. Who were the victims? The people of Ulster, the people of Britain and successive generations of British politicians."

Twice in one Commons debate Powell used the phrase "those who operate the terrorists". I asked him who he meant. "Well, we must ask *cui bono* [who profited by it]? And we know *cui bono*. We know that it is a long-term objective of the United States government and NATO that the island of Ireland should be brought some way or another into the Alliance. And we also know that what the United States thinks is desirable is sought to be brought about by methods not all of which would always bear public examination."

Not even Paisley claims that the British and American governments might be actually controlling the IRA and conniving at killings. But Powell believes in a vast web of conspiracy, decades old and spanning not just the Irish Sea, but the Atlantic also. He believes, for example, that Charles Haughey's government controlled the IRA's hunger strike – it "had it in its power directly or indirectly to manipulate, to switch on or to switch off, according to convenience".

In 1982 Powell produced a sort of South Down Zinoviev letter: an alleged transcript of remarks made by a Northern Ireland Office civil servant who was said to have advocated Irish unity. The document was inherently incredible and did not stand up to more than the most cursory scrutiny. Yet Powell believes in it implicitly. The civil servants in his conspiracy, he has said, work by "subversion, bribery or deceit", and to his mind the document tended to demonstrate this. His faith in the document showed a serious lack of judgement.

Powell's famously logical mind has made an illogical leap. He moved from noting that most people did not accept his views to believing that those who disagreed with him were in league, working together covertly to wrench Northern Ireland out of the United Kingdom. Furthermore, he believes there are no methods, murder included, to which they will not stoop. Perhaps the most telling comment on the impact of his campaign is that no one, with the possible exception of James Molyneaux, accepts his grand conspiracy theory.

The theory may have a psychological base. Powell thinks that all sensible people should see that constitutional certainty is the solution for Northern Ireland, and wonders why the authorities do not accept this idea and act upon it. To attempt to explain why, he has conjured up the notion of huge but invisible sinister forces acting behind the scenes. Governments have not acted upon his advice, he has come to believe, because more powerful influences have forced them not to: NATO and the CIA, acting through the Foreign Office, have thwarted him. Thus is his own lack of success with governments rationalised and explained.

Some thought, when Powell became a full-time recruit to the Unionist cause in 1974, that he might be a figure strong enough to unite Unionism. His intellectual power was obvious, and his speeches on race in Britain showed he knew how to stir populist feelings. But in the event he made no bid for the leadership of Unionism, opting instead to work behind the scenes. From the late Seventies on, he clearly set himself three main targets to influence – James Molyneaux, Margaret Thatcher and the House of Commons in general. With Molyneaux his success was almost complete: he was clearly the biggest influence on the man who, from 1979 on, led the Ulster Unionist Party. Time after time Molyneaux steered the party away from devolution.

Powell brought with him to the Unionist Party the admiration of 30 or 40 Tory right-wingers, almost all of whom he convinced that integration was preferable to devolution. In the longer term, however, this may have been more of a drawback than an advantage in that it helped to create, in the minds of Molyneaux and the other Unionist MPs, the false impression that they were not isolated in the Commons. There were no sustained attempts to forge links with other sections of parliamentary opinion inside or outside the Conservative Party. And Powell's presence among the Unionists helped define Unionism, in the minds of most MPs, as a far-right, old-fashioned and slightly eccentric minority. The respect he commanded as a parliamentarian did not translate into political influence.

This was crucial in 1983–4, as the feeling grew in Whitehall and Westminster that some new Northern Ireland initiative was needed. Garret FitzGerald, John Hume and others were pressing hard for a new London–Dublin arrangement; the Powell–Molyneaux counter-argument was that any significant new move would worsen a situation which, they contended, was improving. They advocated modest changes in the direction of integration, consisting of little more than alterations in parliamentary procedure and extended powers for local councils. This minimalist approach proved unattractive to the Government, which accepted neither their analysis nor their suggested remedy. Powell's arguments proved no match for the nationalist push which convinced first Whitehall, then ministers, and finally the Prime Minister that a new departure was called for.

His greatest mistake was to overestimate his influence with Margaret Thatcher. He and Molyneaux appear to have assumed that she would not depart too far from their advice. They may have been encouraged in this belief by Ian Gow, the Prime Minister's parliamentary private secretary, who made no secret of his personal admiration for Powell. The Ulster Unionist Party invested a great deal in Powell's supposed relationship with Mrs Thatcher, notwithstanding the fact that her changeable policies towards Northern Ireland were the very opposite of the consistency he advocated. As the Anglo-Irish agreement approached, Powell and Molyneaux completely misread the signs. They persuaded themselves that she would never accept anything like the accord, since she was an instinctive Unionist who would not allow Northern Ireland's constitutional position to be placed in doubt. Only a few days before she signed it, they were saying privately that it would not happen: when it did, it came, in the words of a close colleague, as a colossal surprise to them. Powell's bitterness afterwards was great. He regarded it as a betrayal and called the Prime Minister a Jezebel.

The accord was a shattering defeat for Powell's certainty theory and for his strategy of having Unionism, through Molyneaux, place its faith in the Commons and more especially in Margaret Thatcher. Integration made little headway before the Anglo-Irish agreement; and it is difficult, in the wake of a pact which Unionists regarded as such a betrayal, to envisage them ever having complete confidence in any British parliament.

In the last analysis, the largest obstacle in the path charted by Powell is Unionism itself. How can Northern Ireland become the same as Britain when the political and sectarian divide permeates every aspect of life? Powell wants, ideally, a new and non-sectarian Unionism; yet for years he was flanked on the green leather benches of the Commons by two living symbols of division – the Grand Master of the Grand Orange Lodge of Ireland, the Rev Martin Smyth, and the Sovereign Grand Master of the Royal Black Institution, James Molyneaux. The fact is that Powell is a British Unionist in a party of Irish Unionists. His message to them is one of giving loyalty to the Crown in Parliament as the final guarantor of their constitutional position. It is true that most Unionists are indeed attached to Westminster and to Britain – yet almost to a man they also harbour, in a different part of their psyche, deep suspicions about the intentions of "the mainland". The signing of the Anglo-Irish agreement greatly heightened those suspicions.

Powell is for the Union for its own sake, but for most Unionists the Union is not so much an end in itself as a device for staying out of a united Ireland. They put their faith not in British institutions and politicians but in their own strong right arms. When Powell tells Unionism to put its faith in parliament, he is battling against not just the 50-year-old tradition of Stormont but against centuries of believing that God defends those who defend themselves.

The post-election period of 1987 found Unionism confused and divided. There was a good deal of grassroots dissatisfaction with the joint leadership of the Rev Ian Paisley and James Molyneaux, but none of their critics was able to command significant support for alternative policies. Integration, independence and other policies were suggested but none gained ground. Into this vacuum came, in July 1987, the report of a Unionist "task force" made up of three senior politicians. This criticised the anti-agreement campaign as directionless and ineffectual, and called for the reopening of official contact with the Government.

One of the report's authors was Peter Robinson of the DUP. He had switched from the extreme camp to a moderate stance following the outcome of the court case arising from the Clontibret incursion. He lost face among hardliners by pleading guilty before a Dublin court and paying a IR£15,000 fine and IR£2,500 in compensation. The hard men muttered that he should have gone to jail rather than bowing to the Dublin authorities and gave him the contemptuous nickname "Peter Punt". In switching from confrontation to negotiation, Robinson was acknowledging the political fact that Unionist strategy had failed to shift the agreement.

Challenge to the old men of Unionism

T he language of Unionist politics is the language of absolutes, usually pitched in negative terms. To the traditional "No surrender" has recently been added, in response to the Anglo-Irish agreement, "Never, never, never" and "Ulster says no".

A year and a half after the signing of the accord, Ulster – to be precise, Protestant Ulster – still says no. Not a single Unionist politician advocates accepting the agreement. But yesterday saw publication of a Unionist report advocating such a radical change of direction that it may turn out to be the most significant political development since the agreement itself. Instead of the standard denunciation of consensus politics, the report actually advocates it. "The expedient of compromise and barter" is commended. The thrust of the document is the need to open talks – without preconditions – with the Government, on alternatives to the agreement.

The report is the work of a "task force" made up of Harold McCusker and Frank Millar, respectively deputy leader and chief executive of the Ulster Unionist Party, and Peter Robinson, deputy leader of the Democratic Unionists. The extent of the political movement taking place may be judged from the fact that only last winter Mr Robinson, wearing a red beret, was addressing recruiting rallies for a Protestant militia, "Ulster Resistance".

So sudden a change of tack naturally raises the question of the sincerity of the task force in reporting, as it does, that "protest can be no substitute for politics". The indications are, however, that the task force is consciously reflecting a widespread desire for negotiation, after all the months of boycott and freeze. Protestants have shown convincingly that they will not grow to love the agreement – but equally the British and Irish governments have demonstrated that the accord can operate tolerably well without Unionist consent.

The first hurdle for the would-be negotiators will be to get the policy past their own party leaders. James Molyneaux does not favour talks, because the talks would be about devolution, and he is opposed to devolution. The Rev Ian Paisley wants a devolved government, but only on the basis of majority Protestant rule, which is a political impossibility. The suspicion, therefore, is that the two men will privately be concerned either to prevent serious negotiations or to ensure their failure. The question is whether they retain the strength to do so.

The personal stature of both men has perceptibly diminished as it became cruelly clear that they were at a loss as to how to defeat the agreement. Their anti-accord campaign is now seen as a series of ineffective and often counter-productive gestures. Many of the protests have ignominiously fizzled out. At the moment the only policy they advance is the maintenance of an inglorious and unattractive freeze, during which they hope the accord will somehow wither away. The Unionist public is obviously dissatisfied with this long-haul approach, which is implicitly criticised in the title of the task force report, *An End to Drift*.

The two leaders are both probably in the final phases of their careers, and the emergence of the task force was itself a sign of the erosion of their authority. They are keenly aware that its three members are, by no coincidence, the most ambitious men in Unionist politics.

Charges of sell-out and betrayal were made against the task force even before its report was published. These are potent allegations which have destroyed the careers of a series of Unionist leaders – Terence O'Neill, Brian Faulkner, William Craig. But Mr Robinson has hardline credentials and so does Mr McCusker, who recently spent a week in jail for not paying his taxes in an anti-agreement protest. Mr Millar is on his party's liberal wing, but has taken a hawkish line on issues such as the boycott of Westminster. It will be difficult for their opponents to make the allegations stick.

Most Unionists are painfully aware of the weakness of their position in any negotiations. The British and Irish governments, and the nationalist Social Democratic and Labour Party, believe the agreement is working. If talks should break down, the accord would simply continue as before. The onus will be on Unionist negotiators to prevent this happening. It will also be up to them to produce an offer which the two governments, and the nationalists, would find preferable to the accord as currently structured. No one believes that negotiations will be easy. But the task force report raises possibilities which did not exist in the past year and a half. If it has correctly judged the mood of the Protestants, Northern Ireland may now be entering a new phase of political activity.

The main author of the task force report was
Frank Millar, general secretary and chief
executive of the Ulster Unionist Party.
Described by Mr Paisley as a "devious wee
imp", he brought an unusual degree of
articulateness to the Protestant cause.

14 JULY 1987   THE INDEPENDENT

PROFILE

Frank Millar, the modern face of Unionism

Frank Millar is one of the most unusual Unionist politicians in Northern Ireland, and potentially one of the most important. At a time when Unionism is undergoing a catharsis, his has been the clearest voice arguing for its modernisation. He has consistently advocated talks, negotiation and eventual accommodation. Such an approach may be unremarkable at Westminster, but on the other side of the Irish Sea talking is often presented as a sign of weakness, and compromise characterised as sell-out.

The Rev Ian Paisley once told his congregation: "If you compromise, God will curse you." Frank Millar was married in Paisley's church, with Paisley officiating, but his ideas have changed radically over the years. Today Millar is at the opposite pole of Unionism from Paisley. His speeches contain no bluster, no threats. He rules out rebellion against Britain, rules out paramilitary activity, rules out independence for Ulster. Millar's views are also at odds with those of the leader of his party, James Molyneaux, who believes the goal of Unionism should be complete integration with Britain. This Millar dismisses as a chimera, a mirage which can never be reached.

Although neither of the party leaders favours talks, they are shortly due to meet senior civil servants for exploratory contacts. They will be doing so not voluntarily, but under pressure from the Unionist "task force" which recently called for talks. The task force consists of Millar and the deputy leaders of the two main Unionist parties, Harold McCusker and Peter Robinson. Both deputies are senior to Millar and wield more political clout, but the ideas the task force is advancing are unmistakably his. If serious negotiations get under way it will be a victory for Millar and his associates, achieved against the wishes of Paisley and Molyneaux. Paisley recently growled, in an unintended tribute to Millar's political skills: "That's one devious wee imp."

Yet Millar was once among the staunchest of the "no surrender" brigade. Now aged 32, he made his name with a fiery speech denouncing "Westminister interference in the internal affairs of Northern Ireland". That was in 1970 when he was 15 years old. Such views were unsurprising, given his background. His father was, and is, a far-right independent Unionist who has spent his life fighting the twin menaces of republicanism and Catholicism. His father-in-law is also noted for his extreme views.

He was brought up in north Belfast, probably the most murderous part of Northern Ireland. Preoccupied with politics since his early teens, he joined the Ulster Unionist Party and the Orange Order. He left school early, he and his father considering a university education unnecessary for a future MP. The embarrassment is that he lived through his adolescence in public.

Millar was in his early twenties when he began seriously to question the no-compromise philosophy of hardline loyalism. The key period of his development was five years spent at the Commons as research assistant to Unionist MPs. Westminster added polish and perspective. He returned to Belfast as party press officer and soon became general secretary. He was at first an integrationist but switched to the devolutionist wing of the party. He has been a most unusual party officer, regularly pronouncing on policy. Articulate and persuasive, good on television and good with journalists, he has developed a high profile in the media.

When Unionism splintered in confusion with the signing of the Anglo-Irish agreement in late 1985, he took two strong lines. One was the condemnation of violence. A year ago extreme loyalists carried out a systematic campaign of petrol-bombing the homes of RUC officers, believing the police to be the Achilles' heel of the agreement. Many Unionist politicians fell silent, or adopted the formula that they regretted – rather than condemned – the bombings. Millar's condemnation of the campaign was so forthright that, following a string of abusive phone calls, he was given a police bodyguard.

His other theme has been that the accord will be replaced only through negotiation rather than protest. For more than a year he and a few associates urged this line on unresponsive colleagues. Only now, when the protests have self-evidently failed, have others, such as Robinson and McCusker, come to agree.

Though occasionally spoken of as a future leader of the party, Millar has as yet no strong personal following. His message is essentially unpopular: he is telling his party, and his community, that their traditional methods and traditional policies have failed. He also attracts the resentment and jealousy which any able and ambitious 32-year-old can expect, especially when his message to his seniors is that their approach has failed and indeed jeopardised their cause. His critics complain of a certain arrogance; his defenders say that any abrasion he may demonstrate comes from the fact that he is a man in a hurry. Certainly, his analysis is that time is against the Unionists, and that under the agreement the British sense of detachment from them can only increase.

What makes Millar so unusual among Unionists is his readiness, even enthusiasm, to go into negotiations. It is unquestionably the most dangerous course for a Unionist to take: others who tried it have been denounced by their rivals and dumped by their followers. His significance lies in the fact that he is prepared to take the risk of saying that Unionism should respond to the agreement through political action, and in no other way.

The task force report was launched in July 1987: by October it was dead, defeated by a strategy of delay operated by the Paisley–Molyneaux team. Millar withdrew from politics to pursue an alternative career in television journalism in London. The political freeze claimed other casualties among the younger generation of politicians who saw no immediate future in political life: chief among these was John Cushnahan, leader of the small, non-sectarian Alliance Party.

The exit of the young Turks

W hether one approves or disapproves of the Anglo-Irish agreement, it has to be said that the recent leakage of our notoriously scarce political talent is one of its most alarming consequences. Millar, Cushnahan and the Glendinnings [respected Alliance Party husband-and-wife councillors] have gone, and they will not be the last to quit.

The fact is, though, that the agreement was the result – not the cause – of fundamental shifts in Anglo-Irish relationships. London is working out new attitudes towards Dublin and Belfast – the old ways are going. Many of the older generation of politicians have failed to come to terms with this. In the years of flux that lie ahead, the loss of the more adaptable younger generation will be all the more sorely felt.

John Cushnahan was a key figure in the Alliance Party long before he took over as leader: few realise how heavily Oliver Napier depended on his energy. His Falls Road background gave him courage. Unusually, though, he also developed an understanding of Unionist sensitivities. Cushnahan's comparatively short period as leader was extraordinarily eventful. He could do nothing to save the Assembly, but he sheltered the party against perhaps the most traumatic shock wave it had ever encountered.

The agreement cut into the Alliance Party in two ways. The wave of polarisation affected party members. But, more fundamentally, the accord went right against the philosophy of pushing for powersharing within Northern Ireland, while confining the relationship with the Republic to one of good neighbourliness. At a stroke Dublin had been brought in, and the prospects for powersharing had practically disappeared. These developments put Cushnahan in an almost impossible position and threatened, for a moment, to split the party. But he steered it to what, with hindsight, was the only possible position: qualified acceptance of the agreement. Rejection would have placed the party in the loyalist camp.

With his unpretentious approach and his willingness to slug it out with opponents on television, Cushnahan toughened Alliance's middle-class image and preserved its structure. The party's role will always be a limited one, but the fact that it survived the agreement suggests it can survive anything. That was Cushnahan's lasting achievement, but the party will be poorer without him.

If Cushnahan was the leader who could not afford to stay in politics, Frank Millar will be regarded as the leader who never was. Even his opponents and his rivals must admit his formidable political skills – clear-sightedness, television presence and drafting ability. The remarkable thing was that those talents were used as a force for moderation. When the agreement arrived Millar was personally upset but clear on what the Unionist response should be. While he supported the anti-accord campaign, he was anti-violence, anti-strikes, anti-independence and anti-integration. He received a police bodyguard after forthrightly condemning UDA attacks on the RUC, at a time when many other loyalist politicians were ambivalent or silent. As early as March 1986, in a speech in Armagh, he said negotiation was the only way to deal with the agreement. He rose to the occasion, in other words, in a way which James Molyneaux and Ian Paisley have yet to do.

Much of Millar's work went unnoticed or unappreciated. He successfully convinced important sceptical Westminster journalists that the Unionist cause still had merit. He was acutely aware of the weak position of Unionism – without friends, its representatives simply were not thinking or speaking in terms that the rest of the world understood. But he was, at 32, too young to be party leader – not to mention too sharp, too impatient, too liberal and too intelligent. The leadership, and other elements too, were suspicious of this eager young man. When Millar and his associates produced the task force report, Molyneaux and Paisley treated it not as an opportunity but as a danger. In terms of their personal positions they were right to do so: it was clearly an indictment of their anti-agreement performance, a challenge to change their tack and an attempt to seize some of their power.

The weeks before the task force launch were marked by many public calls, from Protestant churchmen and others, for the dropping of boycotts and the reopening of contacts with the Government. Yet when the report emerged the response was muted. Few stuck out their necks to back it: most of the clerical dogs did not bark.

Within a short time it was clear that the forces of reaction were stronger than Millar had calculated. Molyneaux's strategy of delay – the classic tactic used within the Orange Order – did the trick and Millar, disheartened, quit. Paisley and Molyneaux have managed to kill the task force report without producing an alternative policy to put in its place. The anti-agreement campaign is dead on its feet and looks incapable of even partial revival. Paisley has nothing left up his sleeve, either in terms of protests or policy initiatives. Molyneaux, meanwhile, appears to believe that ending Orders in Council and establishing select committees will somehow undermine the agreement.

The Ulster Unionist Party's chief executive was edged out by a more subtle campaign than those waged in the past against Unionists who have endorsed the idea of accommodation. A vendetta of innuendo by the Belfast Unionist *News Letter*, the silence of the clerics and Molyneaux's stonewalling all played their part.

Millar had been the great hope of the Northern Ireland Office and the SDLP. The difficulty was that neither could offer him support in his attempt to reach out. One SDLP man, greatly depressed at his departure, gave him this epitaph: "Millar was good — independent and freethinking. He was different, refreshing. He had a genuinely open mind. Now there's nobody to trade with and nothing to trade about."

Both Millar and Cushnahan made leaps of the imagination: Cushnahan to come from the Falls Road and end up leader of a largely middle-class Unionist party, Millar to transcend the bitterness of the loyalist ghetto and become the advocate of compromise. Both were modernisers — and both were eventually overwhelmed by those forces which prefer the ancient joys of bitter conflict to the uncertainties of accommodation.

In late 1987 the focus of attention shifted from Unionism to the violence of the IRA. Both governments had hoped that the Anglo-Irish agreement's emphasis on cross-border security co-operation would help curb the IRA's activities, but in fact it had launched a new offensive early in 1987. Large bombs exploded in the heart of Belfast and a number of towns, while home-made armour-piercing grenades ("drogue bombs") posed a serious new threat to security force vehicles. A number of loyalist paramilitary figures were shot dead. A wave of mortar attacks was launched against army bases and police stations, coupled with death threats to builders involved in repairing the damage. In April of that year the IRA blew up and killed a senior judge, Lord Justice Maurice Gibson, and his wife Cecily as they travelled through south Armagh.

The offensive was to some extent checked at Loughgall, Co Armagh, in May, when SAS troops ambushed and killed eight IRA members intent on attacking an RUC station. But the violence continued, culminating in the horrific Remembrance Day bombing in Enniskillen, Co Fermanagh. Eleven people – six men and five women – were killed by a bomb as they waited for the annual Poppy Day parade in November 1987.

9 NOVEMBER 1987   THE INDEPENDENT

Bewilderment and pathos at hospital

I was standing outside the Erne Hospital with Mervyn Dane, the local newspaper editor who knows everyone in Enniskillen, when a ruddy-faced man in an open-neck shirt walked over to us. He was middle-aged, stocky and looked like a farmer. "I just heard," he told Mervyn, "my mother's one of the dead."

"Oh, Derek, I'm sorry," Mervyn said. They shook hands. The man seemed dazed, numb. "She wanted to go early and get a good place," Derek said. "I'd just dropped her. I was sitting in the car when I heard the bang." He turned and slowly walked away, clearly uncertain where to go. It was two o'clock. For three hours Derek Quinton had been trying to establish whether his mother was alive or dead.

The hospital grounds were full of people enquiring after relatives or collecting the injured. One of the less seriously injured was brought out. A teenage girl wearing a neck-brace and sitting in a wheelchair was taken to her family's car. At the hospital door, Ken Maginnis, the moderate Unionist MP for the area, had to pause during a radio interview when his eyes brimmed with tears. He managed to say: "I'm bitter and disillusioned at the way we have been

75

The funeral of one of the Enniskillen bomb victims makes its way past the building shattered in the explosion.   CRISPIN RODWELL, *Independent*

abandoned to the terrorists."

I gave a lift from the hospital to Pat O'Doherty, 26, a teacher and environmental scientist whose family home was right opposite the blast. "The explosion itself seemed to last about 15 seconds. Then there was a dead silence for 10 seconds. Then there was sobbing and crying."

People had been waiting in their Sunday best to see the parade and the service, standing around the war memorial in family groups. Mr O'Doherty said: "I'll never forget it. It was chaos. We just rushed to try to get the rubble off the people. Other people were trying to look for their relatives, children were looking for their mothers. I helped to take bricks off and I consoled people. There were two bodies in the street. People were crying, soldiers were crying. The most seriously injured were pressed against a railing by a wall that collapsed on top of them. People knew their relatives were underneath it. Everybody rolled up their sleeves and helped."

A number of people were blown into the O'Doherty house by the force of the blast. "We have a big mahogany door, but it came off its hinges, and two people came through it into the hall. Another one came through a window," he said. "We brought people in, made them tea, and gave them blankets. There's very little you can do, but you do your best."

Two weeks ago he returned to Enniskillen from India, where he was carrying out voluntary work. "I went out there thinking I was from the civilised West, going to help less-fortunate people. Now I'm wondering how civilised we really are. Life is so precious. Why waste it so blatantly? I just hope I never experience anything like this again in my life."

9 NOVEMBER 1987   THE INDEPENDENT

The changing face of IRA strategy

The Enniskillen bombing represents a radical departure from the IRA's general strategy of recent years. For more than a decade the organisation has been attempting to refine its tactics, putting much effort into avoiding civilian casualties and concentrating on military and police targets and those associated with, in their terminology, the "British war machine".

Clearly this description can by no stretch of the imagination be applied to a Poppy Day ceremony attended by Girl Guides and surrounded by onlookers dressed in their Sunday best. The Enniskillen bomb was bound to kill more civilians than military personnel, as well as injuring a great many people on a completely indiscriminate basis.

One theory is that the bombing may represent an outburst of IRA anger against the seizure last weekend of the 150-ton arms shipment on its way from Libya to Ireland. The fact is, however, that the IRA leadership regards past incidents when large numbers of civilians were killed as major setbacks for both the IRA and its political wing, Sinn Féin. Such occasions include the 1978 La Mon hotel explosion near Belfast and the car bomb at Harrods in Knightsbridge in 1983 which badly damaged Sinn Féin's standing among elements of the British left. Yesterday's killings, therefore, broke the IRA's self-imposed rules.

Sinn Féin, in its efforts to build a political machine in both parts of Ireland, has been concerned to project IRA violence as the clinical and carefully directed use of force. There are many nationalists who do not oppose IRA attacks on the police and army but who strongly disapprove of attacks on civilians. Sinn Féin now stands to lose the support of many such people.

In political terms, the incident may lead both the British and Irish authorities to take stronger action against the IRA.

After Enniskillen, the hope arose in many quarters that the horror of the incident might make a lasting difference, and that support for the IRA and Sinn Féin might be permanently affected. Such sentiments were widely voiced just after the bombing, as the Anglo-Irish agreement reached its second anniversary.

---

17 NOVEMBER 1987   THE INDEPENDENT

A bloody step closer to accord

I reland appears to be approaching another watershed. One came in 1981 with the Maze hunger strikes, when the IRA built a substantial political movement on the deaths of 10 republican prisoners. That IRA success played a large part in the genesis of the second watershed, the signing of the Anglo-Irish agreement two years ago last Sunday.

With the accord the Government enlisted the assistance of constitutional nationalism, north and south of the border, in the thankless task of running Northern Ireland. In doing so it defined militant republicanism, and Unionism in general, as problems in the way of progress. It was a historic reversal of the policy, which ran from the 1920s until Stormont fell in 1972, of governing Northern Ireland through Unionism.

The question now is whether the carnage of Enniskillen will turn out to be another such watershed. Despite the almost unprecedented wave of emotion and sympathy, it is by no means certain that it will be a significant turning point: there have been a great many false dawns. Tolerance of paramilitarism and violence has centuries-old roots in Ireland, and public opinion can be startlingly volatile. The IRA could yet salvage something from the wreckage. A retaliatory loyalist outrage or even a recklessly fired plastic bullet could begin to dull the impact of Enniskillen in the nationalist ghettos.

In the meantime there will be no IRA ceasefire, though there will probably be assurances that civilian life will from now on be treated with rather more respect. For there is no doubt that severe damage was inflicted on the organisation by the Enniskillen attack. The IRA and the RUC, in rare agreement, describe it variously as devastating and disastrous. It will take some time for the exact dimensions of the IRA's setback to become clear: a few optimists hope that Enniskillen will mark the beginning of the end. One thing, however, is obvious. Barring unforeseen catastrophes, the IRA and Sinn Féin, its political wing, are now facing a period of contraction. Votes will be lost. Criticism is coming in from America.

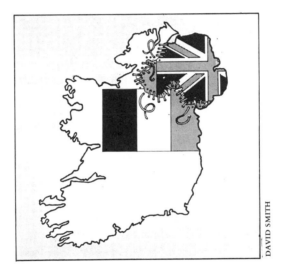

DAVID SMITH

There is a symmetry about the fact that Enniskillen should mark the opening of this new phase. It was there, in 1981, that 30,492 nationalists voted in IRA hunger striker Bobby Sands as the honourable member for Fermanagh and South Tyrone. That election, and the IRA's skilful handling of the ancient emotions stirred by the hunger strike, marked the beginning of the organisation's expansionist phase. In the next few years Gerry Adams became MP for West Belfast, 60 Sinn Féin members were voted into the council chambers, and new links were forged with the British left and others. At one point Sinn Féin had hopes of replacing the non-violent Social Democratic and Labour Party as the principal voice of Northern Ireland nationalists. Irish and British ministers feared the eventual destabilisation of the whole island, since Sinn Féin also looked hungrily towards the Republic and laid its plans to infiltrate and use the political processes there.

Suddenly, post-Enniskillen, the expansionist ambitions have been dashed. The IRA argument that violence could be used cleanly and surgically against the security forces with minimum risk to civilians has been shattered. From now on, each Remembrance Day will serve as an annual reminder of that fact.

As the RUC says, the IRA remains highly dangerous militarily and Sinn Féin may well hold much of its vote. But any hope of increasing its support in Northern Ireland, and of winning significant support among the alienated poor in the Republic, has vanished for years to come.

In the last Westminster election the Sinn Féin vote was under pressure and dropped slightly. But the party none the less collected 83,000 votes, and Adams held his seat. One view, pre-Enniskillen, was that much of this was a bedrock republican vote which could be whittled down only gradually and with a great deal of hard pounding. Sinn Féin's opponents will now be more hopeful of eroding that support in the next few years.

One key fact in the continuing struggle for the hearts and minds of the nationalists is the Anglo-Irish agreement. The existence of the accord permits the SDLP and the Irish government to argue to disaffected northern Catholics that there is an alternative to violence. The accord was designed to demonstrate to the uncommitted that there are better, non-violent ways of dealing with grievances and achieving nationalist objectives. After Enniskillen, the waverers may be more receptive to this point.

Having reached its second anniversary, the agreement has not achieved all that non-violent nationalists had hoped for. They would say the pace of reform has been too slow and too grudging. Some in government would say, in response, that the Irish government could have moved faster and with more determination on some aspects of the security front.

Obviously there are significant differences of approach between the two governments. But the point is that since the signing of the agreement the majority of conflicts have been argued out in private and not by means of megaphone diplomacy. This is important. As recently as May 1985, the RUC and the Garda were prepared to lock horns in bitter and highly public disputes on whether various IRA attacks had, or had not, originated south of the border. For more than a year the heads of the two forces simply refused to meet.

Past security crises, such as the deaths of 12 people in an IRA incendiary bombing at La Mon House hotel in 1978, were followed by public recriminations between British and Irish ministers. This time, as ministers demonstrated in Dublin yesterday, the message is one of joint determination to combat terrorism. With the agreement as the established context for Anglo-Irish relations, the IRA is simply no longer allowed to drive a wedge between the two governments.

All of this is of no immediate consolation to the bereaved and injured of Enniskillen whose lives were shattered by the Poppy Day bomb. But at least it can be said that the Anglo-Irish structures have helped ensure that the IRA is, to the maximum extent, suffering the consequences of its own violent methods.

The assumption made in the above article was that the IRA was at a low ebb both militarily and politically. This idea was widely held at the time; it lay behind, for example, the decision of John Hume to open an unprecedented series of talks with Sinn Féin leaders. But it emerged shortly afterwards that everyone had made a serious misjudgement about IRA strength and that in terms of weaponry at least, the organisation was stronger than it had ever been in its history. The story of how this came about shows up an intelligence lapse of enormous proportions by the authorities in Northern Ireland, Britain and the Republic. The IRA had, in complete secrecy, been supplied with weaponry by Colonel Gaddafi's Libyan regime — weaponry of such types, and in such quantities, that the IRA's campaign of violence in Northern Ireland was transformed.

The first clue about what had been going on came early in November 1987, when a French customs patrol intercepted a trawler, the *Eksund,* off the coast of Brittany. The French, who were looking for drugs, were amazed to find the vessel loaded with some 150 tons of heavy modern weaponry. This included SAM-7 ground-to-air missiles, heavy machine guns, RPG-7 rocket launchers, grenades and mortars. There were also two tons of Semtex plastic explosive and one thousand Kalashnikov rifles, together with fifty tons of ammunition.

The trawler appeared to have come from Libya. Security sources in both Belfast and Dublin, however, at first discounted the possibility that it could have been headed for Ireland. They knew nothing of any arms shipment and nor, when they checked, did the Anti-Terrorist Squad in London or any other intelligence agency. There was no real evidence, they said privately, of an active connection between Gaddafi and the IRA. Besides, they added, there was simply more weaponry on the *Eksund* than the IRA could cope with. They suggested the shipment might have been bound for ETA terrorists in the Basque country.

Even when it emerged that the trawler was crewed by five Irishmen, the RUC and Gardaí attempted to cling to the theory that they had been acting for some foreign terrorist grouping. Only when it was established that three of them were known IRA members did the unpalatable truth sink home.

Six months previously, in May 1987, the *Independent* had reported that Gaddafi had supplied the IRA with large amounts of Semtex explosive, which had been one of the mainstays of its violent campaign. A senior Special Branch source said at the time that the IRA had received some help from Libya but said it was "probably a one-off. There is no indication of anything further."

In the Dáil the former Fine Gael Foreign Affairs Minister, Peter Barry, raised the story in an adjournment debate. He was told by Brian Lenihan, then Minister for Foreign Affairs: "This article was wrongly based. We investigated the facts and it did not measure up. On full investigation the report was found to be inaccurate and without foundation." Gardaí had for some time been reluctant to confirm Libyan connections with the IRA. Even when 130 Kalashnikov rifles, some in crates marked "Libyan armed forces" and "Destination Tripoli" were found in Co Roscommon in January 1986, they took the view that such evidence did not necessarily prove the link.

Relief in Dublin that the *Eksund* had been intercepted soon turned to dismay when realisation dawned that other major shipments had successfully got through. One of the crew, interviewed in Paris, confessed to involvement in a number of other gunrunning episodes. In previous shipments, he said, a total of at least 150 tons had been successfully landed in the Republic. The Dublin government took this seriously and launched the largest search operation in the history of the state, Justice Minister Gerry Collins declaring: "No state can tolerate a situation where arms of this volume and power are held by any group other than the lawful security forces."

But senior RUC officers for some time doubted that the IRA had received previous shipments, and were sceptical of the Paris confessions. It was only when *Eksund*-type material began to turn up in arms finds that they accepted their Special Branch had failed to detect an active Libyan connection which had been in place for years.

The size and nature of the IRA's new armoury had the most profound implications in both the political and security fields. By December 1988 security sources were saying that 5 tons of weaponry had been recovered, which meant the IRA still had an estimated 145 tons at its disposal. Two painful facts had to be faced: that IRA violence was unlikely to diminish for the foreseeable future, and that the intelligence services of both Britain and the Republic had been proved inadequate to the task of establishing the terrorists' intentions and thwarting their plans.

In this perpetual contest between the IRA and the authorities, the former has one obvious advantage: Northern Ireland Secretaries and army chiefs may come and go, but the IRA and Sinn Féin are led by veterans who have close on twenty years' hard experience beneath their belts. And for a decade the chief strategist of the republican movement has been Gerry Adams.

1 NOVEMBER 1986   THE INDEPENDENT

PROFILE

Gerry Adams, guru of gun and ballot box

In 1984 James Prior, then Secretary of State for Northern Ireland, outlined a nightmare scenario to a group of Tory MPs. He warned them that if the rise of Provisional Sinn Féin were to continue unchecked, first in the north and subsequently in the south, then it was just conceivable that the whole of Ireland could become "a Cuba off our western coast". Prior may have been exaggerating for the sake of effect, but both British and Irish ministers take seriously the potential of the Provisionals, acting through the IRA and Sinn Féin, to destabilise society and politics in Ireland. And if there is an Irish Castro in all this, it is Gerry Adams.

The West Belfast MP's capacity for blending cool political analysis and cold military ruthlessness has made him the dominating influence on both Sinn Féin and its military wing, the IRA. He is the leading theoretician of a movement which has three times in recent years elected representatives to Westminster, which has around 60 councillors in Northern Ireland and which regularly commands 10 per cent of the vote there.

Yet at the same time the IRA has been responsible for more than a thousand deaths in the past 16 years; and it almost managed to assassinate the Prime Minister. The Adams strategy has married terrorism and politics in a form acceptable to, at one point, 103,000 Northern Ireland voters.

This weekend in Dublin at the annual Sinn Féin conference he and his supporters will, in the face of a rearguard action from republican traditionalists, seek to change the 60-year-old rule which prohibits its representatives from taking their seats in the Dáil (Irish parliament). They are expected to succeed. The party may win no more than a couple of Dáil seats, but the prospect is an alarming one for constitutional politicians. [Adams succeeded in getting the change through the conference.]

One Irish minister, Barry Desmond, has already spoken fearfully of "IRA Army Council deputies stalking the corridors of Dáil Éireann, holding the balance of power". The central proposition of Adams and his supporters is that the Provisionals can abandon abstentionism and use the political processes without getting sucked into the system and without becoming distracted from the "armed struggle".

Not everyone in Sinn Féin and the IRA accepts this. Adams's traditionalist enemies accuse him of unprincipled pragmatism and of abandoning one of the central tenets of IRA faith. It is certainly true that under his guidance the Provisionals have changed greatly; but his personal republican credentials are difficult for his opponents to fault. The Adams family, based in the Provisional heartland of west Belfast, have been active republicans for decades. In addition, Adams's wife is a Hannaway – a member of one of the city's best-known republican families. A great many of his close relatives have been to jail for IRA activities.

His own career, according to both republican and security sources, began in the mid-1960s and he is believed to have held the ranks of intelligence officer, battalion quartermaster and battalion commander before his internment in 1972. But soon afterwards he was released, specifically to take part in secret talks with William Whitelaw.

Adams rose to the rank of Belfast commander before being arrested again. It was in jail that he made a real name for himself: fellow prisoners still retain vivid images of him dominating discussion groups in the damp, drafty Nissen huts of Long Kesh internment camp. His admirers speak of his air of authority, his debating skills and above all his inner conviction that he knew the way ahead. But he did not impress everyone: one prisoner wrote of his "arrogance and overbearing posture, his sarcastic and devious ways". However, after his release he rose quickly through the ranks and by 1977 he was in control of the Provisionals.

Some IRA sources now credit Adams with saving the organisation from complete defeat at the hands of Roy Mason, then Secretary of State for Northern Ireland, and Sir Kenneth Newman, then head of the RUC. A tough security policy saw a number of IRA men shot dead by the SAS, while robust questioning practices at Castlereagh interrogation centre produced a stream of confessions from IRA members. The organisation was indeed, as Mason said, on the run at that point. But it has survived by contracting into a smaller, more secure cell structure.

An attempt was made to take Adams out of commission in 1979. The day after the "La Mon massacre", when 12 people were burnt to death in an IRA hotel firebombing that went wrong, he was arrested and charged with IRA membership. But after a long and complex trial he was acquitted.

Since the late 1970s the Provisionals have been controlled by admirers of Adams, men in their twenties and thirties. A small group of dissidents who believed Adams was spending too much money on elections was summarily expelled 18 months ago. Meanwhile the build-up of Sinn Féin has continued.

The breakthrough came with the hunger strikes of 1981, when 10 republican prisoners starved themselves to death in pursuit of a campaign to have jailed IRA members recognised as political prisoners. Adams originally disapproved of the tactic and pressed the hunger strikers to desist: some of them were his personal friends. But once the strike was under way he assiduously extracted maximum political advantage from the deaths.

Sinn Féin has subsequently won a substantial following in Northern Ireland, and Adams hopes the taking of Dáil seats will pave the way for a similar infiltration of the Republic's political process. The integrated strategy has wrought changes on the IRA itself. Much of the racketeering has been ended and the violence has become more selective. Killing the innocent costs votes.

Adams has, after five years in the public eye, established himself as a form-idable political figure: the beard, spectacles and pipe reinforce his image as the guru of the Provisionals. His calmness under television questioning; his readi-ness to rationalise and defend the most brutal acts of the IRA; his argument that all violent deaths are the sole responsibility of Britain; his apparent immunity from prosecution – all tend to infuriate his opponents and project him as a hero to the disaffected youth of Belfast.

Alan Dukes, the Irish Justice Minister, recently condemned "the suave sick voice of Gerry Adams" and declared: "No feudal lord ever said 'He shall live and he shall die' more arrogantly than the present lords of the IRA." He is a hate-figure for loyalists too: UDA gunmen put three bullets into him in 1984. The incident added to his stature.

DAVID SMITH

There are obvious contradictions involved for a movement which combines terrorism and political activity. For example, a Sinn Féin councillor in Newry recently complained about the unsafe state of the pavements in a shopping area. The complaint became academic, however, when the IRA blew up the shops and put them out of business. Yet the traditional Irish tolerance of violence helps the Provisionals get away with a great deal. It also helps when they can borrow political credentials from elsewhere: Adams has put considerable effort into forging links with elements of the far left of the British Labour Party.

For Adams, most politics is propaganda. Because Sinn Féin has no definitive position on a great many issues, such as housing, he can plug away in the local media on the need for more resources to alleviate the urban deprivation in his

West Belfast constituency. The line that all problems are caused, at root, by the British presence has an appeal for the nationalist poor.

Although the projection of inner certainty and conviction is one of his personal trademarks, he has displayed uncertainty about the most significant political event of the past decade, the Anglo-Irish agreement. He prophesied, wrongly, that it would lead to the banning of Sinn Féin and the reintroduction of internment. He has said, variously, that it is a most dangerous document; that Sinn Féin and the IRA will not actively oppose it; that its benefits are really due to the Provisionals; and that it has produced no benefits.

Even republicans chronically mistrustful of any deal with Britain suspect there must be merit in something which Protestants hate so much. The Protestants, in fact, represent one of the weakest points of Adams's philosophy. For constitutional politicians such as Garret FitzGerald, the essential long-term task of nationalism is to convince Unionists that they can survive in some future all-Ireland structure.

To Adams, the division between the Irish people, Catholic and Protestant, is simply a function of the British presence in Ireland. He has not wavered from the belief that the solution lies in using force to bring about a British withdrawal. He believes that Unionism, faced with the departure of the British, would simply collapse; alternatively, if it resists, it can be militarily mopped up.

In building Sinn Féin into a real political force, Adams has added a new dimension to the formerly straightforward violence of the IRA. But the reason why he disturbs non-violent politicians so much is that he is power-oriented. Sinn Féin's stated aim is a democratic socialist republic. The Provisionals have never been democratic, but under Adams they have become more and more contemptuous of established political processes. In Adams's new Ireland Sinn Féin and the IRA would not fade away. Rather, they would attempt to take power.

One of the chief weapons of the security forces against the IRA and similar groups is the use of informers within the organisation or on its fringes. Between 1980 and 1987 the IRA killed more than twenty people whom it claimed were passing information to the police and army.

Why 'traitors' cannot be tolerated

When the IRA murders a suspected informer, it goes to great lengths to attempt to justify its action. Its statements of explanation are often several pages long. They are full of circumstantial detail, allegedly revealed by the informer: they will include his codename, the codenames of his RUC "handlers", their rendezvous points and the amounts of money said to have changed hands.

Occasionally, after a suitable interval, the families of the dead are visited by senior figures in Sinn Féin, who produce evidence of the guilt of the murdered person. This usually takes the form of transcripts of interrogations; in some cases they even bring tapes of alleged confessions. Such measures, allied with the traditional Irish disapproval of the informer, have been largely successful in minimising criticism of the killings in the areas where the IRA draws its support. More than one such funeral has taken place without a word of reproach from the officiating priest.

On occasions large sections of the IRA have been effectively paralysed by the real or imagined presence of informers. Sinn Féin says the police and army "trawl for agents" and practise entrapment of vulnerable members of the public. There is a well-established pattern of detectives approaching IRA members, and people on the fringes, to sound them out. A favourite police target, according to observers within republican areas, are taxi drivers who may pick up large amounts of low-level information about the movements of republicans. The classic moment for an approach is when the man has been charged with drunken driving and is thus in danger of losing his livelihood. The classic deal, allegedly, is that the charge will be dropped in exchange for occasional pieces of information.

But the most important informers are within the IRA itself. The security forces are reluctant to discuss the subject, but several court cases have revealed something of the pattern. One Londonderry IRA member, Raymond Gilmour, was recruited as an informer at the age of 17, and supplied information on both the IRA and INLA for years before becoming a supergrass. He claimed he had repeatedly alerted the police to impending violent incidents.

Patrick Murray, an IRA member shot as an informer last year, is said by the organisation to have been in the pay of the police for eight years. His alleged earnings totalled around £10,000, but most lower-level informers appear to receive a standard £10 per week, with bonuses for results. For five years Murray was an important figure in the IRA in Belfast and was responsible for the seizure of weapons and explosives, as well as the arrest of several IRA members.

If the IRA is to be believed, Murray was involved in many acts of violence. But it says the RUC used clever ploys to avoid injury – using Murray to replace real explosives with dummy material, and supplying him with a liquid similar to petrol, but which would not ignite in incendiary bombs. In other cases, informers under police control were used to photograph arms caches, and to plant electronic bugs in stocks of rifles. The police are forbidden under Home Office guidelines from using an informer as an *agent provocateur*, and clearly such operations are at the edge of the law.

At least one key informer figured in the investigation by John Stalker and Colin Sampson into the alleged shoot-to-kill policy operated by the RUC in 1982. It is known that Mr Stalker was unhappy with some aspects of the informer system, and intended to recommend changes in his report.

Some IRA murders of alleged informers have taken place in Belfast, but many of those killed are found along the south Armagh border. The IRA is believed to have a number of "safe houses" in the Dundalk and Castleblayney areas of the Republic, where protracted questioning of suspects takes place. IRA volunteers are always apprehensive about receiving a summons to that area. By tradition, those judged guilty in the kangaroo courts are killed by a single shot to the head. They are then usually dumped on the northern side of the border.

An unusual and revealing insight into the minds of members of the IRA and other terrorist groups was given by a senior Belfast psychiatrist who examined more than a hundred people who had committed murder.

The 'stable, normal minds' of terrorists who kill for a cause

Dr H.A. Lyons has the detached, slightly weary air of a man who has seen, or at least heard, it all. He has listened in prison hospitals as more than a hundred killers told their tales: tales of shootings, bombings, knifings, of murders in hot and cold blood. As a consultant psychiatrist he has, for a decade and a half, examined terrorists and their victims, giving evidence in scores of court cases. He and a colleague, Dr H.J. Harbinson, have compiled a study of 106 people who killed. Its conclusions are surprising and perhaps disturbing.

The study compares 59 "ordinary" killers with 47 "political murderers" who killed as members of either republican or loyalist paramilitary organisations. Dr Lyons found great differences between the categories. The non-political killers tended to come from lower social groups, with generally poor educational attainment. About half had previous convictions. Many had a family history of crime and more than a third showed evidence of personality disorder. Alcohol played a large part in the incidents: half the murderers were intoxicated, and so were 40 per cent of the victims.

According to Dr Lyons: "Many of these were domestic murders within a family. So many crimes are committed under the influence, in fact, that we should be very concerned about the whole question of alcohol. Very often the victim was well known to the person who carried out the murder. Many of the incidents took place at weekends, especially on Friday and Saturday nights – times when, of course, there tends to be an excessive amount of alcohol taken." More than half the non-political offenders were judged by the psychiatrists to be mentally ill.

The 47 political murderers presented a different picture. According to Dr Lyons: "Generally speaking, they were what would be regarded as a reasonably normal group of men. They didn't have significant psychiatric problems or mental illness and they didn't, by and large, abuse alcohol. Most of them are of average intelligence.

"Looking at the political murderers as a group, one found them to be a reasonably stable group of people who committed these acts when they were sober. I think probably the highly unstable person who abuses alcohol is not acceptable to organised paramilitary groups because he can be a risk – he may carry out foolish acts and irresponsible behaviour. Of course, you may say the murderer is highly irresponsible; but the people who plan or carry out these acts wouldn't regard it as irresponsible, unfortunately. And I want to stress that while I have found differences between the two groups, I'm not suggesting for a minute that one crime is less serious, or should be punished in a different way."

The Lyons study does not differentiate between republican and loyalist killers, but other observers have noted significant differences: loyalists may be of slightly lower intelligence and have a less coherent philosophy than republicans: they have less certainty about their goals.

The study noted that political killers as a whole displayed little regret for their actions. Dr Lyons said: "In this group there is a general lack of remorse, because they regard themselves as soldiers or freedom fighters, acting for a cause. Generally speaking, even those sentenced to imprisonment for life don't break down: symptoms of any sort of stress are rare among them. They don't need tranquillisers or night sedation. They have clear ideals and goals, many of them; they have leadership, they get strong support from other members of the group, and that helps to keep them well. It helps to keep any guilt from coming to the surface."

Dr Lyons sees no end in sight to the long stream of young men he interviews in the aftermath of their terrorist killings. "If I see a murderer now who is in his mid-twenties, that means when I started doing this sort of work he was only about 10. So he has seen violence for 15 years, he has been conditioned to it and has seen it achieving results. He thinks that violence is acceptable – maybe, for him, it is a normal way of life.

"I think society would like to think of these people as abnormal because the acts they commit are abhorrent. But when one comes to examine them that is not the case. These are not people who are psychiatrically abnormal."

In 1987 came publication of the definitive work on the IRA, by Belfast journalist Eamonn Mallie and English writer Patrick Bishop – *The Provisional IRA* (Heinemann). Its examination of the organisation's structure and roots helped explain why the IRA has achieved such longevity.

BOOK REVIEW

The mind of a killing machine

T he Provisional IRA is one of the most clinically efficient killing machines in the western world. It has sent well over one thousand people to early graves, defying the best efforts of the security forces to end its 17-year campaign of violence. During that time it has developed into an extraordinarily open terrorist group. We know who its leaders are: they can be seen on the streets of Belfast, and on our television sets. Senior policemen, relaxing at home after a hard day struggling against the IRA, switch on their TVs to watch its leaders justifying their latest killings. The security forces know, beyond reasonable doubt, all the heads of the organisation and most of the rank and file.

These men are on the streets, rather than behind bars, because this is a community-based organisation. Earlier this month 83,000 people voted for its political wing, Sinn Féin. A majority of these voters accept the IRA analysis that a war is going on and that the use of force is legitimate. Within this pool of republican supporters and sympathisers the IRA has built a war machine which has survived all the onslaughts of the Army, the SAS and the RUC, the world's most experienced anti-terrorist police force.

But it could not have done so without the unwitting help of the authorities. One of the keys to its long life has been the dismaying tendency of the security forces, and their political masters, to make serious blunders. The authorities took years to learn that tactics such as internment, the large-scale extraction of confessions and the use of supergrasses were counterproductive, driving wedges between the nationalist population and the security forces. The classic example was the Government's handling of the 1981 hunger strikes. The authorities saw themselves as standing firm in the face of blackmail, but the net result was the creation of 10 martyrs and the expansion of Sinn Féin into a political force strong enough to send dangerous tremors through the political system.

In testing times, such as the hunger strikes, it often seems to observers in London that the answer to the IRA is to respond to its force in kind. In Belfast it is rather clearer that for the organisation to be defeated it must be outwitted, outmanoeuvred and isolated. Its leaders acknowledge that they cannot win by military means alone, and that their campaign must also be waged through

93

propaganda, through the traditional Irish culture and on other fronts. Their strengths lie in their flexibility, their long experience and their expertise in exploiting governmental errors.

Many people make the mistake of dismissing the IRA as an organisation of mindless terrorists: terrorist it is, but anything but mindless. Mallie and Bishop clearly spent many hours with its leaders, who have been surprisingly frank with them. The result is an admirably clear picture of the development of the IRA from a straggling, undisciplined organisation into a steel-hard core of activists.

Mallie and Bishop chart the rise of the northern leadership which has fashioned this durable killing machine. It has enormous problems but it has enough money, guns, men, experience and ingenuity to stay in business. While its leaders are adept at using the political processes, they have not wavered in their belief that they are fighting a war. Because of this, they are untroubled by many of the normal political and human sensibilities. For them it is regrettable but necessary that people should die; they believe that their vision of a new Ireland can come about only after violent upheaval. They are concerned with uniting territory, not communities. And because they have not been beaten, they think they are going to win.

If their strategic thinking was as good as their tactical ability they might realise that their type of enforced Irish unity, born as it would be in bloodshed and bitterness, was an unpromising basis for peace. But the past 17 years have had a callousing effect on everyone in Northern Ireland, and the IRA is set in its ways. Violence is a way of life for the organisation, as it already is for the kids in the ghettos who have never known streets without soldiers and armoured vehicles.

Within the ranks of the IRA lies tremendous talent – people who could be a success in other walks of life. Mallie and Bishop were clearly impressed by the people they met, though they have by no means glorified them. These people with a great deal to offer society are instead willing to kill, and prepared to die, for their cause. It is one of the ironies of the IRA machine that it wastes not just the lives of its victims but the lives of its own people too.

The IRA and Sinn Féin have proved adept at provoking the security forces into what is seen as over-reaction. Such an opportunity presented itself with the funeral of a senior IRA man, Lawrence Marley, in north Belfast. Violent clashes between police and mourners led to the coffin being taken back into the Marley home and two postponements of the funeral. After the ghoulish episode the police admitted: "The consequences, in terms of violence and alienation of the community and disruption of police function, have been disastrous."

9 APRIL 1987   THE INDEPENDENT

Paramilitary funeral tactics: the heavy hand of the law

All the signs are that the IRA's three-day *danse macabre* with the coffin of Lawrence Marley has helped the organisation and harmed the image of the Royal Ulster Constabulary. In the working-class Catholic ghettos of Belfast, the IRA and its political wing, Sinn Féin, have been largely successful in portraying the whole tasteless, grisly affair as the fault of insensitive and vindictive authority.

The episode illustrates the almost impossible task faced by a police force which attempts to take account of the views of both political communities. Unionists are outraged by IRA displays at funerals; many nationalists, in contrast, tend to believe that the RUC's approach to republican funerals represents an over-reaction.

The IRA tradition has always been to give its dead volunteers a paramilitary send-off. Until a few years ago troops and police generally maintained, in the cliché of the news bulletins, a low profile, photographing mourners and attempting to drown out the proceedings with helicopter noise. Occasionally, if the Army saw its chance, a snatch squad would be despatched in an effort to arrest those firing volleys over the coffin. This game of cat-and-mouse ended in December 1983, when the cat decided to move in. A heavily armed police squad plunged through mourners and took the beret and gloves from an INLA member's coffin. Since then the policy has been to saturate republican funerals when a paramilitary display is considered possible. Policemen and IRA mourners now stand side by side in bitter intimacy. The RUC, not the IRA, now provide the honour guard.

Not surprisingly, scuffling and fistfights have been the norm at the two dozen republican funerals since 1983. Each one is a test of strength and almost always the RUC has its way. The IRA is thus prevented from staging morale-boosting shows of force. But there is a political price for the RUC to pay: it is characterised as heavy-handed and overbearing, even by opponents of the IRA.

Cahal Daly, the Belfast Catholic bishop noted for his attacks on the IRA, has warned: "Any unnecessary and disproportionate display of force undermines respect for the law." The SDLP, which will attempt to oust Gerry Adams, of Sinn Féin, from his West Belfast seat in the next election, says police tactics "lack sensitivity and commonsense".

Sinn Féin has twice this week attracted several thousand people – their largest turnouts for a long time – at rallies to protest at the funeral tactics. The issue will be an electoral boost for Gerry Adams.

The Marley funeral has some significant special characteristics, which show up a weak point in police policy. Marley was shot dead, in his north Belfast home, by gunmen from the illegal Ulster Volunteer Force. Six months ago the IRA, in similar fashion, shot dead UVF leader John Bingham in another part of north Belfast. The Bingham home was visited by several Unionist MPs, including the Rev Ian Paisley. Hooded UVF men with guns posed for photographs beside his coffin. A black beret and gloves were carried on the coffin and large UVF wreaths were on display during the funeral. Yet the police stayed in the background and made no attempt to interfere.

Sinn Féin use the contrast to argue that nationalists and loyalists receive very different treatment. The police explanation – that the UVF promised not to have a paramilitary show, then broke its word – carries little weight in Catholic north Belfast.

The Catholic Church disapproves of paramilitary displays, but the IRA and Sinn Féin have sought to avoid a clash on the issue. When another Catholic bishop took a firm stand against guns in church grounds, they backed off. In Belfast, however, they have been more critical of Bishop Daly, whom they judge to be less popular among the working class. Sinn Féin makes carefully calculated

judgements on such issues, and has made maximum use of the publicity surrounding the Marley funeral. The RUC succeeded in its aim, but Sinn Féin has
made useful political capital.

The episode demonstrates the difficulty of dealing with a movement which
uses violence and politics as twin tools. The IRA may have suffered a military
defeat at the hands of the police, but Sinn Féin has scored a propaganda victory.

The man at the centre of security policy right
through the 1980s was Sir John Hermon, who
stepped down in the spring of 1989 after almost
a decade as Chief Constable of the RUC,
the most demanding policing job in
western Europe.

30 MAY 1989   THE INDEPENDENT

PROFILE

Sir John Hermon, an unpopular neutral in a divided world

E xactly a quarter of a century ago Sir John Hermon was among the
policemen caught up in a series of disturbances in west Belfast which are
still remembered in the city as the "Divis Street riots". The episode began when a
republican election candidate displayed an Irish tricolour in the window of his
election headquarters in the Falls Road district. Display of the flag was technically illegal, but no one paid any attention until a vociferous young clergyman

called Ian Paisley began to proclaim loudly that the Stormont government had gone soft on republicanism. The Unionist authorities, always sensitive to such claims and anxious not to be outflanked by Mr Paisley, reacted by sending in a force of RUC to seize the flag. Fierce rioting lasted for several nights, with many injuries and much destruction of property. The law was upheld, but at a cost of transforming a peaceful district into a battleground.

Political interference of this kind was the norm rather than the exception in the first 50 years of the RUC, and it left Sir John Hermon with a deep distrust of politicians in general – together with a marked aversion to Mr Paisley which the passing decades have done nothing to reduce. As Chief Constable, he jealously guarded his independence – so much so that one of the most commonly heard complaints against him was that he carried it to the point of arrogant autocracy. He was certainly intensely unpopular with the Northern Ireland Office, the Police Authority and the Police Federation.

The force today is almost unrecognisable from that which he joined as a raw recruit, after a brief and unhappy apprenticeship in accountancy, back in 1951. The RUC that Sir John leaves behind, as he retires to a heavily fortified new home tucked away in Co Down, is still 90 per cent Protestant, with all the difficulties that this implies for the policing of a deeply divided community. But it has more than quadrupled in size – to 13,500 – and is much better trained and equipped than it was. It has been through numerous traumatic episodes, and lost many officers to terrorist attack. Its record is, by common consent, a mixed one: most of its critics would amount that improvements have taken place; most of its supporters concede that mistakes have been made. Many of the improvements and many of the mistakes are the responsibility of the departing Chief Constable, who held that post for a record nine and a half years.

Much of Sir John's early career was marked by large slices of luck. He came to the fore during the IRA campaign of the 1950s, and rose steadily through the ranks. One particularly fortunate stroke was his appointment, in 1969, as head of RUC training. This meant he missed the rioting and deaths of that August, when the RUC's performance established it, in British eyes, as a badly led, discredited sectarian force. Many senior officers of the time were henceforth regarded by London as incompetent or anti-Catholic and found their promotions blocked. Sir John Hermon, however, quickly became identified not just as a talented policeman but as one of the newer breed who accepted that far-reaching reforms were essential. From that point on he was marked out as an officer destined for the top. More luck came in the late 1970s, when he was seconded to Scotland Yard for a year. This meant he missed most of the heated controversy over the alleged ill-treatment of terrorist suspects in Castlereagh interrogation centre. It was therefore with a comparatively clean record that he took over the top post from Sir Kenneth Newman in 1980.

Sir John Hermon, inspecting the spot in south Armagh where two of his senior officers were shot dead by the IRA. PACEMAKER PRESS INTERNATIONAL

The decade that followed was extraordinarily eventful and studded with major crises, including the 1981 hunger strikes, the Stalker affair, the death of nine police officers in an IRA mortar attack on Newry RUC station, the Anglo-Irish agreement and many more. The Stalker saga overshadowed his decade as Chief Constable. The controversy began in 1982, rumbled on through court cases and media revelations and flared again in 1988–9 with the Attorney General's decision not to prosecute RUC wrongdoers. Sir John attacked the memoirs of John Stalker, who alleged the RUC had systematically obstructed his investigations, but Stalker's version was given widespread credence. His stock rose in nationalist eyes, however, following the signing of the Anglo-Irish agreement in 1985, when his force held up well against angry loyalists.

RUC Chief Constables are to be judged on their performance in two related fields – their effectiveness against terrorism and the public acceptability of their force. Sir John hit the IRA hard on a number of occasions, but at no point did he appear to come close to actually defeating the organisation. It is now smaller but better armed than it has ever been. Loyalist groups also retain their menace. There are few indications that the force is much more acceptable to Catholics in 1989 than it was in 1980, when Sir John assumed command. The Stalker controversy, the supergrass system, the use of plastic bullets, and other episodes have remained obstacles to nationalist support for the force.

In a divided community Sir John Hermon will be remembered by many as too tough and by others as too soft; he will be commended as independent or condemned as imperious. Just as there is no consensus on policing itself, so there is no consensus on the merits and demerits of the record of Northern Ireland's longest-serving Chief Constable.

The Stalker affair, which had its origins in 1982 and which continues to have a deep effect on perceptions of justice in Northern Ireland, was one of the most divisive episodes in modern policing. It led a British Attorney General, Sir Patrick Mayhew, to announce that in the interests of national security a number of policemen suspected of wrongdoing would not be prosecuted. That decision raised fundamental questions about the nature of the rule of law. John Stalker's memoirs (*Stalker*, Harrap) were published in early 1987.

26 MAY 1987   THE INDEPENDENT

BOOK REVIEW

Justice and time passing

In Northern Ireland John Stalker took the line that justice should be done though the heavens fall. People who adopt such an attitude, especially in a situation as complex and as dangerous as in Northern Ireland, can cause great anguish to those around them. They can appear naïve; they can damage reputations; they can even put lives at risk. None the less, they are right.

The policemen who killed the terrorist suspects, and the senior officers who ordered them to tell lies to colleagues, may have acted from the best of motives. They may have believed they were doing what was necessary to defend the state from deadly terrorist attack. None the less, they were wrong.

There is a strong and understandable instinct within the RUC to say that the force should not be impeded in its battle against the IRA and other paramilitary groups. This developed, however, into arguing that some of its actions and procedures should escape proper scrutiny. John Stalker took the opposite view;

hence his protracted struggle with the RUC for access to its most sensitive secrets, which ended not in disclosure but in his removal from the inquiry. We have yet to hear the RUC's line-by-line responses to his views, and it is unfair to reach a final judgement without them. But with this book Stalker has captured the high moral ground: this weekend he was canonised by nationalist Ireland, welcomed in Dublin as a hero and an honest cop.

His style is lucid and straightforward, though there is evidence of excisions at key points, probably made for legal reasons. He concludes that there was "a police inclination, if not a policy, to shoot suspects dead without warning rather than to arrest them". He judges that all three controversial shootings might have constituted murder or unlawful killing.

During his inquiry he was amazed by the extent of the power of the RUC Special Branch and disturbed by the vast amounts of money – in one case £30,000 – being paid out to informers. There had been a cover-up. Earlier internal inquiries had, in his view, been either incompetent or deliberately misleading. Furthermore, another cover-up was being employed against him.

He recommended prosecuting 11 officers, ranging from constables to a chief superintendent, on charges including conspiracy to pervert the course of justice and perjury. He indicates that he was considering recommending charges against even more senior officers when his inquiry came to an abrupt and unexpected halt.

Stalker's belief is that the Chief Constable, Sir John Hermon, waged an unremitting war of obstruction against him, arguing that he was straying into areas which were not his business, where he might do serious damage and put lives at risk. Sir John and Stalker disagreed fundamentally on how the Manchester policeman should go about his inquiries. Stalker clearly believes he was improperly impeded; Sir John's defenders argue that his concern was to protect his force and its most sensitive security practices.

Stalker has some bad news and some good news for conspiracy theorists. The bad news is that MI5 was not, in his judgement, behind the whole thing: they supplied a bugging device to the RUC, but he appears to exonerate them from involvement in his downfall. The good news, however, is that he does believe he was removed through a conspiracy. In his view it involved senior police figures, but also probably went as far up as the Cabinet.

It comes as a shock to find, on the last page of the book, Stalker's opinion that the passage of time means that deciding not to prosecute the 11 policemen is "a perfectly proper legal and moral stance to take". He argues that sprats would be taking the blame while whales escaped. But chief superintendents and superintendents are not sprats. And if he believes in justice for all and above all, why should the passage of a few years change that?

If the affair had happened in England, there would surely have been prosecutions, and Stalker would surely have approved. By arriving at this extraordinary conclusion he has put himself in the same camp as the authorities who decided not to prosecute: that there is one version of justice in Britain, and quite another in Northern Ireland.

Developments in the Stalker affair were quickly followed by the decision of the Court of Appeal to reject the appeal of the Birmingham Six, the Irishmen convicted of the bombings which killed twenty-one people in Birmingham pubs in 1974. Over the years a campaign to have the affair reopened had gradually gained support from political and legal figures in both Britain and Ireland, and the case was eventually referred back to the Appeal Court by the Home Secretary, Douglas Hurd.

An Irish Catholic bishop, Edward Daly, wept in court when the verdict was announced and the Irish Justice Minister, Gerry Collins, said he was amazed and saddened by the result. The Anglo-Irish agreement's honeymoon period was now well and truly over.

Unsmiling Irish eyes on Britain

T he British may have great confidence in their system of justice: the Irish disagree. Following the outcomes of the Stalker affair and the Birmingham Six case, it is no exaggeration to say that, at this moment, nationalist Ireland regards British justice as a disgrace. Since last week's developments – the decision not to prosecute officers of the Royal Ulster Constabulary in the Stalker case, and the failure of the appeal in the Birmingham bombing case – the Irish air has been thick with criticisms and even abuse of British politicians and British judges. The unanimity has been striking and sustained.

Leading members of all the Irish parties have condemned the decision not to take RUC men to court despite evidence of attempts to pervert the course of justice. The Appeal Court judges who threw out the Birmingham case have been thoroughly condemned: the view heard in every pub in Dublin is that the judges opted to protect the system rather than dispense justice. The Appeal Court's certainty that the Six are guilty is matched by the Irish public's implicit belief in their innocence. The gap between Irish and British perceptions is enormous, and can only be explained in historical terms.

British troops may have vacated Dublin more than 60 years ago, but in many ways post-colonial sentiments are still fresh. The principal reason is the question of Northern Ireland, which Irish nationalists regard as unfinished business. The belief that Ireland will some day be one country has proved ineradicable. No one, however, has come up with a feasible scheme showing exactly how Ireland could be united, and how the southern polity could comfortably accommodate not just Ian Paisley but Gerry Adams also. Consequently, the continuing British presence in Northern Ireland has been accepted, though never welcomed. The years of violence have, in fact, helped shift the southern aspiration towards unity further off into the future. The Republic expects some day to inherit the north – but not yet, Lord, not yet. There can be few politicians in Ireland who expect to see unity in their political lifetime. Given this effective shelving of the historic aspiration, attention has shifted to the question of making improvements to the existing state of Northern Ireland. The chief result of this switch has been the Anglo-Irish agreement.

It has been argued, by Conor Cruise O'Brien and others, that the agreement is perceived by many nationalists as a significant step towards Irish unity. The opposite is probably the case: most southerners see it as a useful device not for drawing Northern Ireland closer, but rather for keeping it at bay. The emphasis now – readily adopted by former Taoiseach Garret FitzGerald, more reluctantly by his successor Charles Haughey – is on improving the lot of northern nationalists. This has been defined, to a large extent, as helping reconcile them to the Northern Ireland security forces and system of justice.

Dr FitzGerald took a historic leap in signing the agreement with Margaret Thatcher. Thousands of republicans were taught at their mothers' knees never to trust the British, that Albion was forever perfidious. The traditional republican proposition is that the British presence is imperialist and therefore illegitimate, and that Britain is prepared to resort to illegitimate means to hold on in Ireland. This is the argument which the IRA and Sinn Féin use to justify terrorism. No deal can ever be done with the British, they say; the only thing they understand is force. The Anglo-Irish agreement struck at the heart of this ancient but forceful argument, since it appeared to be a successful synthesis of two historically opposed views. Britain has tended to hold that the problem is primarily a security matter, while Ireland views it as a political question. The agreement seemed to cover both perspectives. It has been popular with nationalist Ireland because the two governments agreed to tackle the IRA by persuading northern Catholics that the justice system was fair and equitable. Reforms seemed to be in the offing. In the event, the agreement has been increasingly concerned with security rather than with political change, since the Unionist rearguard action slowed reforms, and the upswing in IRA violence concentrated minds on joint security responses.

It is against this background that the Irish cries of outrage against the Stalker and Birmingham affairs should be judged. In both cases the general view is that the British establishment has closed ranks when faced with awkward problems, and that justice has not been done in either case. As a result IRA sympathisers, who had the grace to show some shame after the Enniskillen Poppy Day bombing, are suddenly noticeably more jaunty. One explained happily: "It puts Enniskillen into some sort of context." Their argument is that Britain has demonstrated it will always place its own interests before the cause of justice in Ireland. It helps illustrate, they say, that the agreement is little more than a ruse to enlist gullible nationalists on to the imperialist team.

In the agreement the British government specifically said that if a majority wanted a united Ireland, it would support legislation to that effect. This was a blow to the IRA argument that Britain's motivation was imperialist. The Irish government's problem now is that the Stalker decision in particular is widely perceived as being in the bad old imperialist mould. It would argue, though, that its own attitude is not simply governed by nationalism. It points to the support in Britain for its arguments, from senior public figures, newspapers and the Labour Party. Excusing senior members of the security forces from prosecution, having admitted that serious offences took place, has led nationalist Ireland to conclude that Britain puts security matters ahead of political progress.

This perception has important implications for future co-operation between the two governments, especially on security. The Irish government is not about to pull its troops off the frontier; but it is indisputable that cross-border co-operation is always easier to sell to the doubters in Dublin when Britain appears in a non-imperialist guise.

Although the whole episode is damaging to the spirit in which the agreement was signed, the accord itself is not at the moment in question. The gloss may have gone, but both sides regard it as a useful instrument. It helps communication, for example, in times such as this, when tensions run high. In one sense the Stalker and Birmingham cases are hangovers; one dates back five years, the other thirteen. Both illustrate the problems posed by the terrorist threat, for both stem from security force reaction to IRA violence. In both cases the Irish believe the British got it wrong. In Britain the view may be that the Appeal Court verdict was correct, and that the public interest is best served by not prosecuting errant policemen. But on the other side of the Irish Sea those decisions are perceived as little short of an affront to Ireland's national dignity. Britannia, they are saying bitterly, still waives the rules.

A series of Anglo-Irish meetings brought no narrowing of the gulf between the British and Irish viewpoints, and March 1988 saw an almost incredible sequence of violent events. In Gibraltar three members of the IRA were shot dead by the SAS. They had clearly been intent on attacking British service personnel on the Rock, but a controversy arose when it was revealed that they had not been armed and, contrary to what was originally claimed, had not planted a car bomb in Gibraltar.

The three bodies were brought back to Northern Ireland for burial in Belfast's Milltown cemetery. As the first coffin was being lowered into the grave a lone loyalist gunman, in full view of television cameras, attacked mourners with hand grenades and guns, killing three men and injuring fifty people. Pursued by an angry mob, his life was saved when he was arrested by the RUC.

Two days later, at the funeral of one of those killed, IRA member Kevin Brady, a car drove into the procession of mourners. Its two occupants were armed and the mourners, believing this to be another loyalist attack, surrounded the vehicle and dragged out the two men. They were in fact plain-clothes soldiers, members of the Royal Signals Regiment, who had simply blundered into the funeral. The mistake was fatal: they were beaten and shot dead.

22 MARCH 1988   THE INDEPENDENT

A tragic place apart

S aturday's horrifying attack on an army car in Catholic west Belfast is a metaphor illustrating how the area has become a place apart, even within Northern Ireland. Captured in terrible detail by television and newspaper photographers, the incident will linger long in the public memory as a graphic example of man's inhumanity to man. Many people who live there condemn it without equivocation. A mother of two teenage sons, who has put a great deal of effort into keeping them out of republican groups, said yesterday: "It was

Minutes from death: a soldier confronts a republican crowd after driving into the path of an IRA funeral.   PACEMAKER PRESS INTERNATIONAL

barbaric, utterly barbaric. It was animal – they were like monkeys in cages. They were on that car like lunatics. It was utterly and totally revolting. Watching it on TV just made me sick."

There are others, however, who disagree with that view and attempt to justify the incident. Both these factions have a common view of how it happened, which demonstrates how perceptions in west Belfast are now, after almost two decades of violence, utterly different from those of the rest of the world. Their perspective runs as follows: on Wednesday last, the funeral took place of the two IRA men and an IRA woman shot dead by troops in Gibraltar. The almost universal view is that they were murdered by the SAS, and should have been captured rather than killed. Their funeral, the first to be left unpoliced by the RUC in years, was attacked by an extreme loyalist who used guns and grenades to kill three people and wound 50 others in Milltown cemetery. One of the victims, IRA man Kevin Brady, was being buried on Saturday in an atmosphere of high emotion and tension. Nearby cars were checked and mourners frisked by Sinn Féin stewards in case a copycat attack was launched by loyalists as lunatic as the one in the graveyard. Feelings were running high against both the security forces and the loyalist community.

It was into this situation that the silver car drove. It must have been clear to the driver that he was approaching a large gathering: for several hundred yards he passed knots of people waiting for the funeral to appear. The car drove past a Sinn Féin steward who motioned it to turn about. It mounted the pavement, scattering mourners, and tore into a small side road. It then reversed at speed, ending up within the cortège itself, sealing the fate of its occupants. The immediate reaction was that this was another suicide attempt by loyalists, probably armed again with pistols and grenades. Most of the crowd who engulfed the vehicle were probably not members of the IRA or Sinn Féin.

The key point here, lost to most people outside the area, is that the mob believed itself to be defending the funeral against attack. People in the district who disapprove of what happened none the less view it in that context. One man, not a supporter of the IRA or Sinn Féin, described local sentiment in this way: "Feelings are pretty mixed. A lot of people think it was just awful, and it was a barbaric thing. But you can see how it came about. If the car had turned away, or just sat quietly at the side of the road, nobody would have taken any notice of them. I don't understand why the soldiers did it. They must have panicked. The crowd thought it was another loyalist attack and moved in on them. That's what all the anger was about. Emotions were very high. That guy in the graveyard injured men, women and children, and people weren't going to let that happen again. I wouldn't for one minute try to justify it; I'm just trying to explain it."

But there are those who approve of the savagery. Many youths in the district hate the security forces like poison, and cheer when policemen or soldiers become casualties. The same man said: "The younger element think it's a great coup." And the woman added: "They think it's great. They're rejoicing in the fact that they got two Brits."

Many of these young men will not go on to join the IRA. The current Troubles have created an anarchic underclass of young men who regard the IRA as just another form of authority. These are the joyriders, the petty thieves and drug-takers who appear destined for a life of total indiscipline. Some have been shot by the security forces; some have been shot by the IRA. But neither force nor prison seems to have any effect.

Many parts of west Belfast have always been one huge poverty trap. The area has the worst unemployment, the worst housing, the worst health, of any place in Northern Ireland. It holds around 90,000 people. The 1981 census put unemployment at 32 per cent for males, with some notable blackspots: the jobless figure in Whiterock ward, for example, was 56 per cent. Since then things have not improved. It is a huge ghetto, almost totally Catholic, bounded by mountains, swamp, a motorway, and hostile loyalist districts. Its heartland, the Falls, has been the scene of clashes, with both Protestants and the police, for almost two hundred years. It saw serious rioting more than a dozen times in the last century. West Belfast was always a place apart, scarred by sectarian confrontation points, which experienced serious disturbances with monotonous regularity.

It was here that British troops first strode, bayonets at the ready, on to the streets in 1969 after the riots which marked the start of the present Troubles. The Protestant Shankill had won the latest exchange, extreme loyalists petrol-bombing whole streets. The Army was welcomed at first, being regarded by most Catholics as a saviour. Only a few traditional republicans in those early days argued that the soldiers were the enemy. But friction between the troops and the civilian population steadily worsened; the welcome ended completely with a large-scale curfew in 1970 and the internment the following year of more than one thousand men, many of them from west Belfast.

It is not a no-go area, but it cannot be said that policing there is anything like normal. Last week I watched the police carrying out house-to-house inquiries following a shooting in Ballymurphy. Detectives knocked at doors in the usual way, but surrounding them, for protection, were five armoured vehicles and a patrol of a dozen troops. Estrangement from authority is almost complete in this the most dangerous part of the United Kingdom.

To understand west Belfast, the difference in perception has always to be remembered. For soldiers on patrol, this is a place which can hold sudden death, a place of total hostility. But the belief of most of the inhabitants is that the aggression comes from outside: from loyalists, from the security forces themselves, from poverty. It is this feeling which leads to the continuing support for, or at least toleration of, the violence of the IRA.

Another outbreak of violence occurred in west Belfast when a local IRA man, Robert Russell, was extradited to Northern Ireland from the Republic. In protest, the IRA staged a wave of hijackings and burnings right across the area.

Belfast stoical after violence

S ome of the burnt-out lorries and buses strewn across the roads were still smouldering in west Belfast yesterday, little flames licking the remnants of paint on the vehicles' skeletons. There were few people around, and an incongruous peace pervaded the area in the pleasant sunshine. A boy poked the ashes with a stick while his bored dog looked on listlessly.

"It was like Beirut around here on Saturday," one local resident said. "From the Whiterock right down the Falls Road was just one burning lorry after another." The first round of trouble came at lunchtime when a wave of hijackings swept the district. There was trouble elsewhere too – in Londonderry, Newry and Strabane, in north Belfast and in the city centre. It was carefully co-ordinated. "This wasn't hoods," the local man said. "This was the proper authorities, if you know what I mean." He meant the IRA.

At Mackies foundry on the Springfield Road two commandeered vans were rammed through the shuttered gates of two loading bays and set alight. The vehicles were destroyed but the fire had not spread into the factory buildings. Many locals would not have lost too much sleep had the blaze caught on and caused job losses: the Mackies workforce is predominantly Protestant, consisting in the main of people who live elsewhere and venture gingerly into work each day. The vans stayed wedged into the loading bays until, yesterday morning, salvage workers with impassive faces arrived with a mechanical digger to tug them out. That expression of carefully cultivated neutrality can be seen all over west Belfast in the aftermath of trouble. People do not point and they do not stare. They walk stoically up the road, offering no outward clue of whether they approve or disapprove of the fact that the bus that usually takes them home has been slung across the road and is on fire.

Next day the Royal Ulster Constabulary press office tots up the statistics of violence – dozens of shootings and bombings, scores of other attacks on the security forces – but the locals do not need to be told that their district has been in the wars. They know what the different weapons sound like: they can differentiate between high- and low-velocity bullets, and between army and IRA rifle fire.

On Saturday night the Provos, they say, brought out something new to attack New Barnsley security base: "You should have heard it. It was something very

Aftermath: life goes on amid the debris of IRA violence.

loud, and it went on for ages." This appears to have been a heavy machine gun, which fires hundreds of rounds per minute and has a range of several miles. West Belfast is a densely populated area and the New Barnsley base, which looks like Fort Apache, is surrounded by little council houses; but nobody around accused the IRA, even privately, of being irresponsible. Not far away a bullet grazed a two-year-old child – but again this had not become a major issue.

Some locals approve of the violence and some do not; but all have grown accustomed to it and regard it as a familiar part of life. They get used to weaving their cars around the blackened lorries, crunching over the shattered glass; they get used to the machine guns and the mortar attacks. Many people who do not support the IRA, and would not vote for Sinn Féin, have little time for the security forces or the authorities either: once your house has been damaged by an unnecessary army search, and your wife spoken to less than politely, your attitudes may no longer be black and white.

"I don't agree with this stuff, but I don't agree with extradition either," one man said. "They shouldn't have handed Russell over." The same man would thrash his son if he ever found him having anything to do with the IRA.

A million miles away meanwhile, in middle-class south Belfast, well-dressed women at a Saturday night party talk quietly of the threat posed by the return of city-centre bombings. Some will continue to shop downtown, though they will be wary and on edge in future; some say they will not be going back. Belfast's consumer boom – fuelled by government salaries and subsidies and aided by low housing costs – has been going strong for years. Its Marks and Spencer store sold more food than the company's branch in London's Oxford Street last Christmas.

Big new stores have opened and more are being built. Belfast, the slogan goes, is buzzing. The big fear is that IRA car bombs will put a stop to it all. The terrorist aim is disruption, though it remains to be seen how frequent the bomb attacks will be. At worst, it would be a return to the bad old days of the mid-Seventies with mothers anxious about their daughters going shopping and families sick with worry when they hear a bomb has gone off downtown.

A lot of people have been working towards normality of a kind, but a few explosions can wreck years of work and hope. In one small example, to-morrow's venue for a European Community function in Belfast has had to be switched because of bomb damage. The occasion is the launch of a new Northern Ireland tourist brochure.

The situation in west Belfast makes normal policing impossible, giving rise to immense discipline problems. One of those which has proved most difficult to deal with is that of kids who steal cars for pleasure.

Life-and-death defiance of Belfast's joyriders

Almost two decades of civil disorder in Belfast have produced a new breed of joyrider, boys and young men who defy both the security forces and the IRA. The Catholic housing estates of west Belfast are plagued by youths speeding recklessly in stolen cars. Up to a score of people have died in recent years.

About 1,500 cars are stolen in west Belfast each year. A further 1,500 stolen elsewhere are recovered in the area. The police and army operate with great difficulty in this IRA stronghold. The IRA, whose punishment squads frequently shoot persistent joyriders in the knees or elbows, has not deterred them.

Police and local people say offenders can be as young as 10. They take cars for the sheer excitement. But older boys have progressed to selling cars or parts stripped from them. Youths regard joyriding as one of the few "kicks" in a deprived area of high unemployment – up to 80 per cent in some pockets – which is also a battleground between the IRA and the security forces. According to one community worker: "A lot of these kids just feel they have nothing to lose. They see fast cars on TV and they realise they'll never have the opportunity to drive these things legitimately."

According to one local estimate, the IRA "kneecapped" about 80 joyriders last year. Such punishments are administered at several well-known spots, one called locally "Kneecap Alley". Some of the victims stop joyriding but others go back to it within weeks of leaving hospital. A few have been permanently disabled when the punishment has gone wrong.

The risks of joyriding are enormous. Pedestrians have been knocked down and joyriders killed and injured in crashes. Eighteen months ago five drunken youths involved in an 80-mph chase with the police crashed into a tree. Three were killed, the severed head of one found some distance from his body; the fourth was paralysed from the waist down and the fifth suffered brain damage.

Joyriders have been shot dead when police or troops opened fire on vehicles which crashed through road checks. Security force standing orders have been changed, however, and shots are not usually fired. Joyriders sometimes use "sandbaggers" to stop their cars being fired on. These are children as young as seven or eight who are taken along for the ride and placed in the back window to deter security force gunfire. Police may give chase, but their armoured Land-Rovers have little chance of catching fast cars.

Joyriders come in several categories. One set, possibly 200 strong, are known as "hoods". Although some steal cars for kicks, their main interest is in selling car radios, wheels and other parts. Hoods are also involved in burglaries and muggings. These are the youths most often beaten or shot by the IRA. The IRA has issued public threats, sometimes naming them and warning them to leave the district. The hoods have responded with their own threats: one group of 21 joyriders, in a letter to a local newspaper last year, said they were fed up with IRA beatings and would fight back. They said: "It is up to you, Provies. Stop or action will be taken." One member of Sinn Féin is in hospital after remonstrating with a group of hoods who had gathered in Dunville Park in the Falls area. He was stabbed in the throat, stomach and back.

Another type of joyrider tends not to become involved in other crime, concentrating on fast driving. They will often taunt the Army or police into chasing them. They have been known to play "dodgems" on open spaces. In one cemetery joyriders playing "chicken" knocked down a large number of gravestones as they swerved to avoid each other.

Two of the most notorious joyriders in the Divis Flats are aged 10 and 11. One local councillor said: "All you see is a car flying round the streets. You can't even see anybody in it." Police tell of finding two extremely small children driving a stolen car: one was steering while the other, lying on the floor, operated the pedals.

Some parents admit their sons are out of control and say that beatings and severe punishments have no effect. Others simply refuse to believe their children could be involved.

Taking cars can become an overwhelming compulsion: one 20-year-old joyrider was imprisoned last year after admitting 130 offences. People in Divis Flats say three well-known joyriders were released from prison just before Christmas; since then more than 30 stolen cars, many of them burnt out to remove fingerprints, have been abandoned in the area.

Jimmy's story

Jimmy has a reputation as one of west Belfast's most notorious car thieves and joyriders. A skinny, pale man in his early twenties, he talked freely about his experiences. This is his story.

"First I started missing school and going downtown to play the slot machines. When I ran out of money I started stealing. I was about 10. I got caught a couple of times and got a caution but I didn't think much of it. I kept doing it. When I was 13 I started drinking. There was about 12 of us used to do it. We were sitting one night over in the park when a stolen car came in, the first we'd actually seen. The boys in it, older boys, were doing handbrake turns, hanging out the window and all, then they just jumped out and walked away. We got in it, started and away we went, up and down all over the park. That was the start of it. We heard there was big money to be made, so we took the wheels of a car and sold them. We got £40 and immediately drank it.

"Just after I stole my first car – it was an Escort – I was arrested. But they'd no evidence and they didn't charge me. Then my mate got out and we started doing it together. The paramilitaries [ie the IRA] spoke to us and told us to stop. But next day we went off again. The IRA got annoyed with our gang and one night they picked four of us, took us round the corner and beat the shit out of us.

"My mate – he's totally mad, doesn't care about anything – he went straight downtown, got a motor and started doing handbrake turns, spinning the wheels and so on. The IRA came round again, slobbering away, saying you're gonna get shot if you don't stop this.

"Kneecapping stops some people but others just don't care. One pal of mine has been kneecapped, and another got shot in both knees and both elbows, but it hasn't stopped them. When my mate got caught in a motor and got six months, that started me thinking: did I really want to go to jail? But it's hard to stop, when all your other mates are at it, so we continued. One night I slipped up and got caught. Two CID men grabbed me, pulled me in. They put on this act, hard guy and soft guy, same as on TV; but they didn't have the evidence they needed to charge me. I must have been 14 at the time.

"Quite a few joyriders have been shot dead by the police or the Army, though it doesn't happen as much now. When you're stopped at a checkpoint you wait till the cop walks round to the window, then you stick the boot down and you're away. Into first, hit the accelerator. Then you put your head down and wait for shots. I got fired at a few times. Once a bullet went clean through the headrest. I was lucky I had my head down.

"One cop said to me: 'If ever I'm at a checkpoint and you crash through it, you're dead meat.' He never got me, but some of the boys have got killed. My mate was grazed in the back, leg, neck and arm. I bandaged him up. Shrapnel in his shoulder kept him bleeding for two days.

"At the start it was just pure fun – it was the joy of being able to go away, maybe even go to Dublin. Then the money part came into it. We'd be going for flash cars with big wheels and big stereos. You get a hell of a lot of money for them. But joyriders are different from hoods, and people understand that. Hoods break into houses, steal things, mug people. Joyriders just do cars. Sometimes people would ask us to take their car and burn it for the insurance. Other times they would ask us for car parts and we'd go and steal that particular type of car for them.

"The first time I was up in court my mate got six months and I got probation. The next time I got six months. But as soon as I got out, I went buck mad, cars and cars and cars. Most joyriders wind up in jail but some never get charged. One jammy bastard has never been inside, and he's been in three accidents where people have been killed and injured. Every time he's walked clean away.

"I got caught again and got another six months. After that I met a girl and gradually stopped. Then I met my old mates one night, we went to a club and got totally blocked. I woke up in Newcastle [a seaside resort] in a stolen car with a big cop standing right beside the window. Bang, six months again.

"That finished it for me. I stopped it and I'm in voluntary work now, helping kids, showing them how to weld and that. I haven't lifted a car for three years. But a lot of my mates are still at it. The cops shooting them won't stop it, and the IRA kneecapping them won't stop it. I don't know if anything will."

The battle for most parents and teachers in west Belfast, which is probably the poorest and most violent area of the United Kingdom, is to bring up children as normally as is possible in such circumstances. One man who does daily battle with security and economic difficulties is local headmaster John Watson.

A Catholic education

To get to John Watson's school you drive up the Falls Road, passing Divis Flats and the Sinn Féin offices, and fork left at the heavily fortified RUC–army base which overlooks Milltown cemetery. Keep straight on, past the spot where two soldiers were lynched in March, which is now busy with shoppers. Drive on past another security force base with its 20-foot-high anti-mortar walls, and you reach the sprawling Twinbrook housing estate.

Six army and police vehicles sit by a large open green area; the soldiers, relaxed on this sunny morning, are experimenting by a stream with two remote-controlled robots which they use to dismantle bombs. St Colm's High School is 200 yards further on, beside a huge modern social club bedecked with security fencing and cameras, where local republicans drink.

The first surprise is the sight, in the school grounds, of a minibus bearing the name of a state (ie, Protestant-attended) school from a peaceful part of the city: what on earth is it doing in west Belfast? Watson – tall, bearded, intense and talkative – is reluctant to go into details and asks several times that the Protestant school's name should not be used.

"We have a very strong commitment to peace and community relations. We're linked with a number of Protestant schools, and today we're staging a five-a-side football tournament. It's education for mutual understanding. Parents generally, on both sides, are quite happy with cross-community activities, but too much publicity can bring thunderbolts from the Protestant hardliners down on us. It's not the parents who will object – it's some of the politicians, some of the clergy. So please don't mention names."

Most of the children at this secondary school have not passed the 11-plus, which still exists in Northern Ireland. They are working class and generally poor: 75 per cent of them qualify for free school meals. Discipline, according to Watson, "is not a major problem: there is trouble with break-ins and there are many joyriders on the estate, but within the school our problems are not as bad as those I read about in some schools in Britain".

Party politics is kept at bay. "We don't have politics in the school: that's a deliberate policy of all schools here. We'd have difficulties about bringing in political studies – there'd be a fear that you'd start creating something you couldn't control. In any event, the older teenagers seem more concerned with world politics – the arms race and East–West relations – than with the local thing.

"It's almost a community decision to keep politics out. People accept schools as stable places where authority is still in control, where rules and regulations make for an ordered society. Nobody wants to damage that, so schools generally have been left alone." He reports few problems with the security forces: there has been friction on the estate in the past, but it is currently quiet. None the less, this is not normality.

"If the police come, for example, to look at a break-in, they can't just drive up in an ordinary police car. Here it's two army jeeps and a police jeep to bring the detectives in – a full-scale military operation. Some of them keep watch outside; meanwhile, I'm walking down the corridor with two or three detectives plus uniformed policemen with sub-machine-guns."

Watson guesses that west Belfast unemployment stands at 50–60 per cent. This is actually an underestimate: the Government cannot supply a precise figure, but official sources put the male unemployment rate at between 60 and 80 per cent. Clearly many of the children from St Colm's are destined for the dole.

Watson was born on the Falls Road, has taught in west Belfast for many years and has a Belfast Catholic's characteristically strong sense of justice. He firmly believes that his pupils, when they leave St Colm's, are not given a fair chance. Anti-Catholic discrimination, he says, is widespread. "There are different types of discrimination and sectarianism. The old Unionist government located most of the factories in Protestant areas, places which are still not conducive to Catholic employment. A lot of our people are wary of even considering applying to the big engineering concerns. Some of these places have been bedecked with sectarian symbols and emblems."

Technically, St Colm's pupils should attend the Jobcentre in Lisburn, scene of Wednesday night's IRA attack on military personnel, but they flatly refuse to do so. Watson says they regard it as an unfriendly area and prefer to go into Belfast instead.

"The Twelfth of July is one time when sectarianism flares, though there are other occasions. Who wants to be the first Catholic or the first small group of Catholics into a massive workplace where banners and flags are waved and drums are beaten? It takes a brave person." (New legislation aims to outlaw the use of provocative or intimidating emblems in the workplace, while laws in preparation will strengthen the penalties for discrimination.)

"The situation is improving in the professions – the law, medicine, accountancy, architecture. But state industries do not have a good record, the civil service still has a long way to go and local councils have a lot to answer for. Hopefully the situation will improve in state and semi-state industries, and areas

John Watson and his young hopefuls

CRISPIN RODWELL, *Independent*

where the state has financial muscle in terms of possibly withholding contracts. The Government hasn't done that so far, but hopefully they will do it.

"I see private industry, especially small firms, as the area most difficult to tackle, because there it's based very much on individuals and the Government may not have as much influence. In many cases management backs down or looks for the easy solution – that is, to keep the existing workforce pacified. What manager is going to risk annoying 300 workers to bring in a 15-year-old Catholic youngster on work experience for a week? It's very difficult to go against sectarianism; but as long as management tolerates it to the extent that it has, it's never going to go away.

"It can be very subtle. We had a case where we encouraged a lot of our youngsters to get application forms for a semi-state industry. They got as far as the gate lodge and they found a large Union Jack pinned up on the wall. They turned back. The children said, 'This is not for us.' We had quite a job persuading them to go back. The Union Jack, and to a large extent the tricolour, are sectarian emblems in certain circumstances – they're displayed in defiance or in triumphalism. The clear message from that Union Jack was 'Protestant ascendancy, we are the dominant group.' That's the way Catholics would see it."

But for all the difficulties, Watson is determinedly upbeat and displays that other Belfast Catholic belief, a faith in the value of education and of persistence.

"We try to equip pupils with the intellectual, academic and, I suppose, the emotional ability to be optimistic, not to be easily put off. Apathy is a problem with some youngsters and some parents but we try to send them out with optimism. The message we impart is that there are jobs there; and if they're not there, then they can be created and you can help to create them. The opportunities of the future will be in smaller industries and a lot of self-employment."

Watson's hope for improvement rests largely on an element of economic regeneration. "If there were jobs to be had, and there was fair competition, we may well find that in such a climate it might be easier to create cross-community links and greater harmony. But at the moment people are literally fighting for jobs. It's difficult to be generous and stretch the hand of friendship across the peaceline when the hand you're shaking may be the one that has taken the job away from you."

John Watson described the very real difficulties involved in achieving equality of job opportunity in a society where patterns of inequity persist. This problem increasingly exercised the minds of government ministers, in large part due to the Irish-American "MacBride Principles" campaign which, it was feared, would scare off potential American investment. I accompanied Tom King, the Secretary of State for Northern Ireland, when he toured the US in an effort to counter the campaign.

Battle for the minds of Irish America

T he traffic stopped for Tom King in New York. It had to. Mr King's six-car motorcade zoomed at high speeds through the city streets, its cacophony of sirens intimidating other vehicles out of the way. The drivers, men from the State Department's security section, sat with pump-action shotguns by their side. Mr King travelled in the back of a huge black-windowed Lincoln equipped with television and a private bar. One such journey took him from the World Trade Centre, where he hosted a lunch for businessmen in the 107th-floor restaurant, downtown to meet the editorial board of the *New York Times*. The trip was both exhilarating and exhausting.

Mr King may have been comfortable in his limousine, yet it was clear that his political position in the States was less so. For in spite of his intensive 11-day, nine-city swing through America, the British government is not winning the propaganda battle there. That battle is primarily with supporters of the MacBride Principles, who say Catholics in Northern Ireland are still suffering from the effects of discrimination.

The principles set out an affirmative-action approach, designed to give Catholics equal opportunities in job recruitment and promotions; at first glance unexceptionable, they have none the less formed the basis for a campaign which is causing the British government major political and presentational problems.

The campaign has been endorsed by five states, a dozen cities, American trade unions, church bodies and various Irish-American groups. Its supporters systematically raise the issue at shareholders' meetings of American firms. It is also supported by a number of powerful financial figures such as Jay Goldin, Comptroller of New York city. Mr Goldin, an ambitious politician keen to attract Irish votes, is worth watching: he administers a pension fund totalling $30 billion. The fund has money invested in most of the two dozen American firms with a presence in Northern Ireland.

Mr King has defined his task as stopping the MacBride bandwagon. His position is that the philosophy behind the principles is totally acceptable – the Government, after all, shares the aim of promoting more Catholic employment. But, he argues, the campaign is harmful in that it could scare off much-needed new investment from the States. Potential investors would be put off by the political controversy generated by the campaign itself: and you can't correct imbalances without first obtaining more jobs. Mr King also says the principles are probably illegal under Northern Ireland law, arguing that they amount to advocating reverse discrimination and quotas.

The Government has powerful allies. John Hume of the Social Democratic and Labour Party, whose influence in Irish America is tremendous, strongly opposes MacBride. So, largely because of Mr Hume, do powerful Irish-Americans in the Senate, centring on Teddy Kennedy. The Irish government is remaining studiously neutral, while the US administration is firmly against.

Underlying the British government's arguments is its view of people prominent in the MacBride campaign. Ministers see some as well intentioned but misguided and naïve, some as American opportunists cynically chasing the Irish vote, and some as totally malicious saboteurs, secretly intent on driving potential investment away. In this last category can be included Sinn Féin (the only Northern Ireland party to back the principles), and Noraid, which sends money to the IRA.

The Government is also suspicious of the motives of the Irish National Caucus which launched the campaign in 1984. Its leader, Father Sean McManus, born in Fermanagh, has led previous campaigns to stop US government contracts going to Shorts aircraft factory in Belfast, and to stop the sale of American guns to the Royal Ulster Constabulary. From the Caucus's Washington headquarters, a house on Capitol Hill not far from Congress, Father McManus sends out computerised letters and requests for funds. Send dollars, his latest mailshot pleads, "for the memory of our ancestors and for the Catholics in Northern Ireland today who are still denied their birthright".

He is unabashedly an old-style nationalist: "I want to see justice in Ireland. I want to see basic freedom, basic democracy, respect for human rights, the ending of discrimination. I know that can never happen under English rule. There will never be genuine democracy in Ireland for so long as the British maintain that statelet." Father McManus says he does not favour American disinvestment, but adds that if it happened, the sole responsibility would rest with the British government.

One of the features of the campaign, however, is that it has combined disparate elements in a loose coalition; not everyone involved is as implacably anti-British as Father McManus. Many of the others, in fact, have a very clear idea of what they wish to achieve. That does not include disinvestment, and nor does it include a simple wish to embarrass the British government.

One example is Sister Regina, a Catholic nun with Irish parents, who is "corporate responsibility co-ordinator" of the Sisters of Charity of New York. Her order has shares in many American companies. She says: "We, as part-owners of corporations, have a responsibility for what those corporations do. We're getting a monetary benefit, so it's incumbent to take the moral and social responsibility for what they're doing."

The principles do not, she says, mean reverse discrimination or a quota system, and are probably not illegal under British law. She is against dis-investment and says there is no evidence of a potential investor being scared off by the campaign. Her central point is that the British government, for whatever reasons, has not succeeded in achieving equality of opportunity in Northern Ireland. The lesson she draws is that continuing American influence will be necessary for improvement.

Her argument is echoed by Jay Goldin's assistant, Pat Doherty, who has energetically promoted the principles. He puts his case with American direct-ness. "The forces of internal reform are too weak. US pressure will be needed to get new laws and to make sure they are enforced."

The same message comes from Frank Costello, who handles Irish affairs for Raymond Flynn, the mayor of Boston. Of Mr King's visit he says: "The days are over when British ministers could come over here and satisfy us with fancy brochures. The fact is that they haven't done their job. There's still a lot of discrimination over there."

Flynn, Costello and other pro-MacBride figures in Boston cannot be accused of seeking disinvestment because they are involved in an ambitious venture to bring American entrepreneurial skills and investment to the cities of London-derry and Galway. Mr King has given their scheme his enthusiastic support.

A senior trade union leader who met Mr King in the States was unimpressed with his arguments. His perspective is this: "Look, I was where King is now. A lot of people in my union were against affirmative action to help blacks. But we had to do it, we had to make accommodations. We cleaned up our act. No matter what the difficulties, it's the only way."

Mr King has two main difficulties. First, although John Hume has neutralised much of Irish America on the issue, it is very difficult to persuade state legis-latures not to back a set of principles which seem so innocuous. Second, and more seriously, the facts are that the figures are not on Mr King's side. Eleven years after the passage of Northern Ireland's fair employment legislation, government figures clearly demonstrate that significant Catholic disadvantage remains.

No one is in serious doubt that the recent flurry of government activity on the fair employment front is due almost entirely to the American pressure. From this, the Irish-Americans draw the lesson that their pressure will have to be maintained. Unless the Government takes action to pass and enforce strong new laws, the MacBride bandwagon is set to keep on rolling.

The Government pressed on and brought forward a bill which, it said, would help stamp out discrimination and guarantee equality of opportunity in Northern Ireland's workplaces. Critics claimed, however, that the measure contained flaws which would render it defective and would perpetuate, rather than lessen, the problem.

31 JANUARY 1988   THE INDEPENDENT

Jobs law hopes to heal the divide

The fair employment question is one of the most important and most difficult issues in Northern Ireland today. Politically, economically and socially a great deal hangs on the handling of it: if it is mismanaged, the consequences could include new divisions in the workplace, major obstacles to inward investment and the perpetuation of inequities which help fuel support for Sinn Féin and the IRA.

The Government's case is that the proposed new law will significantly toughen the anti-discrimination legislation which came into operation in the mid-Seventies, but which has clearly made little impact on a situation where Catholic male unemployment is today still two and a half times that of Protestants. The existing Fair Employment Agency is to be replaced by a larger and better-funded Commission. The highly complex legislation will, according to the Government, tighten the law on a series of points. Employers will, for example, be legally required to make annual returns showing the religious breakdown of their workforces, and erring employers may face serious sanctions such as the denial of government contracts.

To the outside observer it may appear axiomatic that it is in almost everyone's interests to create equal job opportunity and hence a fairer society in Northern

Ireland. Such an approach appears not only morally correct but also pragmatically advisable, in that it should help to cut away at support for the Sinn Féin argument that the entire Northern Ireland state is unfair, unreformable and should be abolished by violent means. It should also help draw the sting of the vociferous Irish-American MacBride Principles campaign, which aims to put US political and financial pressure on Northern Ireland companies to hire more Catholics. The Government believes the campaign has a considerable nuisance value which could scare off potential American investors.

There are, however, strong forces ranged against reform. Unionist politicians resent the new measure, which they see as implicitly alleging that Protestants continually discriminate against Catholics. There is also the fear that at the end of the day attempts to provide more employment for Catholics will inevitably mean fewer jobs for Protestants; and many employers genuinely feel it is offensive to be required to carry out a sectarian headcount of their workforces. The Government has, however, paid rather more attention to the business lobby which has pressed, with some success, for a watering down of the new provisions. Businessmen – Catholic as well as Protestant – tend to view the new measure as another government-imposed distraction from economic activity. And many, especially those with a religious imbalance on their workforces, fear the new headcount may amount to the opening of a most unpleasant can of worms, bringing unwelcome government attention and causing ill feeling among employees.

Arguing from the opposite corner are elements which contend the new law will not go far enough; some of these allege the measure has been designed not to make a real difference at home but primarily to derail the MacBride campaign across the Atlantic. Certainly a great deal of government effort has been put into combating that campaign: one source claims the Northern Ireland Office spends more money flying supporters to the US to argue against the campaign than it does on actually promoting fair employment in Northern Ireland. This lobby tends to suspect the Northern Ireland Department of Economic Development, whose approach to the bill is seen as being over-influenced by the views of employers. One of the features of the new law will be that many of the actual regulations will not be in the legislation but will be drawn up later by the Department – an arrangement which the critics say will tend to give the business perspective too much leverage.

Those pressing for a stronger measure include Kevin McNamara, Labour's Northern Ireland spokesman, and a number of lawyers and academics. In the bill, they argue, the devil is in the detail; and in crucial areas, such as the scope for affirmative action by employers wishing to adjust imbalances, there are said to be serious inadequacies and ambiguities.

From the Northern Ireland perspective one thing is clear enough: there are considerable forces and lobbies who are opposed to attempts at improvement. Often this is done covertly rather than in public. If there are any loopholes or weaknesses in the new law, they will certainly be found and exploited, undermining the stated objects of the bill. And a perpetuation of inequity creates the type of fertile ground in which paramilitarism can continue to flourish.

1 FEBRUARY 1988   THE INDEPENDENT

Economic rift widens as Catholic fortunes improve

There is no doubt that the employment position of the Catholic community, taken overall, has improved significantly in the past decade and a half. A rising proportion of Catholics is to be found in areas such as the civil service and the health services. At senior levels in business, the civil service and the police, more Catholic names are to be seen. It is widely remarked in Belfast that much of the city's entrepreneurial thrust now comes from the growing Catholic business sector, rather than the Protestants who once prided themselves on their work ethic. The most expensive residential area of the city, Malone, is becoming more and more Catholic.

But the fact is that the improvement in the Catholic position has taken place in an uneven and unhealthy fashion. Government and government-related jobs are now more open, but there are large areas of the economy – major firms and some whole industries – which are still essentially Protestant. Most banks, for example, employ largely Protestant workforces. This is not necessarily due to active anti-Catholic discrimination, but has much to do with patterns and structures established under the Protestant Stormont government, together with the "chill factor" which prevents many Catholics from applying for jobs.

Northern Ireland appears, in fact, to be experiencing a process similar to that affecting blacks in America. There has been a rapid growth of a black middle class in the US; yet it is also apparent that many working-class blacks still hold low-status jobs as janitors, cleaners and cooks. In his book *The Declining Significance of Race,* Professor William Wilson noted a "deepening economic

126

schism developing in the black community, with the poor falling further and further behind middle- and upper-income blacks". Something similar appears to be happening in Northern Ireland. The Catholic middle class has done increasingly well but this process has left untouched those at the lower end of the economic scale. Their position has in fact worsened, with Catholic unemployment rising from 17 per cent in 1971 to 31 per cent in 1985. Some blackspots have up to 80 per cent joblessness. One Catholic politician said this week: "The division between the Catholic middle class and the poor unemployed Catholic is total. The experience of the two types is now completely different." This fact may go some way to explaining why various representatives of the Catholic community have given a comparatively low priority to the fair employment issue. Interest increased in the run-up to the bill, but over the past decade and a half the issue has not been an important item on the political agenda.

Neither of the nationalist political parties, the Social Democratic and Labour Party and Sinn Féin, has treated it as an issue of primary importance; nor has the Catholic Church, the Irish government or Catholic businessmen and trade unionists. Each is formally in favour of fair employment but none has emphasised it. The political push which produced the new bill was largely external, originating in Irish America and from Kevin McNamara of the Labour Party.

The SDLP's base is in the rural west of Northern Ireland, where unemployment is so high that the central problem is seen as one of employment rather than fair employment. The party has therefore defined the answer not as fairer employment but as more jobs. The Catholic Church has not, in Northern Ireland, developed the role of social conscience which it has done in the Irish Republic. It has, rather, put much more energy into defending its own institutional concerns in, for example, the field of education.

Catholic businessmen view the issue as potentially divisive for their workforces – and some, who employ more Catholics than Protestants, fear that this fact may lead to them being penalised under the new bill. Trade unions are in general nervous about dividing their religiously mixed memberships; and they tend to reflect the distribution of employed working-class power which, being largely Protestant, tends to frown on the whole topic of fair employment. In addition, the Catholic unemployed tend to count themselves out of the arena of political influence by the way they vote. Well over half of them appear to vote for Sinn Féin, whose position on the issue will, almost as a matter of principle, be ignored by the Government.

There is a great deal of fatalism among Catholics. One man said he would dissuade his son from applying to work in a particular large firm because "that's Apache territory". There is a tendency for Catholics to stick carefully to their traditional sectors of the segregated economy, avoiding those areas where they believe they will encounter resistance. Others emigrate.

The feeling is widespread that attitudes are so entrenched that little can be done to make a real difference. The test of the new bill is whether it will be strong enough to break down not only Protestant resistance but Catholic apathy as well.

In the spring of 1988 the idea grew up among some commentators that, in the pause which followed events in Gibraltar and west Belfast, a new chance for political progress had suddenly arisen. An analysis of the situation revealed, however, no real grounds for assuming that the deadlock was about to be broken.

8 APRIL 1988   THE INDEPENDENT

Northern Ireland: the window of opportunity is barred

Suddenly the atmosphere in Northern Ireland is upbeat and optimistic. There is talk of breakthroughs, rumours of fundamental reassessments, reports of light at the end of the tunnel. Hope is blooming with the daffodils. After months when political action took second place to horrifying murder, the emphasis is now on dialogue – even, perhaps, serious negotiation – between bitter foes. There is, it is said, a window of opportunity. Politicians now regularly proclaim their readiness to talk to opponents. The theory goes that recent violence has been so dreadful that people of goodwill are recoiling from such glimpses of the abyss and have been forced to contemplate living together.

There is, however, a problem with all this. It is that the hope exists not in political circles but in journalistic quarters. The apparatchiks of the important parties and paramilitary groups are bemused by the view that something is stirring. Yet, interestingly, the slightly starry-eyed approach is having an effect. That is why the language of dialogue is being used by politicians who, privately, do not believe for a moment in the window of opportunity. If they found such a window, many would set about closing and barring it with some determination. But open intransigence is momentarily out of fashion and dialogue is, ostensibly at least, the name of the game. There are politicians, nationalist and Unionist, who hope to see meaningful contacts established: they may even succeed in opening new forms of talks. The hard fact is that the political implacabilities are still in place, as rocklike as ever.

Tom King, the Secretary of State for Northern Ireland, and the Irish government are jointly responsible for some of the wave of false optimism. Mr King and Dublin have been eager to claim that the Anglo-Irish agreement is functioning well. The irony is that both Mr King and Charles Haughey, the Taoiseach, had deep misgivings about the agreement when it was signed in November 1985. Now they both cling to it, with something close to desperation, as a defence against paramilitarism. That is, of course, an excellent reason for backing the agreement; in Ireland, it is necessary to assert continually that politics is preferable to violence. The problem is that the accord, while sound enough in London and Dublin, is in trouble in Belfast. A recent poll indicated that 81 per cent of northern nationalists believe they have gained no benefit from it. This may hide as much as it reveals, because respondents were not asked whether they thought the agreement should be scrapped. Most would probably have voted to retain it. None the less, it shows that the accord has a serious credibility problem.

Southern nationalist opinion, horrified by northern violence and the possibility of its spilling over the border, appears ready to forgive and forget, or at least forgive and minimalise, on many of the contentious issues of recent months. The two governments, in other words, are prepared to drop or hide many of their disagreements.

North of the border the perspective is very different. London, the bitter complaint runs, simply did not give a damn for nationalist feelings in a series of keynote issues such as the Stalker–Sampson affair. The agreement was supposed to take account of nationalist sensitivities; instead it has appeared meaningless as Britain went its own way. It will need time and effort to demonstrate that London sees it as more than a device to reduce nationalist criticism of security policy.

Sinn Féin, the same poll indicated, lost support after the Enniskillen bombing but got it back with the Stalker and Birmingham Six decisions. It probably gained from the shootings of the three IRA members in Gibraltar, but dipped again after the deaths of the two soldiers who drove into the IRA funeral in Andersonstown. Violent death and political swings often go together.

The signs are that John Hume's exploratory talks with Sinn Féin will fail, in that there will be no IRA ceasefire. The IRA has had a mixed year: Enniskillen, the loss of eight men in the Loughgall ambush and the seizure of the Libyan arms on board the *Eksund* were severe blows. Fewer IRA members are coming before the courts, but more are being killed in action. Some become martyrs, but the high attrition rate must be a worry for the organisation. A ceasefire, however, can only be expected when the IRA feels its position is extremely strong or extremely weak. Neither of these conditions applies at the moment. Despite its losses, the IRA is still armed to the teeth with Libyan weaponry and explosives. The difficulty for the authorities, north and south, is that they underestimated the IRA's capabilities. Security sources will privately admit that they simply did not believe it could sustain the number of shootings and bombings of the past two and a half years.

One of the hopes for the agreement was that a reduction of violence would help local politicians come together in a new devolved government. Much of the current hope stems from the theory that this could still happen, but the signs are all against it. The SDLP, traditionally an advocate of devolution, is now faced with powerful arguments against it. The attitude of Unionist parties is confused: not all senior Unionists want devolution, and not all of those who do want it see it on a basis of partnership, with nationalists at the top level of government.

On the other flank, Sinn Féin would use any new assembly in the most divisive and disruptive way possible, denouncing SDLP compromises as sell-outs. A devolved administration would inevitably function with whatever resources Westminster decides to allocate. Furthermore, the feeling is general that the SDLP could not remain as members of a British-sponsored administration through the sort of security crises we saw recently. With the IRA continuing its campaign and the security forces reacting in ways that the SDLP finds unacceptable, its representatives would have to resign.

All of this suggests that devolution would be a force for instability rather than cohesion. The Unionist side remains a confusion of bickering factions, lacking in consensus. The agreement, as its architects hoped, began a debate among Protestants on their future in Ireland, but it is nowhere near resolution. There are few advocates of a new partnership arrangement, and none at all who say the accord should be accepted. James Molyneaux, of the Ulster Unionist Party, is not about to reverse a political lifetime spent opposing devolution, and Ian Paisley, of the Democratic Unionist Party, is not about to countenance Catholics in government. Mr Molyneaux will do nothing to differentiate Northern Ireland from the rest of the United Kingdom; and Mr Paisley, whose role models are

Protestant martyrs who went to the stake for their beliefs, will not compromise now, in the twilight of his career.

The devolutionists have not the power to overthrow these leaders. None of this rules out new talks, but it does explain why the notion of a breakthrough coming from them is so remote. Some may think false hope is better than none at all, but pretence is always a bad idea; and false dawns ultimately retard rather than accelerate the possibility of real advance.

Within a few months the springtime optimism had been dispelled, to be replaced by increasing cynicism about the political process. With none of the major parties having any substantial achievements to offer their supporters, and no negotiations under way, the mood of disillusionment grew.

14 SEPTEMBER 1988   THE INDEPENDENT

Northern Ireland: a failure of politics

The late Sean Lemass, when leader of Fianna Fáil, Ireland's largest party, once wrily described it as "a slightly constitutional party". Everyone knew what he meant: it is a familiar idea that the political process is not the only way to settle disputes. The thousands of people who use the Falls Road, for example, pass a huge mural which includes the words of Mairead Farrell, the IRA heroine killed by the SAS in Gibraltar. It proclaims: "I have always believed we had a legitimate right to take up arms and defend our country and ourselves against the British occupation."

Some, such as Sinn Féin and the IRA, have opted for violence rather than politics, though they will make cynical use of the electoral process. Others are primarily involved in political activity but will, at certain times, move easily enough into paramilitary mode: the Rev Ian Paisley has perfected this technique.

The use of force, or the threat of it, is usually a subtheme except in times of extreme crisis. There is currently a security crisis in Northern Ireland as a ruthless and heavily armed IRA attempts, in the words of the RUC, to provide a horrific remainder to 1988. And there is a real question mark as to how well the security forces will be able to cope. But there is also a political crisis which has been little remarked on, partly because of the violence and partly for other reasons. Political activity has rarely been held in such low esteem, and that is a dangerous state of affairs. This is, of course, what the IRA wants. It is at its happiest when the only real news concerns its violence and the security forces' response. The coverage it prefers is that of IRA v Brits, the hammer and the anvil, with local politicians irrelevant.

It used to be the case, in the early and mid-Seventies, that those attempting to find agreement on devolution were fixated with the problem of what to do with Mr Paisley. The conundrum was this: it seemed impossible to conceive of an arrangement which included him since he was more interested in protest than power. But it also seemed impossible to establish a workable arrangement without him, since he had the capacity to bring it down. That particular puzzle has never been solved. Some people believe that Sinn Féin and the IRA are now in the process of demonstrating that they exercise a similar veto. It goes without saying that they cannot be brought into the system, since they use violence and since their political demands are to all intents and purposes simply non-negotiable. Yet from their position outside the system they have inflicted more damage on the Anglo-Irish agreement than it has on them.

The talks between Sinn Féin and John Hume, leader of the Social Democratic and Labour Party, established once and for all that the republicans had no interest in joining the political system and attempting to change it from within. Their attempts to alter it are being made with Semtex and Kalashnikovs.

And what, meanwhile, is happening within the system? Some of the politicians are gamely seeking to give the appearance of being busy men, but actually the picture is one of stagnation. There is activity but no action. Publicly it is business as usual but, in private, politicians of all parties are prepared to say the situation is bleak, and deteriorating.

"I think it has never been so bad," an SDLP man said. "There aren't any politics at all. It's a matter of battening down the hatches." According to a Unionist representative: "Protestant opinion is all over the place. I can't detect any common threads in what people are saying, though the comment I hear most is 'Huh, you people [the politicians] aren't much use, are you?' They're fed up,

132

they're confused and they're pessimistic."

In theory, the temptation of devolution offers the best prospect of finding common ground between Protestant and Catholic. In practice, however, the idea has lost much of its attraction. On the Unionist side, the party leaders, Ian Paisley and James Molyneaux, are dead against talks. Starry-eyed speculation about them contemplating talks with Dublin has disappeared, leaving a number of depressed and disillusioned former optimists. Nor are meaningful inter-party talks any more likely. Mr Paisley and Mr Molyneaux made it very clear, within hours of the ending of the Sinn Féin–SDLP talks, that this did not mean the way was open for them to meet Mr Hume. Mr Paisley said the agreement would have to be suspended first; Mr Molyneaux said talking would only be a distraction from the battle against the IRA and felt they should wait until terrorism had been eradicated.

To Mr Paisley, religion is more important than politics: his career is a fight not against Irish nationalism but against Catholicism. He is simply not interested in coming to terms with the Catholic minority: that, for him, would be a deal with the devil. Mr Molyneaux is an integrationist: he believes devolution is dangerous because it would set Northern Ireland apart from the rest of the United Kingdom. This desire to become British has over the years developed into an antipathy towards many of the usual forms of political activity. This in turn has led him to conclude that discussion is an intrinsically risky business. "Why the insistence," he asked a year ago, "that talking is the most important function of elected representatives?"

Some of those in the ranks of their parties favour talks – principally Mr Paisley's deputy, Peter Robinson, and Ken Maginnis, the Unionist MP – but they face an uphill struggle to push their own leaders to any conference table. Mr Robinson's stock is not as high as it once was amongst loyalists and Mr Maginnis, though a genuine advocate of accommodation, lacks strategic political skills.

The reputations of the two party leaders have been severely battered by their failure to shift the Anglo-Irish agreement, but almost by default they remain in charge. Although the agreement is still in place and is now approaching its third anniversary, it has proved a major disappointment to the SDLP and other non-violent nationalists. Originally sold as a vehicle for reforms to help Catholics, it is increasingly regarded as a device almost completely concerned with cross-border security co-operation. The reforms have not materialised. An SDLP source said glumly: "If I went into a working-class district in my area and mentioned the benefits of the agreement, they'd laugh at me. They'd ring Purdysburn [a Belfast psychiatric hospital]."

The Irish and British governments, however, are not so critical of the accord. In Dublin, Charles Haughey keeps a personal oversight of every detail of its working, to the extent that work has been considerably slowed down. The northern nationalist criticism – muted, since the SDLP does not want to display divisions with Dublin – is that Mr Haughey is allowing the agreement to wither. His policy, the private allegation goes, is one of indifference or even antagonism to the accord – because it was not his creation, and because he believes it simply props up a Northern Ireland state which he has in the past described as a failed entity.

The final factor in the subterranean crisis affecting politics is the Secretary of State for Northern Ireland, Tom King. Holders of this post fall into two categories: the activists (Whitelaw, Prior, Hurd) and the passivists (Rees, Atkins and now King). Mr King has presided over the current deterioration, and has seen no point at which he might make a decisive intervention. Perhaps there never was such a point; but the net effect of his approach, and the attitude of most of the other players, has been to leave the field clear for the IRA to exploit.

The only real political forums in Northern Ireland at this time were the monthly meetings of the twenty-six local councils. Rather often, however, these meetings were characterised by a certain lack of moderation and goodwill.

---

4 JUNE 1988   THE INDEPENDENT

Protest tactic that paralyses Belfast council

" I would like," the Sinn Féin councillor said, "to raise item B572 of the minutes." All 30 Unionist councillors immediately rose to their feet and headed for the door. "We object to the proposed closure of St George's Market," the Sinn Féin man said. One of the Unionists, Alderman Sammy

Wilson, turned and shouted: "Gunman, gunman, that's what he is." His colleagues joined in: "Gangsters, IRA men, get them out." Some banged desks.

A councillor, on a point of order, asked: "Is it in order for him to appeal to keep the market open when his party blew it up?" Alex Maskey, the most outspoken of the Sinn Féin people, retorted: "You never know, it could be bombed again." After some minutes of bedlam, Alderman Wilson could be heard proposing that the Sinn Féin councillor "be no longer heard". A quick show of hands and the Sinn Féin microphone was cut off and business moved on.

After a few minutes, Sinn Féin councillor Sean McKnight stood up. The Lord Mayor, Nigel Dodds, called everyone else who wanted to speak, then finally pointed to him and said: "You." "What's my name?" Mr McKnight demanded. The Lord Mayor repeated: "You."

Throughout the evening Mr Dodds, a young solicitor who is one of the Rev Ian Paisley's closest aides, would not name him or any of the Sinn Féin councillors. When a Sinn Féin man called for more recognition of the Irish language and spoke a few words in Irish, the Lord Mayor called him to order: "It's not in order to speak in a foreign language in this chamber. You'll not be allowed to say that as long as I'm in this chair."

Unionist councillors, who had left their seats and were chatting over at the door, quickly resumed their seats, proposed that the Sinn Féin man not be heard, and voted him down. Rhonda Paisley, her father's daughter in every way, said Sinn Féin used the Irish language as a political weapon. "It drips with their bloodthirsty saliva," she said. For Ms Paisley the choice lay between the IRA and democracy.

Members of Sinn Féin's non-violent nationalist opponents, the Social Democratic and Labour Party, argued in vain that the two sides should tolerate each other's traditions and culture. "For heaven's sake, grow up," an SDLP man told Alderman Wilson. "Show a bit of political maturity." The said alderman, undaunted, continued to deliver taunts about what he termed "leprechaun language".

"Come on over here and heckle, Sammy," Mr Maskey invited menacingly. He is the most belligerent of the Sinn Féin people, possibly because last year he was shot in the stomach by loyalists. Across the chamber, perhaps 20 feet away, sits Elizabeth Seawright, whose husband was last year shot dead by republicans.

Alderman Wilson is, in real life, a cheerful and intelligent teacher. The purpose of it all, he said outside the chamber, is to get the Government to ban Sinn Féin, and to frustrate its councillors. He explained: "If they propose anything – it doesn't matter what it is – we defeat it. They haven't got one thing through in three years. There is no question of the merits. If Sinn Féin raise it, it's dead. By our protests we are demonstrating that while they are here there will be no normality." Until quite recently the Unionists employed an even more effective tactic; they simply never called Sinn Féin to speak at all. The threat of High Court action, however, meant this had to be dropped.

The fact is that Sinn Féin has more than 50 councillors throughout Northern Ireland. In Belfast, where 30 Unionists are faced by nine Sinn Féin and six SDLP members, and on a number of other councils, it is the largest non-Unionist party. In a few councils Sinn Féin is actually the largest party and it holds a couple of council chairmanships.

Brian Feeny of the SDLP, in defending his party's recent talks with Sinn Féin, summed up the problem. Eighty-five thousand people, he said, voted for Sinn Féin; they and the IRA were not going to go away, so the talks were aimed at finding out if they could be weaned away from the gun and brought into the political process.

In the meantime, Sinn Féin councillors say they will not be driven out. Unionists, on the other hand, say they will never be acceptable. The two sides sit, implacable and irreconcilable, just feet away from each other, each regarding compromise as defeat. Together they make up a bitter, frozen little tableau, a microcosm of political life in Northern Ireland.

The autumn 1988 conference of the Democratic Unionist Party would, it was suggested, be the occasion for a major initiative from Ian Paisley. It failed to materialise.

Paisley party piece fails to dispel mood of Unionist apathy

E ven though he had billed it as "probably the most important speech I will ever make", there was a smaller than usual media turnout for the Rev Ian Paisley's address to his Democratic Unionist Party conference on Saturday. In the event, he did come up with one or two intriguing lines; they aroused, however, only tepid interest in Belfast and in Dublin. Try though he might to come up with something novel, the feeling seems to be growing that the old dog has no new tricks to show.

That is not to say for a moment that he has had his day electorally. On the stump, the Big Man, as he is known, is hard to beat; his electioneering is endlessly entertaining and loyalists enjoy voting for him. But his credibility has been affected by a series of failed campaigns and called bluffs. His own faithful, of course, are still with him: nobody is more free from doubt than a Paisleyite. Thus they may well have believed him when he told them on Saturday that the Government appeared to have banned the Bible. Under new Public Order legislation, Mr Paisley warned: "It is possible that to possess in your home a copy of the Holy Scriptures could make you guilty of an offence."

His problem, however, is that he has to reach a wider audience than those who clapped and laughed as he ridiculed popes and priests. Next spring brings local government and European elections, and the latter are particularly important to him. In previous European contests, Mr Paisley has amassed an enormous vote: a drop next time would be a sore blow to his pride and his party morale. Thus he needed to take an initiative to improve his standing and begin the formidable task of dispelling the rampant apathy currently afflicting Unionism.

His new position, however, turned out to be much the same as the old one: a call for the suspension of the Anglo-Irish agreement, followed by the election of a new assembly charged with coming up with ideas for political progress. No one has expressed surprise at the speech, and no one expects the Government to take up the suggestion.

In the past, a Paisley initiative might have taken the form of a protest, a street

137

stunt or perhaps the announcement of some shadowy force of irregulars. But the loyalist appetite for the dramatic has been blunted by the collapse of a succession of such moves: the bombast is losing its effect. Now the move takes the form of a speech, studded with coded hints that if only the agreement could be put into cold storage, then new movement might be possible. Once or twice, past Northern Ireland Secretaries of State have nibbled at such bait from the DUP leader; they have wound up, months later, sadder but wiser men. For Tom King, the calculation is how much reliance might be placed in a party leader stuck without much of a policy and worried about forthcoming elections. There is little evidence that Mr Paisley is thinking of future movement rather than clinging to the past. The family Jaguar which delivered his wife and grandchild to the conference bore the licence plate MOI 1690 – the date of the Battle of the Boyne.

August and September brought a large-scale escalation of IRA violence, in particular the killing of eight soldiers in the bombing of an army bus at Ballygawley, Co Tyrone. The dimensions of the IRA menace were now becoming clear.

Security forces fear big push by IRA

T owards the end of last year, the authorities in Northern Ireland began to realise that they had a grievously incomplete picture of the strategy of the IRA. During 1987 the organisation had significantly raised its general level of violence: the statistics of shootings and bombings rose markedly and the assassination of Lord Justice Gibson represented a major morale-boosting success for the terrorists. On the other hand, the deaths of eight IRA men in an ambush by the SAS at Loughgall early last year was a serious setback; and the Army's new border watchtowers and the death of a leading IRA figure, Jim Lynagh, at Loughgall seemed to show that the Army was getting results in south Armagh.

The official view was that the IRA, with some difficulty, was trying to raise its profile to attack the Anglo-Irish agreement. Intelligence sources were, in the middle of last year, surprised by the extent to which the IRA had managed to increase the number of its attacks. That was the first surprise, but not the last.

The momentum of violence was not only maintained but increased. The Enniskillen Remembrance Day bombing hit Sinn Féin's support badly, but did not affect the IRA's capabilities. And late last year everybody's perception changed with the discovery that the terrorists had received well over 100 tons of weaponry from Libya and carefully stockpiled it for future use.

The IRA still has political aspirations through Sinn Féin, its political wing, but most of the attention is now focused on military activity. There are a number of reasons for this – one being the organisation's possession of such a stock of explosives and modern weaponry.

The development of Sinn Féin as a political party has brought dividends but these have their limits, many of which have been reached. Support for Sinn Féin in Northern Ireland seems stuck at around 12 per cent, and the party's vote in the Republic remains insignificant. At one point the Sinn Féin president, Gerry Adams, was successful in forging links with elements on the left of the Labour Party, but the Harrods and Brighton bombs largely wiped out such gains.

There are no important splits within the IRA or Sinn Féin today; certainly, there is debate and argument, but it is about tactics and timing, not aims or methods. Both organisations are concerned with blasting Britain out of Ireland.

A Garda officer carries away heavy machine guns discovered in an IRA arms dump on a Co Donegal beach. PACEMAKER PRESS INTERNATIONAL

The aim is to break the British political will to stay, and there is unanimity in the ranks that the use of force would be the major factor in achieving this. The only questions are exactly how, and when, resources should be used.

One security force theory is that a big push will now come quickly, to cash in on the current high level of public attention achieved by the Ballygawley coach bombing last Saturday and recent attacks on the Continent and in London. "They have geared themselves up," according to one security source. "The next six weeks in particular are likely to be very difficult." The unknown factors are how hard the IRA will try in the coming weeks, and what the results will be.

Experience shows that the IRA does not gamble everything on one throw, so there is no question that everything will be used in an all-out assault. The possession of the kind of weaponry the terrorists now have, however, carries its own imperative, and the best guess is that the next two years will see a sustained attempt to put their campaign on an entirely new plane.

The problem for the security forces is that the IRA has so many options. Its target list includes security force personnel, judges, loyalists, those who work for the security forces and others. Its weapons include anti-aircraft guns, missiles and rockets. The IRA has always recognised the value of diversification. Only this week, it declared two more categories to be at risk – naval officers and "commercial targets" in town and city centres. Faced with such threats, the security forces have been compelled to change patrolling patterns, strengthen vehicles and alter helicopter tactics – and the IRA has yet to use the bulk of its heavy weaponry.

Last year the security forces thought the IRA was in top gear; in fact, it was only in second. Today it is in third gear; the real test will come if and when it shifts into top.

The violence of the late summer resulted in a high-level security review directly involving the Prime Minister. At one point it seemed as though the reintroduction of internment without trial was a real possibility.

---

22 AUGUST 1988   THE INDEPENDENT

Internment: will the trauma return?

All those involved in the internment debate, on either side of the argument, agree on one point: it would transform the security and political situation in Northern Ireland. The disagreement lies in whether that change would be for better or for worse.

It is also common ground that when last used, between 1971 and 1975, internment proved disastrous and traumatic. It is difficult to underestimate its lasting effect on the Irish nationalist psyche: the anniversary of its introduction is still, more than a decade on, one of the major dates in the republican calendar. The memory of internment endures because it has never been just another security measure. Symbolically and in practice it would mark a new era in government policy in Northern Ireland. It would represent an admission that the rule of law is inadequate to deal with the IRA, and signal a reversal of the policy adhered to, through many difficulties, for more than a decade.

The first Operation Demetrius swoops in the early hours of 9 August 1971 netted more innocent men than IRA activists. The files of the RUC Special Branch, it soon became obvious, were obsolete and inaccurate. Within hours street disorders were widespread. Hostility between the security forces and much of the Catholic community reached a new pitch, and polarisation between the communities heightened dramatically. Those released told tales of casual brutality in the interrogation centres.

Internationally the image of British justice was considerably harmed – particularly in America, where the IRA benefited from a new wave of support. The dollars rolled in. Anglo-Irish relations plummeted: the Republic accused Britain of torture. Years later the European Court of Human Rights found the UK guilty of inflicting "inhuman and degrading treatment" on a number of internees.

Internment triggered off the bloodiest days of the Troubles. Gun battles became nightly occurrences. Up till 9 August that year 30 people had died violently. In the remainder of 1971, 143 were killed. The following year, by far the worst of the Troubles, 467 died.

The second tier of IRA leaders, who took over after the first swoop, employed indiscriminate no-warning car bombing. Even so, the IRA gained greatly in recruits and support. Some working-class Catholic districts became "no-go areas" for the security forces. I recall, during an exploratory drive along the Falls Road, having to produce my press card to two youths in a hijacked Jaguar. One examined it, while his friend, who looked about 16, sat comfortably in the back seat watching me. I shall always remember his piercing blue eyes and his sub-machine-gun.

Thousands embarked on rent and rates strikes; many Catholics withdrew from public life as a protest. Internment was seen as anti-Catholic since it was the work of the then Unionist government, and since no loyalist paramilitaries were held.

Many Protestants, far from being reassured that the IRA was finally being engaged, were alarmed by the dramatic increase in violence. Tens of thousands joined underground militias such as the Ulster Defence Association and the Ulster Volunteer Force. Loyalist assassinations, of the type which still persist in Belfast, began in earnest.

The key question now is whether something similarly calamitous would happen again, or whether everything would be different this time. The basic thesis of the pro-internment faction is that the security forces are more experienced now and wiser; that almost all IRA activists are known and on file, and that internment could be introduced with a degree of selectivity, professionalism and sensitivity which was missing in 1971. This lobby includes almost all Unionist political opinion: the near-unanimous view among loyalists is that internment should be accompanied by a ban on Sinn Féin and the reintroduction of capital punishment. Some Unionist MPs also favour detaining violent loyalists; others, including the Rev Ian Paisley, say that only republicans should be held.

Others in favour include a number of journalists, notably Conor Cruise O'Brien, and the Northern Ireland Police Federation. The latter group appears to represent a large body of opinion in the middle and lower ranks of the RUC, though not the views of the force's commanders. Advocates of internment can point out that fewer important IRA men are coming before the courts; that the IRA, with its Libyan-supplied weaponry, is now more heavily armed than ever and intent on raising the level of violence even higher.

Nationalist opinion is without exception strongly against internment. The list of opponents includes the Irish government, the Social Democratic and Labour Party and the Catholic hierarchy, together with the Labour Party, the SLD and civil liberties groups. Most of the nationalist argument is based not on the moral ground that locking people up without trial is wrong, but on the fear that Sinn Féin and the IRA would once again be the beneficiaries. Moderate elements would suffer. The SDLP, for example, has based much of its recent approach on the belief that Britain regards the problem as political and not merely as a security issue. Internment would be seen as demolishing that argument.

It is also most unlikely that the Irish government would bring in internment south of the border. Charles Haughey's administration is more likely to condemn the policy than copy it. Internment in the north alone would probably not work and might well mean the break-up of the Anglo-Irish agreement – an important incidental result which would delight Unionists.

The worst nightmare is that something as bad, or almost as bad, as the 1971 experience could happen again. Nationalists, north and south, could again become completely estranged from the authorities. The IRA and Sinn Féin could be strengthened rather than weakened. Britain's image abroad would suffer.

And the likelihood is that public disorder and IRA violence would increase. The IRA has made contingency plans, and violence would also probably become more haphazard and arbitrary, as it did in 1971–2, with less of the relatively tight political control over terrorist activity.

To date the British government has accepted this analysis. Of course, none of it can be stated with absolute certainty: it is conceivable that internment in 1988 could succeed where internment in 1971 failed so dismally. What is certain is that the risks can hardly be overstated. If internment is tried again and fails, it could result in the regeneration of the IRA – an error of historic proportions.

September 1988 brought the twentieth anniversary of the first civil rights march, from Coalisland to Dungannon in Co Tyrone. The march and rally held to commemorate the event highlighted the divisions within the Catholic community.

5 SEPTEMBER 1988   THE INDEPENDENT

Marching to the beat of the Armalite

One thousand people took part yesterday in a march from Coalisland to Dungannon in Co Tyrone to commemorate the first Northern Ireland civil rights march 20 years ago. Although the number taking part in the march was roughly the same as in 1968, the crucial difference was immediately apparent. The foot band in the parade had a drawing of an Armalite rifle on the bass drum. The people on this march did not share the belief in non-violence held by most of those on the first protest. The best-received speaker at the rally in Dungannon town centre was Gerry Adams, Sinn Féin president, who said the state of Northern Ireland was terminally ill. It was being maintained on "a life-support unit of British repression" and would never recover.

The original march, one of the organisers recalled yesterday, was non-violent. "We thought we could do a Gandhi. We all sat down in the road, to start with.

But really, we should have known that we are just not Indians."

None the less, the Unionist government of the day, prepared as it was to meet IRA force with force, was completely outflanked and confused by the non-violent approach. It could not cope with the argument that if Irish nationalists were to be classed as British citizens, then they should have full British rights. That argument drove a wedge between the Unionists and their former allies in the British government; it also split Unionism into factions which believed civil rights demands should be conceded and those who adamantly opposed all reform.

Although the civil rights movement was non-violent, some in its ranks, principally republicans and revolutionary socialists, believed even then in the use of force. Others who were present at yesterday's march would say they did not originally think violence could be justified, but have been changed by the experience of the past 20 years.

The original civil rights coalition of working class and middle class, republicans, nationalists, and socialists, broke up quite quickly into those who favoured political means and those who opted for stronger measures. This is still the key division in Irish nationalism today.

The marchers yesterday supported, or could tolerate, the IRA's "armed struggle". This was a part of the Catholic population which has decided, in the words of the main banner, that there can be "no civil rights without national rights". They believe a solution can be found only after a British withdrawal. They are opposed by the majority of Catholics who believe, in line with the policy of the non-violent Social Democratic and Labour Party, that Northern Ireland can be changed and improved without violence.

Mr Adams and other speakers condemned official "repression"; the other view is that most of the controversy generated today – disputed shootings, security policy and so on – has its roots in the Government's response to the IRA's campaign of violence.

There are two versions of what happened to the original civil rights movement: the SDLP view is that it was hijacked by extremists who sought confrontation and eventually turned to violence; the speakers yesterday, by contrast, portrayed the SDLP as middle-class elements who had betrayed and deserted the original movement.

The speakers yesterday said the violence of the past 20 years was tragic and unnecessary but essentially the responsibility of the British government. The other side of Irish nationalism argues that the IRA cannot so easily shrug off any blame for the two decades of turmoil.

During the late 1980s the authorities made efforts, none of them particularly successful, to clamp down on the racketeering and other activities used by the terrorist groups to finance their campaigns. The problem was highly complex and difficult to tackle.

The business of terrorism

D espite official attempts at a clampdown, paramilitary organisations in Northern Ireland – both republican and loyalist – continue to net very large amounts of money through racketeering. The Government is in the process of introducing laws to curb paramilitary finances. But terrorist organisations, in particular the IRA, have countered by switching resources into legitimate or apparently legitimate businesses.

The authorities believe – and paramilitary sources confirm – that both sides extract thousands of pounds each week from the construction industry alone. In addition, the organisations run drinking clubs and collect money from taxi operators, among other activities.

The Government is planning tighter controls on public money and new laws to impose stricter regulations on clubs and to limit the number of gaming machines they have. A further measure is aimed at outlawing bogus security firms which give cover for paramilitary extortion. An amendment to anti-terrorist legislation will ban all security firms not certified by the Secretary of State for Northern Ireland. In another development, the Northern Ireland Office has withdrawn funding from a number of community organisations suspected of having paramilitary links.

The IRA's main sources of income are the building trade and the major drinking clubs it controls, especially in Belfast. On the loyalist side, paramilitary groups make money from the building industry, from taxis and from crude but effective protection rackets. The loyalist protection business, which dates from the early Seventies, grew with the major Belfast slum-clearance programmes of

146

the past five years. Firms which refused to pay tended to be heavily hit by vandalism, theft and malicious damage. Before long, paying protection became the norm on building sites in loyalist areas. Sometimes firms hand over several thousand pounds as one-off settlements. In other cases amounts ranging from £100 to £500 are paid weekly. Businesses are also asked for occasional "bonus payments" for the families of imprisoned group members.

One businessman, who would not be named, said: "Two of these men came into my office and explained, very civilly, that I needed protection for my business. When I said I didn't want any, they replied that accidents could happen, that fires could start."

[One of these two men was Jim Craig, the UDA's chief racketeer who was later shot dead by his own organisation. *See* "Jim Craig: death of 'public enemy number one'".]

"I went to the police and told them about the threats. They showed me mugshots and I picked out the two men immediately. They asked me if I would give evidence in court but they made it very clear they couldn't protect me or my family if I did. Some firms hold out against them, but people are frightened for their families' sakes. One friend of mine received in the post a photograph of himself, his wife and children leaving church. Another had a phone call to his home saying, 'Your son looked well getting out of school today.'"

That sort of thinly veiled threat is typical, according to a security source who said: "They call at a site, or at a man's home and talk to his wife. The most effective thing they do is to mention his family; very often that's enough. They don't need guns or hoods."

In some cases firms are given receipts from the bogus security firms. These are registered companies making tax returns, but little attempt is made to conceal their purpose. One such firm, listed in the Yellow Pages, has the same address and phone number as the Belfast office of a loyalist paramilitary group.

Another source of steady income for one loyalist group, the Ulster Volunteer Force, is collections from taxis operating in loyalist areas. In west Belfast, according to authoritative sources, 70 taxi drivers each pay £29.20 a week, netting the organisation more than £100,000 annually. Such groups also control social clubs which provide revenue but are neither as well run nor as profitable as those controlled by the IRA.

There is no doubt that loyalist and republican groups handle millions of pounds each year; yet there are signs that the profit is lower than might be expected. One large and constant drain on their resources is prison welfare payments. The major organisations make weekly contributions – typically £5 to £10 – to the families of their imprisoned members. Northern Ireland's jails hold approximately 1,300 prisoners on terrorist-related offences, and the families of most receive welfare payments which mount up to an annual expenditure for the organisations which is almost certainly in excess of £500,000. Another drain is that referred to by one paramilitary leader as "internal theft". When organisations keep false accounts – or no accounts at all – money easily goes into private pockets.

The key problem for the Royal Ulster Constabulary is producing evidence which will be acceptable in court. The RUC has a special rackets squad, designated CI3. The unit receives many complaints, but those who are intimidated generally will not testify. Privately, the authorities say businessmen who will not give evidence must bear a measure of blame for their own problems. The businessmen reply that it is the authorities' function to protect them, and they are not doing so. While such arguments continue, so does the racketeering.

30 DECEMBER 1986   THE INDEPENDENT

'Acceptable' face of IRA rackets

The Provisional IRA's well-developed fundraising structure is based on a carefully worked-out philosophy. Its guiding principle is that it should be broadly acceptable in those Catholic working-class areas from which it draws support. Its methods illustrate how the search for votes for its political wing, Sinn Féin, has changed the IRA and led to the streamlining and refinement of its illegal activities.

The IRA's methods are, in general terms, no great secret to most people in the republican ghettos; the emphasis is on ensuring that the techniques of raising money do not alienate actual or potential supporters. Thus the general public is largely untroubled by demands for money; strong-arm tactics are rare; and in some cases the IRA actually provides a service as it raises its funds. The most obvious example of this can be seen in the IRA's social clubs, particularly in Belfast. Clubs controlled by paramilitary groups have been in existence for almost two decades. At first most of these were crude, unlicensed shebeens, but over the years a number have developed into fully licensed premises. Several dozen of Northern Ireland's 600 social clubs, including some of the largest, are

148

under paramilitary control. A great deal of money is spent in these establishments: according to government statistics, members spent £34 million on alcohol in clubs last year.

The IRA controls several very large clubs in Belfast, as well as many smaller establishments. According to official figures, the larger IRA clubs have a combined annual turnover of more than £1 million. A number of the clubs are among the largest and best-appointed in the city. They often feature cabaret by very well known artists.

One of those who inspects the clubs said: "They provide luxurious surroundings, first-class entertainment and cheap drink. They are, on the face of it, completely legitimate. The police go in by appointment to check the books – and the books are always in order. The police are courteously received, often offered a drink. These people employ accountants, solicitors and professional stewards and managers."

The authorities have announced new measures designed to tighten up clubs legislation. The new laws will make life difficult for some smaller clubs, but no one believes they have any hope of putting the larger paramilitary establishments out of business. The authorities are concerned that profits from the clubs will shortly be used to buy, through front men, respectable bars outside the ghettos of Belfast in trouble-free areas of Co Down. Furthermore, the Royal Ulster Constabulary's Special Branch is investigating a report that IRA funds are being channelled to a large pub-owning partnership.

An incidental but surprisingly substantial source of income lies in the gaming machines installed in many clubs. Although the machines take only 10p and 50p coins, they are often in heavy use and in some clubs can net several thousand pounds in a week. The IRA appears to supply and service these machines in its own clubs. In other cases, it may put its machines in non-IRA establishments. New regulations aimed at cutting down paramilitary finances will limit the number of machines to two per club.

At the beginning of the Eighties the IRA hit a real jackpot – the building trade. Groups such as the IRA had been making money from housing work for years; 10 years ago a confidential police report concluded that terrorist organisations had probably skimmed off around £1 million from building contracts in 1974 and 1975. New controls were introduced but the problem was never entirely eradicated. The large-scale slum-clearance effort of the Eighties meant a great increase in demolition, new building and rehabilitation work, much of it in those working-class areas where groups such as the IRA are strongest.

The most profitable area was the use of tax-exemption certificates. Large building firms pay sub-contractors holding such certificates a lump sum for carrying out agreed work. The sub-contractors take over all tax liability. The IRA and other groups moved in and intimidated legitimate certificate-holders.

Under the deals they dictated, the organisations kept a share, commonly 15 per cent, of the lump sum. The site workers handed over some of their wages to the IRA — usually 25 per cent — but many recouped the money through illegally claimed unemployment benefit. When the tax became due many of the certificate-holders simply declared themselves bankrupt. In other cases the certificates turned out to be forged.

The heyday of this particular racket has now passed, but even the authorities can only guess at the total sums involved. In the past few years the RUC has charged 180 people in this field, mainly in connection with the misuse of tax-exemption certificates. Around 60 have been dealt with in the courts and the rest are still being processed. The amount of money involved comes to just under £55 million. About one third of this is owed in tax. A great deal of such missing money is simply pocketed by various criminal elements unconnected with paramilitary outfits; some is taken by other groups.

The Provisional IRA has, in fact, a major though hardly ever publicised rival for funds. This is the "Official IRA", a group which broke with the Provisionals in 1969–70. The Officials, as they are known, declared a ceasefire in 1972 and have since then only rarely indulged in overt violence. For years the organisation has issued no public statements; in fact, it no longer acknowledges its own existence. Yet members and former members have been deeply involved in racketeering.

The Provisionals dislike the Official IRA but treat them with wary respect. They — and the authorities — have good reason to believe that the Officials maintain a highly sophisticated up-to-date armoury, largely as insurance against attack from the Provisionals. A security source said: "In fact, if there was ever a power struggle between the groups, we think they are strong enough to put the Provos out of business." As far as fundraising is concerned, the two groups (together with a third, the much smaller and more fragmented Irish National Liberation Army) uneasily coexist, often sharing the same territory. The tax-exemption fiddle, though it still goes on, has been reduced in scale and profitability; but these organisations have other sources of power and profit, especially in the building trade. The rehousing programme, which at its height ran at 7,000 new homes a year, has been cut back. But the paramilitary groups now have an interest in city-centre commercial developments and in road building.

On one site the Provisionals might provide, say, the bricklayers and the Officials the plasterers. The organisations hold regular meetings to carve up new projects. The actual workers involved are not necessarily members of paramilitary groups. "You don't have to become a member," a building worker said. "You do your work, and don't ask questions, you accept the going rate." The organisation, of course, takes a cut of the worker's wages as the price for providing him with the job.

For the major contractors, arrangements with paramilitary groups have their advantages. The Officials in particular are known to provide superior quality work. The jobs are usually completed on time, there are few if any incidents on site, and pilfering and vandalism is low. The large firms who go along with such arrangements are the despair of the security authorities. "They are sheep, weak and ineffective," one source said. "They'll complain to us, but none of them will give evidence against these people."

Although the Officials are involved in protection rackets, the Provisionals have in recent years tended to keep clear of such activity. "They're anxious to gain acceptability," a security source noted. "If they desperately need a lot of money they will go to big businesses in republican areas, but they try to avoid that where possible."

As for money from Irish-Americans, it is regarded as a useful (and morale-raising) bonus rather than a lifeline. Last year Noraid, the New York-based fundraising organisation, sent around $150,000 (just over £100,000) across the Atlantic, according to US Justice Department records.

But for all the large sums of money involved, the IRA is not rich. It needs a great deal of money to keep going: arms are expensive, prison welfare costs are high and the political activities of Sinn Féin are costly. Within the IRA there has recently been a revival of the periodic friction over how much money should go on votes, and how much on weapons.

The RUC suffers from the classic police dilemma of having intelligence but little evidence which will stand up in court. A solution is instead sought through new legislation. Such laws take time to formulate and to pass through the parliamentary process. Because their thrust is visible in advance of their enactment, the organisations have time to find loopholes and change tactics. This helps explain why some people in security and in politics doubt that the rackets can be eradicated.

The public identification of loyalist groups, in
particular the Ulster Defence Association, with
the crudest forms of racketeering helped
reduce Protestant support for such
organisations. But it did not eliminate them
entirely, for their historical roots run deep.

18 MARCH 1988   THE INDEPENDENT

The centuries-old tradition of Protestant paramiltarism

A glossary of loyalist paramilitary organisations compiled in the mid-Seventies listed no fewer than 35 groups. Many were tiny and some were entirely fictional, but up to a dozen were real – that is, with at least a rudimentary command structure and access to weapons. Today the ranks have thinned out, leaving two dominant groups actively engaged in violence, the Ulster Volunteer Force and the Ulster Defence Association. Other groups, such as the Red Hand Commandos, are by comparison minuscule and highly localised.

The existence of these organisations carries on a tradition going back for centuries. From the seventeenth century both Protestants and Catholics have shown a tendency to band together in unofficial sectarian gangs. Early groups had names such as the "Hearts of Oak", the "White Boys" and "Peep O' Day Boys". They would publicise their terror tactics by signs pinned to trees with claims such as: "The Hearts of Oak burnt this house down – signed Captain White." The folk memory of the aliases used to claim responsibility for acts of violence has lasted for centuries: in the early 1970s UDA claims were often signed by a "Captain Black".

The Orange Order, which includes in its ranks most leading Unionist MPs and politicians, had its origins in such organisations. In times of crisis, working-class loyalists have often felt the need for paramilitary back-up for their politicians to counter republican aggression or the possibility of a British "sell-out". The

The tradition of sectarian secret societies goes back for centuries.

justification is one of defence, but such organisations have often extended this original concept into attacks on republicans and Catholics.

The paramilitary tradition was strengthened by the circumstances of the creation of the Northern Ireland state in 1921. When it became apparent that home rule – independence for Ireland from Britain – was a possibility, Protestants in the north-eastern counties banded together in the first Ulster Volunteer Force. This bore no resemblance to today's UVF. It brought together all sections of Protestantism in a large, well-organised private army.

A hundred thousand men drilled and marched, and were inspected by large industrialists and landowners. Strong support came from the Tories and from senior elements in the British Army. The UVF imported 25,000 rifles into Northern Ireland to display its determination to oppose home rule, and pronounced that the north-eastern counties would declare independence rather than go quietly into a new all-Ireland state outside the British Empire. The stratagem worked. Home rule was granted to the rest of Ireland but six counties were allowed to remain, albeit at arm's length, within the United Kingdom. The new state set up a variety of official militias, known as the A, B and C Specials. The B Specials, an exclusively Protestant force, were abolished only in 1970.

Although the Ulster Defence Regiment was formed to replace them, Protestant mistrust of Westminster was strong and the emphasis switched to militias outside the control of the authorities. By the mid-Seventies, however, these groups had lost the confidence of Protestants in general. They developed a reputation for ill-discipline, incompetence, ineffectiveness and involvement in criminal activity. Although they professed to be the enemies of the IRA, it became clear their main activity was the sectarian murder of Catholics, often chosen at random simply on the basis of their religion.

Today only the UVF and UDA remain as significant forces. Although their numbers have dwindled, they probably still have up to 10,000 men in their combined ranks. Comparisons of imprisoned loyalists and IRA prisoners indicate that the loyalists tend to be of slightly lower intelligence, with a less coherent political philosophy and less certainty about their aims. Many loyalists have taken drink before carrying out shootings. Those who carry out armed robberies expect a cut from the organisation. More money goes astray in loyalist groups than in the IRA, and organisation is much looser. One observer said: "The IRA is political, with a sectarian tinge. The loyalist groups tend to be purely sectarian."

The UVF and UDA are regarded in most loyalist circles as being less than respectable. When their representatives stand for election they tend to receive derisory shares of the vote. None the less, they remain a significant force in communities such as the Shankill in west Belfast. Many Unionist politicians are in frequent touch with such groups on matters such as prison welfare, but they generally keep these contacts private, if not furtive.

The contrast between the original UVF and the groups of today is immense. The UVF, UDA and Red Hand now send a shudder through respectable loyalists. Hundreds of their men languish in prison, often in a confused state about the exact aim of the violence they committed. Their goal is partly to terrorise the Catholic community and partly to warn the British government against the violent consequences of attempting a withdrawal. To an extent they have succeeded; but in the process they have increased community polarisation, caused many civilian deaths, and helped create more volunteers for the IRA.

In the years following the Anglo-Irish agreement the Ulster Defence Association experienced a period of upheaval. Between December 1987 and October 1988 no less than five members of its ruling eight-man "inner council" were removed, by factors ranging

from illness to gunfire. The first to go was John
McMichael, who was in charge of the UDA in
south Belfast and acted as the organisation's
political spokesman. He was killed by the IRA,
who placed a boobytrap bomb underneath his
car. His death was condemned by a number of
Catholic politicians and churchmen, who had
seen McMichael as a man who might be
weaned away from violence and into the
political processes.

John McMichael: killer with political ambitions

J ohn McMichael was a violent man whose confused and erratic attempts to
develop politically were abruptly and brutally cut short by Tuesday night's
IRA boobytrap bomb. His startling changes of opinion and direction were
symptomatic of the confusion within loyalist paramilitary groups about their
role and their aims. He could not decide whether Protestant Ulster should fight
or negotiate, and whether its goal should be to remain British or to break the link
and strike for independence. He swung alarmingly from violent deeds to political
thought and back again.

At the same time as he picketed Irish parliamentarians in Dublin, he was
helping assemble teams of firebombers to attack the city. As he was holding
secret meetings with leaders of the Catholic Social Democratic and Labour Party
to discuss sharing power with nationalists, his men were shooting innocent
Catholics in Belfast. McMichael saw nothing inappropriate about pursuing two
contradictory policies at the same time.

A highly impressionable man, his views often changed with bewildering
speed. Within the Ulster Defence Association he was not necessarily a force for

moderation. He functioned as the organisation's military commander through-out 1986, when UDA members were responsible for a string of sectarian killings. According to reliable security and loyalist sources, McMichael was involved in the wholesale intimidation of Catholics from his home town of Lisburn, Co Antrim; in attempts abroad to buy guns for the UDA; and in protection racket-eering. At the same time he had grandiose political ambitions for himself and the organisation. Although he polled fewer than 600 votes in a 1982 Westminster by-election, he had visions of expanding the UDA into the political arena.

He was the principal author of a UDA document which last January called for powersharing with Catholics. Delighted by the positive response to the booklet, he launched into a series of private meetings with nationalists; at one stage he had plans to meet the Catholic Primate, Cardinal Tomás Ó Fiaich.

Most of the nationalists who met him had few illusions about his background of violence; they tended to hope that such contacts might help steer him and the UDA away from the gun and into political activity. That hope was always a faint one, but with his violent death it has faded completely.

The spring of 1988 saw the removal of Andy Tyrie, who for a decade and a half had been one of the most important figures of the loyalist paramilitary underworld. He had been chairman of the UDA since 1973. His departure was peaceful: he lost a vote of confidence and was forced to stand down. His critics within the organisation said he had lost touch with rank-and-file opinion and had presided over a series of major setbacks for the organisation in recent years. These were cited as the seizure by the RUC of the UDA's biggest-ever arms shipment, the toleration of notorious gangsters within the organisation and the lack of a coherent political philosophy. Tyrie was widely regarded as something of a moderating influence within this violent organisation and in some respects he probably was. But although he attempted to develop a political wing, it would be simplistic and inaccurate to classify him as a dove among hawks.

12 MARCH 1988   THE INDEPENDENT

Andy Tyrie: formidable errors of the UDA's unlikely leader

Andy Tyrie's departure as leader of Northern Ireland's largest loyalist paramilitary organisation follows months of rising pressure from its ranks. The quiet 48-year-old Belfast man with the Zapata moustache has, for a decade and a half, been one of the key players in the violent paramilitary underworld. But the writing has been on the wall for some time. Dissident Ulster Defence Association members recently attempted to set fire to his office and tried to blow up his car.

Earlier this week one of his critics appeared in silhouette on BBC 2's *Newsnight,* warning Tyrie his time was up. He did not expect to go, and asked for the vote of confidence himself, apparently believing he would win it. The move comes after a long series of disasters suffered by the UDA, for which Tyrie attempted to disclaim personal responsibility. The list is formidable. The organisation imported its largest arms consignment, only to see it seized by the RUC. Money was poured into ventures such as the development of a "commando elite", the Ulster Defence Force. Other funds went missing. The organisation also failed to use the crisis over the Anglo-Irish agreement to expand its support.

Tyrie ran the UDA through a small clique of "brigadiers" within the ruling inner council. But circumstances removed his staunchest supporters. One was disgraced after appearing on television demanding money with menaces; one

157

was imprisoned; one, John McMichael, split from the coterie and was subsequently blown up.

Some of Tyrie's appointments have been regarded with dismay. Notorious gangsters were given key positions. One well-known UDA man, who can only be described as a psychopath, was promoted by Tyrie to the inner council. He later stabbed three men in a drunken rage in a bar. Urged to discipline him, Tyrie warned him not to do it again.

But the worst blow to the UDA has been its public identification with racketeering and gangsterism, in particular the crude extortion of "protection money". Television exposés such as *The Cook Report* pinned such practices on the UDA but Tyrie appeared complacent in the face of attacks. He also airily dismissed reports that senior figures in the organisation had colluded with the IRA in the murders of a number of UDA officers, in particular John McMichael last year.

Tyrie was always an unlikely paramilitant: he is smallish, tubby and slightly asthmatic. A former landscape gardener and machinist with Rolls Royce, he first became involved with the paramilitary world in the late 1960s. He was a middle-ranking figure in the west Belfast brigade – probably the UDA's most militant section – until 1973, when he was unexpectedly elected chairman. He was a compromise candidate, and at first had little real power until misfortune overtook the two major leaders. Tommy Herron, east Belfast commander, was murdered, then Charles Harding-Smith, west Belfast commander, was shot six times and fled to England.

From the beginning, Tyrie was more adventurous than Unionism's conservative political leaders. In 1974 he sent a UDA delegation to Libya and he always hoped to add a political movement to the UDA's paramilitary activities. In recent years, however, his judgement seemed to desert him. In 1972 the UDA had 26,000 members: today there are well under 10,000, and its standing in the loyalist community has never been lower.

More changes followed at the top of the UDA. Eddie Sayers, the mid-Ulster inner council member who had unwisely allowed himself to be filmed demanding money with menaces from television investigator Roger Cook, received a ten-year sentence for extortion. The Antrim commander, Alan Snoddy, died from cancer of the throat.

Then in October 1988 two UDA gunmen walked into an east Belfast pub and shot dead Jim Craig, Northern Ireland's most notorious loyalist gangster. He was killed principally because of his alleged co-operation with both the IRA and INLA in the deaths of loyalist paramilitary leaders over a six-year period. He had been a marked man for many months. His notoriety and range of enemies was such that he could have been killed by almost any of Northern Ireland's paramilitary groups, loyalist or republican.

For years he had been the prime target of C13, the RUC anti-racketeering squad. No one, however, would give evidence against him in open court, and a series of charges brought against him failed.

---

17 OCTOBER 1988   THE INDEPENDENT

Jim Craig: death of 'public enemy number one'

James Pratt Craig, who met his violent death in an east Belfast bar on Saturday night, was one of the most remarkable characters thrown up by Northern Ireland's two decades of troubles. Deeply involved in killings and extortion, he was an extreme loyalist, yet he enjoyed apparently cordial relations with republicans who were supposed to be his sworn enemies.

When the history of recent years comes to be written, Craig will be seen to have had a small but significant part in the wider political picture, for his notoriety as a racketeer played a large part in discrediting his organisation, the Ulster Defence Association, in the eyes of many working-class Protestants. In 1974 the UDA had played a major role in the Protestant strike which brought down the Sunningdale agreement. But by 1985 the organisation's reputation for gangsterism meant it was unacceptable to the mass of Protestants. This notoriety, which was almost entirely due to Craig's activities, helps explain why, when the crisis of the Anglo-Irish agreement arrived in 1985, loyalists shrank from attempting to use the UDA's paramilitary muscle to break the accord.

Craig, who came from the loyalist Shankill Road district of Belfast, was a personable drinking companion with a ready smile and a fund of jokes. Stocky and with very broad shoulders, he had a strong physical presence. He was street-wise but not particularly intelligent. He could convey friendliness or menace as the occasion demanded.

When the Troubles began he was in jail for criminal offences, but quickly established himself as "UDA commander" first in Belfast's Crumlin Road prison and later in the Maze, taking charge of the growing number of imprisoned UDA members. In the early 1970s he made it clear that he was prepared to work with IRA prisoners, arguing that the authorities were their common enemy. In the Maze he was a member of the "camp council" of paramilitary leaders who met regularly to work out a co-ordinated approach to the authorities.

The late David Morley, who was IRA commander in the Maze, once privately recounted a conversation he had with Craig and Gusty Spence, UVF leader, comparing notes on how they kept order among the men in their compounds. Craig, according to Morley, outlined his approach to man-management thus: "I've got this big fucking hammer and I've told them that if anybody gives me trouble I'll break their fucking fingers."

On his release in 1976, he immediately became active at a high level in the UDA. He was involved in at least two killings, one of which was the murder of another leading west Belfast UDA member suspected of being a police informer. The second killing was unintentional: he was examining a gun in a Shankill Road pub when it went off accidentally. The shot went through a window, killing a passer-by. At the time Craig was full of remorse, even talking to associates of giving himself up to the RUC.

The racketeering began in earnest in 1982, when Craig and three associates realised that a great deal of money was to be made through demanding payments with menaces, particularly from building contractors. By 1984 he was receiving payments from 72 different firms. He cashed in not only on the large-scale slum-clearance operations in Belfast and elsewhere, but also on the attempts to regenerate commercial and social life in the city centre. He became the prime target of CI3, the RUC's anti-racketeering squad, who received many complaints from businessmen about his activities. A senior detective said of him:

"He's public enemy number one." Although the police knew exactly what he was doing, they were unable to prove a case in court, since his victims were afraid to give evidence.

One attempt to surmount this obstacle failed in 1985 when a number of businessmen agreed to testify in court, provided their identities were concealed. They appeared in court muffled in anoraks and balaclava helmets, but this proved unacceptable, the case collapsed and Craig was freed.

Until this point he had operated his rackets almost entirely for self-gain, passing on to the UDA itself only a very small proportion of the money he collected. Far from disciplining him, however, the organisation recruited him in an official capacity as its chief collector, and his activities were resumed. But even then he held on to much of the funds.

Throughout his career he appears to have kept up the contacts he made in prison with republicans of various hues. In the early 1980s there was a series of UDA shootings of republican activists which appeared to be based on unusually accurate intelligence. The rumour was that the Official IRA was giving information to Craig which would allow the UDA to remove some of its republican rivals.

A very different pattern, however, began to emerge in 1982, as republican groups targeted loyalist paramilitary leaders. Suspicions grew over the years as it was noted that at least four UDA and UVF men killed by the IRA and INLA had previously had financial disputes with Craig. First to go was Lennie Murphy, leader of the UVF's "Shankill Butchers" gang, who had been involved in a dozen or more particularly gruesome murders. He was shot by the IRA. Craig was superficially friendly with Murphy, but it was common knowledge that the UVF man had encroached on his territory by attempting to collect money from building sites in west and north Belfast. The pattern persisted with the INLA killing of Billy "Bucky" McCullough in 1981 and last year's IRA killings of Billy "Frenchy" Marchant of the UVF and John McMichael of the UDA. All of them had quarrelled with Craig over money.

Craig's extortion activities and the suspicion of collusion with republicans caused concern in UDA ranks, but for years no action was taken against him. This inaction contributed to the downfall of the organisation's chairman, Andy Tyrie, earlier this year.

Anti-racketeering legislation being prepared by the authorities will represent a fitting epitaph for Craig, a man whose patriotism, if he ever had any, became perverted by a lust for cash.

Two weeks after Craig was murdered, another well-known UDA leader, north Belfast commander Davy Payne, was sent to prison. For years the RUC had attempted without success to link him with a series of murders of Catholics in Belfast in the early 1970s.

2 NOVEMBER 1988   THE INDEPENDENT

Davy Payne: jailed UDA leader enjoyed sadistic reputation

A Protestant paramilitary leader associated with some of Northern Ireland's most gruesome killings was jailed yesterday for 19 years after being caught with the largest-ever haul of loyalist arms.

Davy Payne, 40, became a paramilitary legend in Belfast during a career spanning more than two decades. He was suspected of being a member of a gang which tortured and stabbed to death a series of Catholic men and women in the early 1970s, and he served for many years at the top of the largest loyalist paramilitary grouping, the Ulster Defence Association. His activities in the early 1970s made him possibly the most feared man in Belfast, and earned him a lasting reputation as a psychopath with a taste for sadistic murders.

Far from resenting that reputation, he revelled in it. He enjoyed instilling fear by thrusting his face into another's and declaring: "Do you know who I am? I'm Davy Payne. They say I killed Senator Paddy Wilson." Paddy Wilson was an SDLP politician killed with a woman friend, Irene Andrews, in 1973 on a lonely road in the hills overlooking Belfast. Senator Wilson was stabbed 30 times and had his throat cut. Miss Andrews was stabbed 20 times.

Payne was interned without trial on suspicion of involvement in these and other murders, but police lacked the evidence to bring a charge against him.

Since then he has served two spells as a member of the UDA's ruling inner council, but although questioned many times had not been convicted of any offence.

He was finally arrested last January when police stopped two cars which were carrying 60 rifles, 30 pistols, 11,000 rounds of ammunition and 150 grenades. At first he planned to contest the case but he surprised everyone by pleading guilty and making an extraordinary statement from the dock. He claimed he had left the UDA 14 years ago, that he was shocked when he saw the weapons, and that he had been framed by two members of the inner council who had since twice tried to poison him in prison. The judge did not believe him.

Payne was a member of two other loyalist organisations, the Ulster Volunteer Force and Tara, in the Sixties before joining the UDA. On his release from internment in 1974 he was appointed brigadier in charge of the organisation's north Belfast area, but left after allegations that he had pocketed UDA funds.

Some time later he re-emerged as the darling of the now-defunct Peace People, and made a speech denouncing paramilitary organisations in general and the UDA in particular. He helped run a mixed community workshop but once again there was trouble over missing funds. One night he answered a knock on the door of his home and was hit by a blast from a shotgun: the UDA was settling old scores.

He returned to the organisation as north Belfast brigadier in 1985, though some sections in that area refused to accept his authority. His technique was one of management by terror: earlier this year he is said to have stabbed three men in a pub. There were more fights over money and the proceeds of racketeering, and dissatisfaction within the brigade grew. His free-spending habits and his expensive carphone strengthened the belief that UDA funds were again being misappropriated.

Payne was quite right that attempts were made to poison him while on remand. Members of the north Belfast brigade, unsure whether he would beat the rap, decided to try to make sure he would not return to take command for a third time. In loyalist paramilitarism, colleagues can sometimes pose greater danger than enemies.

The loyalist attack on the funeral of three IRA members shot dead in Gibraltar later had its sequel in court. There was no question about the guilt of Michael Stone, who had been televised tossing grenades and firing shots at mourners: none the less, he pleaded not guilty. The prosecution presented its evidence, but he instructed his defence counsel not to challenge it. This approach, explicable only as a tactic to gain maximum publicity for his activities, meant the court heard full details of a career which prior to Milltown had included three other murders and a series of attempts to kill republicans. To no one's surprise, the judge found him guilty and sentenced him to life imprisonment, recommending he serve at least thirty years in jail.

4 MARCH 1989   THE INDEPENDENT

Michael Stone: the graveyard killer

Michael "Flint" Stone, according to his former colleagues, made one crucial mistake in Milltown cemetery: he forgot to count to four before tossing his grenades. They were Russian-made anti-personnel fragmentation grenades, fitted with a time delay so that they go off some seconds after being primed. Stone pulled the pin and immediately tossed the grenades: they hit the ground and exploded. But the idea is to count to four and then throw them so they blow up in mid-air, raining lethal shrapnel over a wide area. Had he followed the proper drill, his associates complain, he would have killed a lot

Televised murder: Michael Stone in the act of killing three men at an IRA funeral

more republicans and might even have got away from the graveyard.

Stone is undoubtedly a celebrity to some, as the fan mail and gifts delivered to his prison cell demonstrate. The younger, more reckless paramilitary elements clearly look up to him. A song has already been written about his exploits and admiring graffiti can be seen on ghetto gable walls: in some parts of Northern Ireland society violence is not only tolerated but revered. Yet the myth-makers will find it difficult to elevate Stone into a Homeric figure. He is, in fact, living proof of the banality of evil. Anyone who kills half a dozen people and plots to kill half a dozen more should by rights be an intriguing character. Michael Stone, frankly, is not.

The product of a broken marriage, he was born in Birmingham in 1955 but spent most of his life in east Belfast where he was brought up by an aunt and uncle. Between 1972, when he was 16, and 1977 he was continually in trouble with the law, twice going to jail for a string of offences including stealing cars, burglary, joyriding, causing grievous bodily harm and a minor firearms charge. His petty criminal record came to a sudden halt in 1977: after that anyone glancing at his RUC file would have concluded he had pulled himself together and settled down.

He married a Belfast woman and had three sons, but complained his wife was overbearing and they divorced. He later remarried, apparently happily. Michael Stone liked watching television documentaries, taking his wife for meals in hotels, sitting in the sun, and breeding his Staffordshire bull terriers. He drank little and did not smoke. Friends describe him, variously, as generous, quiet, witty, inoffensive and polite – in short, unrecognisable as the gunman in Milltown cemetery. He never seemed to be well off. He worked as an unskilled labourer on local building sites, often "doing the double" – collecting wages and simultaneously drawing the dole.

Between 1977 and 1984 Stone's life appears to have been unexceptional. He looked to be an unskilled, not particularly intelligent man from a broken home, who with his second marriage had left his criminally inclined teenage years behind him. But somewhere along the way he changed from an unremarkable building labourer into a remorseless and almost nerveless stalker of republicans. His violent activities between 1984 and 1988 fit into no previously known pattern. He attempted to join the east Belfast brigade of the Ulster Defence Association, the largest Protestant paramilitary outfit, but he was suspected of being involved with drugs and rejected as unreliable and unpredictable. According to one source: "He seemed a loner, he didn't want to work with anybody. The UDA just didn't want him. He was chased." Undeterred, he surreptitiously established links with others in the organisation. One of his contacts was John McMichael, the UDA leader assassinated by the IRA at Christmas 1987. Three other senior UDA officers who dealt with him have, for reasons unconnected with Stone, since been deposed from their positions.

Within the UDA Stone's activities were known only to a few at the top of the organisation. The UDA's current leaders, who did not know Stone, were amazed to discover after the Milltown incident that he had connections with their organisation. Killings claimed by McMichael as the work of his south Belfast brigade were suddenly shown to have involved an unknown outsider. None the less, the UDA is now prepared to take him into the ranks of its jailed members in the Maze prison – another indication of his high standing in the loyalist community.

Stone also had connections with the other main violent loyalist group, the Ulster Volunteer Force, in particular linking up with one of its semi-autonomous components, the Red Hand Commandos. The grenades and possibly the Browning pistol used in the Milltown attack are thought to have reached him from the UVF, via a well-known Red Hand member who is now in prison. But again his existence was known to only a few members of the organisations. One loyalist source said: "I remember one of our leaders saying he knew a man who would do absolutely anything. He must have meant Stone." It is not known whether Stone had associations with the only other significant loyalist paramilitary group, known as "Ulster Resistance".

The UDA, UVF and Ulster Resistance jointly organised a major arms shipment which included the grenades Stone used at Milltown. This arrived in Northern Ireland in early 1988, financed largely by a £325,000 bank raid which members of the three groups staged in Portadown, Co Armagh, the previous year. The RUC seized all of the UDA's guns and grenades almost immediately, and picked up much of the UVF's quota in later raids. Ulster Resistance's share appears, however, to remain untouched, while part of the UVF's remaining arsenal found its way to Stone.

His activities extended to almost every part of Northern Ireland. He believed his targets were all active republicans, but only one, so far as is known, was a member of the IRA. Other victims could, however, be classed as republican sympathisers, a category which extreme loyalists regard as "legitimate targets".

Prior to Milltown, his actions were marked by an attention to detail uncharacteristic of loyalist assassins. He studied documents and photographs of his targets and carried out careful reconnaissance of their movements. In one case he loaded the back of the car with concrete blocks and improvised sandbags to protect himself from any return gunfire. Even at Milltown he did not quite abandon the instinct for self-preservation. He went armed with two particularly powerful modern handguns, a Browning automatic pistol and a Ruger revolver, both of which are used by the security forces. He wore gloves with the tip of the right index finger cut away to allow better trigger control; and those who caught up with him on the motorway said he had a sticking-plaster on his exposed finger so as not to leave fingerprints. He gave himself an escape route of sorts. He decided against shooting Gerry Adams at the church where the funeral service took place because, he said, "I had no chance of getting away from there." His grenades fell short of the Sinn Féin leaders because he had positioned himself too far away from the graves.

None the less, his attack on the IRA funeral was unique in that he was almost certain to be caught, either by republicans or security forces. The men of violence on both sides have often taken high risks, but few have been prepared to leave themselves such a slight chance of eluding death or imprisonment. Michael Stone now faces the prospect of decades behind bars; but as he goes he leaves behind important unanswered questions for the authorities.

Sinn Féin has alleged there was collusion from some elements of the security forces, pointing in particular to his statements that he was shown documents and photographs of his intended victims. This is a familiar, indeed a standard, republican charge: but there have been too many recent convictions in the courts, especially of members of the Ulster Defence Regiment, for it to be lightly dismissed as groundless. Stone's mentions of being shown dossiers on his victims have left lingering suspicions that some people in the security forces were guiding, or contributing to, his activities.

The other question concerns the proficiency of the intelligence services. It is often said that the security forces know virtually all the major paramilitary players, both loyalist and republican. The facts are that for four years Stone was an extremely active loyalist assassin, operating in the cities of Belfast and Londonderry and at least five of Northern Ireland's six counties. He was responsible for a sizeable catalogue of attempted and actual murders and during that period was in touch with major figures in the UDA, UVF and Red Hand – people who are well known to the security forces and are presumed to be subject to surveillance. Yet the police say that before Milltown he had last come to their attention in 1977, for non-terrorist offences. Such a gap in the knowledge of the authorities is alarming and will presumably lead to a review of how such an active assassin could completely escape the notice of the Special Branch and army intelligence.

Michael Stone now joins in the Maze prison several hundred loyalists who, like him, viewed the use of force as a historically sanctioned and morally permissible activity. Some will look up to him – but not all. In the words of one loyalist paramilitary leader: "Because of the Milltown business there's a bit of a myth about him. He's a hero figure to some people. To me he's a lunatic."

Events in a Paris hotel in April 1989 provided firm evidence of the source of the weaponry which had reached loyalists in December 1987, bringing to light an extraordinary tale of illicit international traffic in arms. What happened demonstrated that the Libyans were not the only African power involved in shipping guns to Northern Ireland

A South African diplomat, an arms dealer and three loyalists were arrested in Paris, and missile equipment manufactured in Belfast by the Shorts company was seized.

South Africa, it emerged, was involved in a remarkable plot aimed at procuring Britain's missile secrets for Armscor, its state-owned armaments manufacturer. It hoped to obtain hardware or blueprints of Shorts-made weapons for Armscor to copy, and was particularly interested in the brand-new Starstreak ground-to-air system, which Shorts was developing for the Ministry of Defence under a £225 million contract.

In return South Africa was prepared to supply weapons or money to loyalists. Its agents had already been involved in the December 1987 importation of weapons, channelling it to Northern Ireland via Lebanon. It was part of this shipment which UDA leader Davy Payne had been caught with in Co Armagh, while grenades from the consignment had been used by Michael Stone in the Milltown attack. Loyalists had been prepared to hand over material stolen from Shorts and from the Territorial Army, some of whose units used guided missiles. At least two items were stolen from Shorts, and another taken from a TA base in Co Down.

The Paris arrests were an indication that negotiations for an important arms swap were at an advanced stage. Had the whole conspiracy succeeded as planned, the South Africans could have obtained the latest in British military technology while extreme loyalists could, for the first time, have come to rival the IRA in terms of weaponry. Britain would have lost millions in potential arms sales, while Northern Ireland would have become a much more dangerous place.

Three loyalist groups co-operated in the
venture – the UDA, the UVF and Ulster
Resistance. The first two were long-
established, but the third came into being
specifically to oppose the Anglo-Irish
agreement.

24 APRIL 1989   THE INDEPENDENT

Citizens' force set up with backing of loyalist politicians and businessmen

U lster Resistance represented, at its creation in late 1986, an attempt
by loyalist politicians and business elements to harness the potential
paramilitary muscle of the Protestant majority in Northern Ireland and use it to
bring down the Anglo-Irish agreement. Political and street protests had failed to
budge the Government from the idea of involving Dublin in the decision-making
processes in Northern Ireland. Loyalist opposition had proved ineffectual and
was badly organised and badly led.

A one-day stoppage had brought much of the province to a halt, but was
characterised by intimidation and disturbances. The existing paramilitary
groups, principally the Ulster Defence Association and Ulster Volunteer Force,
were relatively inactive and had shown themselves unwilling to respond to
directives from Unionist politicians. A grouping known as the Ulster Clubs, led
by Alan Wright, a religious zealot from Co Armagh, had attracted some support
but was badly organised.

Ulster Resistance brought together the Rev Ian Paisley and Peter Robinson,
the Democractic Unionist Party leaders, Mr Wright, and a collection of minor
loyalist politicians and businessmen who hoped to create an organisation
capable of forcing the Government to scrap the agreement. It was referred to by
those involved as an army and a military force, though the impression was that
its main role would be street protests and confrontations rather than para-

170

military warfare or the type of sectarian killings which have been the stock-in-trade of the UDA and UVF.

Mr Paisley and Mr Robinson prepared the way for the emergence of the new body with speeches indicating that the use of force was proper when all other means had been exhausted.

The group was officially launched in November 1986 at a rally attended by 2,000 men in the Ulster Hall, Belfast. With Democratic Unionist leaders flanked by a colour party carrying flags and wearing military-style uniform and berets, the new organisation declared itself ready to use "all means which may be found necessary to defeat the Anglo-Irish agreement". This was followed by recruiting rallies throughout Northern Ireland, featuring appearances by the colour party and militant speeches.

Mr Paisley and Mr Robinson urged able-bodied men to come forward for training, the latter warning that Ulster Resistance was not for "the faint- or half-hearted". Mr Paisley said: "There are many like myself who would like to see the agreement brought down by democratic means, but wouldn't we all be fools if we weren't prepared?" They were widely criticised by other politicians and church figures for inciting the impressionable and encouraging militancy. The main loyalist party, the Ulster Unionists, refrained from supporting the new organisation. Its leader, James Molyneaux, said the problem with such a citizens' army was ensuring control in the long term, adding: "I have always been very careful not to incite or encourage people who engage in activity which will end up putting yet another generation of young loyalists in jail."

Mr Paisley and Mr Robinson were undeterred: when the Royal Ulster Constabulary warned that wearing uniforms might constitute a public order offence, they defiantly donned Ulster Resistance berets at the rallies. Ulster Resistance claimed it was vetting, training and drilling thousands of recruits, but once the initial series of rallies was over the organisation fell silent. Within months reports emerged of internal wrangling and disagreements, and it became clear that the organisation's attempt to become a mass movement had ignominiously fizzled out. Mr Paisley and Mr Robinson stopped mentioning it. The DUP leader, it was rumoured, had become nervous about its militancy and distanced himself. Other senior party figures have maintained links. With local government and European elections due in May and June, the DUP has of late been tacking towards the middle ground in the hope of attracting as many moderate Protestant votes as possible. The missile episode will represent something of a political embarrassment.

In November last year, on the same day that Ulster Resistance berets were discovered in a Co Armagh arms dump containing Shorts missile parts, Mr Paisley and Mr Robinson took part in a DUP rally in Larne, Co Antrim, in which an Ulster Resistance flag featured prominently. Five days later, after details of the discovery were made public, a DUP statement said that while the party had encouraged recruitment for Ulster Resistance, its leaders had never been members of the organisation. The statement added: "Some time later we were informed that the organisation had been put on ice and our association and contact ended. At no time during our association was anything done which was outside the law and no member of the movement was ever charged with an offence."

The Social Democratic and Labour Party called yesterday for the banning of Ulster Resistance and said the RUC should question the loyalist politicians who had been associated with it.

The close of 1988 saw the agreement reach its third anniversary intact, though battered by various political controversies. As this three-part series pointed out, neither nationalist hopes nor Unionist fears were fully realised.

12 NOVEMBER 1988   THE INDEPENDENT

Unionists wait for something to turn up

U nionism erupted when the Anglo-Irish agreement was signed three years ago. All Unionist MPs resigned their seats and boycotted government ministers; most local councils came to a standstill; ministers encountered protests whenever they ventured out from behind Stormont Castle's barbed wire. More than 100,000 Protestants assembled at Belfast City Hall to utter a collective primal howl of betrayal. The sense of abandonment was deep and genuine.

It is true that some parts of Unionism, notably the Rev Ian Paisley and the loyalist paramilitary groups, often act in the most un-British of ways. It is also true that Unionists have always known, deep down, that Britain's commitment to their cause is less than wholehearted. But the agreement was particularly hurtful in that it set down, in black and white, that the Irish Republic was to have a guaranteed say in the running of Northern Ireland, with Irish civil servants permanently based in Belfast. The agreement defined Unionism as one of the problems, aligned London with its ancient enemy, and seemed to say that the future belonged to Irish nationalism.

There were marches, rallies, riots, by-elections, Protestant attacks on the RUC, threats, warnings, alarums and excursions. Ten MPs went to jail. There were unsuccessful attempts to raise private armies to fight, or at least threaten, the British.

Three years on, Unionism has calmed down. Ministers have, tentatively at first and then with growing confidence, ventured out into the community again. Many councils are meeting; MPs are back at Westminster and talk to ministers, and it was recently judged safe enough for Mrs Thatcher to visit Belfast. The agreement has not been the catastrophe Protestants feared and there is now, for the most part, a reluctant acquiescence in its existence. The temperature has dropped, but the pressure remains. The accord does not look as menacing as at the start, and the reforms it promised (or, in Unionist terms, threatened) have not appeared. But it remains a standing constitutional affront to them, by providing Dublin with a foothold in Northern Ireland.

It has, in fact, been a terrible and traumatic three years for Unionism. The agreement, though much reduced in scale, has acquired an appearance of permanence. It also serves as a constant reminder of Protestant political impotence in that everything Unionism could throw at it failed to shake it. If the accord should crumble, it will not be because of the Unionist opposition, which has managed, at most, only to help slow the pace of reform.

Unionist strategists privately and glumly admit that this fact has important long-term consequences. It had always been assumed that Unionism possessed the strength, in determination and in numbers, to stop in its tracks any British initiative of which it did not approve. But this time, in the words of a senior Unionist: "We showed we couldn't fight our way out of a wet paper bag. The Foreign Office and our other enemies will certainly have noted that fact for future reference."

It was not just loyalist muscle which failed this time, but Unionist politics also. Its leaders, James Molyneaux and Ian Paisley, had built careers on the respective propositions that London could be either befriended or bullied. Neither approach prevented the signing of the agreement and neither has since shifted·it. As a result, Protestants hold politics in dangerously low esteem. Both Unionist leaders have lapsed into something close to inactivity, leaving the spectacle of an entire community with pathetically little say in its own destiny.

However, happily for all concerned, working-class Protestants have not turned to paramilitary activity: groups such as the Ulster Defence Association and the Ulster Volunteer Force have deteriorated into gang warfare over money and collusion with their republican enemies. None the less, they remain sporadically dangerous and are reasonably well armed. Their menace would have increased tenfold had not the security forces seized 800 home-made but well-crafted machine guns two months ago.

As its architects hoped, the agreement has started a debate within Unionism on the future. But this has been unstructured and inconclusive and there is no real steam behind any of the options canvassed – powersharing, majority rule devolution, integration, independence and so on. Not one Unionist advocates acceptance of the agreement, but the protest campaign has collapsed and none of the alternatives has won wide support. Powersharing does not appeal to many; independence is judged frightening; majority rule and integration are simply not on offer. Most Unionists – and that includes most MPs – have lapsed into a trough of listless dissatisfaction.

The debate has slowed as the agreement has run into difficulties and the hope has reappeared that outside forces might somehow bring about its downfall. So long as that faint hope remains alive, the signs are that Unionism will resist the pressures to redefine its relationships with London, Dublin, and northern Catholics. That may be Micawberism elevated to a political policy, but this alienated, resentful community has come up with no better idea.

---

14 NOVEMBER 1988 THE INDEPENDENT

Nationalist jury delays verdict

For nationalists, the story of the Anglo-Irish agreement is one of expectations unrealised. When the accord was signed, the non-violent Social Democratic and Labour Party was hopeful while Sinn Féin was apprehensive. Three years on, neither the hopes nor the fears have been borne out.

The two factions of nationalism in Northern Ireland are still intact and, as far as can be judged in advance of next year's elections, appear to command roughly the same proportional strength as before. That is to say, John Hume's SDLP can expect around 65 per cent of the nationalist vote with Sinn Féin taking 35 per cent. But the arguments between the two sides have intensified in the wake of the agreement. John Hume's long series of talks with Gerry Adams over the past year has clarified positions in a way which has not happened on the Unionist side. That clarification has not, of course, brought nationalist unity any closer: the fundamental differences on the use of force remain as stark as ever.

One of the central aims of the agreement was to demonstrate to nationalists that Britain was prepared to have some regard to their concerns. It would be shown that the authorities regarded the nationalist tradition as legitimate and that Britain responded to political argument. The moral would be that violence was unnecessary and counterproductive.

The expectation was that non-violent nationalists would find a range of attractions in the accord. The first was the very fact of its existence, recognising and institutionalising the Irish dimension as it did. Second, there would be attempts to make the security forces, the courts and the justice system in general more acceptable to Catholics. The first part worked well enough: nationalists drew cheer from the sight of London doing serious business with Dublin – and drew pleasure too from the obvious discomfort of the Unionists. But the second part has not worked at all. The anticipated reforms failed to materialise and security policy became tougher.

As a result, moderate nationalists are expressing disillusionment and disappointment that the accord has failed to produce the results they hoped for. This feeling has been illustrated by opinion polls showing that up to 80 per cent of northern Catholics feel the agreement has not benefited their community.

The agreement seemed to commit the British government to consult Dublin on major matters, yet on a number of occasions London has simply given the Irish a couple of hours' notice that major announcements were imminent. Thus, ironically, nationalists can now make the same complaint as Unionists did when the agreement was signed – lack of consultation. One Unionist commented: "At the start I thought the Brits were going to run Northern Ireland without the Protestants. Now they seem to have decided they don't need the Catholics either."

But the key question is whether nationalists think the agreement is so useless that it should be scrapped. The answer to that is, in general, no. It is judged to be an important first step towards alleviating Catholic grievances. It may not be delivering at the moment, but it may do so at some stage in the future; and scrapping it would be a victory for Unionism and extreme republicanism.

In any event, John Hume is still strongly in favour of the accord, and his stature within nationalism is so high that most are prepared to accept his arguments even when they are unsure where he is going. Mr Hume has the reputation, more than any other Irish politician north or south, of possessing the capacity to think not just years but decades ahead. His contention is that the accord represents a historic agreement, the dimensions of which are not yet fully apparent, and which signifies that Britain is neutral about maintaining its presence in Ireland and is not, as Sinn Féin and the IRA assert, a colonial power.

This is, of course, a rerun of the traditional argument within nationalism. The intention of the agreement's architects was that it would by this stage be producing results which would demonstrate that the British presence was not colonial, thus undermining Sinn Féin's position and, in time, eroding its electoral support. So far that has not happened. Most Catholics are not happy with the arrangement, but are prepared to try it for a while longer in the hope that it will improve. In essence, the jury on the nationalist side is still out.

Deal fails to live up to government expectations

There are two main approaches to the Northern Ireland problem. One holds that it is a security issue, a question of how to put down terrorism. The other maintains that violence is not in itself the issue but rather a symptom of an underlying political problem. The Anglo-Irish agreement, according to the highest hopes of those who formulated it, represented a unique synthesis of the political and security analyses. The two governments were to make determined efforts on both fronts at once: cross-border security co-operation would be increased, while Dublin would be given a say in the running of Northern Ireland.

The deal offered the prospect of a new era of co-operation between two countries whose relations have frequently been disrupted by events in Northern Ireland. But the three years since its signing have not brought about its declared object of achieving peace, stability and reconciliation: nor have they introduced any new warmth to Anglo-Irish relations. There are many reasons why. Margaret Thatcher regarded Garret FitzGerald, her co-signatory, as an honourable and decent politician with whom she could confidently do business. He has been replaced by Charles Haughey, whom she does not like. A senior diplomat said: "There is a very deep distrust on both sides." As a result, there has been an unusually long period without a prime ministerial summit. Tom King, Secretary of State for Northern Ireland, gets on well enough with Brian Lenihan, his Dublin counterpart, but that is hardly a substitute for good relations at the highest level.

Mr Haughey has not been pressing wholeheartedly for political reforms in Northern Ireland, and part of the reason for this may well be that he fears a push on his part would be met by a public rebuff from London. The one area in which Mrs Thatcher thinks Mr Haughey is doing well is in security co-operation. It is not viewed as perfect, but London is more inclined to attribute any defects to the limited capabilities and resources of the Gardaí than to lack of political will on the part of the Irish government.

The idea of the agreement was sold to Mrs Thatcher by the Foreign Office and Lord Armstrong, the former Cabinet Secretary, on the basis that it would eventually help reduce the level of violence. But the number of deaths and injuries has in fact risen. This came about because the agreement coincided with the IRA's procurement of a substantial arsenal of modern weaponry, including Semtex plastic explosives, from Libya in 1985 and 1986. The IRA has used this *matériel* to launch a campaign against the agreement, killing soldiers in incidents such as the Ballygawley bus bombing and civilians in incidents such as the Enniskillen Remembrance Day attack.

In the face of such ferocity, the Government's approach has also shifted: the current emphasis is on making security policy tougher. In other words, despite the rhetoric of the agreement, the political theory has for the moment at least been abandoned and the issue redefined as a straight terrorist problem. This suits Mr King and the Northern Ireland Office, who administer the agreement on a day-to-day basis. Their view from the start has been that the accord should be seen as a modest way of putting Dublin–London co-operation on a more sensible and better-regulated basis.

For Mr Haughey this is not a satisfactory state of affairs, but his objections to it are not so great as to lead to an abandonment of the agreement. He has many reservations about its underlying philosophy. But the accord is still regarded by most nationalists as an instrument which may yet contain great potential. The reality is that public opinion would not allow Mr Haughey to scrap it.

Thus the agreement has not worked out as either government envisaged, yet has proved useful enough to keep. Ending it would be claimed as a major victory by both the loyalists and the IRA. In the circumstances, and unless the Thatcher–Haughey relationship can somehow be significantly improved, it seems destined to continue at a low level. The unanswered question is whether the two governments might some day attempt to revive the original concept of the accord as a far-reaching and possibly historic compact.

A nglo-Irish relations, which were clearly not in a particularly healthy state, reached a new low in late November 1988 with the Father Patrick Ryan affair. Britain wished to extradite the Irish priest to stand trial on terrorist charges, alleging possession of explosives and conspiracy to murder. The Irish Attorney General, John Murray, ruled out extradition, however, on the grounds that comments on the priest by British politicians and newspapers had made a fair trial in Britain impossible. A major Anglo-Irish storm followed. British opinion tended to believe that Father Ryan should have been handed over, while the generally held Irish view was that "trial by tabloid" had irretrievably prejudiced potential English jurors. The whole issue of extradition had become highly politicised.

30 NOVEMBER 1988   THE INDEPENDENT

Extradition issue touches sensitive Irish nerves

D uring the recurring extradition controversies, such as the case concerning Father Patrick Ryan, it must be appreciated that the Irish government tends to regard itself as not just the recipient of a legal request, but also the target for a concerted wave of political pressures. The belief within the government, in all the major parties and other sections of opinion, is that this is a campaign wholly or partly orchestrated by the British government. This widespread perception is certainly regarded as an irritant to Anglo-Irish relations in general: it may also act as a hindrance in extradition cases themselves.

The underlying Irish opinion is that the Northern Ireland problem is at root political, and that security measures which are heavy-handed, or which can be characterised as such by the IRA, can be counterproductive and help the terrorists.

Extradition has always been an emotive issue in that it touches directly on a most sensitive nationalist nerve – the relationship between the Republic, now an independent country, and Britain, the power which formerly ruled it. This has lately been made even more delicate by the fact that the question of the quality of justice available to Irish people in Britain has become an issue of growing concern in the Republic.

The past 12 months have seen a succession of incidents and episodes which have increased Irish unease. The list includes the decision not to prosecute in the Stalker affair and the holding of a severely restricted inquest; the failure of the Birmingham Six appeal; the release from prison after less than two years of a soldier convicted of murder; the recent curbs on broadcasting; the removal of the right to silence of suspects in custody; and cuts in prison remission. The standard British justification is that the state must take exceptional measures to protect itself and its citizens from terrorism. The standard Irish rejoinder is that when justice is not seen to be done there can be grave consequences for public confidence in the security forces, the courts and eventually the whole system of government.

This is not merely an academic debate. It has measurable political effects, the most immediate being a growing unease about extraditing Irish citizens to stand trial in what is perceived as a less than fair system. A year ago an *Irish Times* opinion poll showed that 40 per cent of people in the Republic approved of the extradition arrangements. Last month, another poll showed this had dropped to 31 per cent.

One of the political problems for the Irish is that London, in pursuing the Ryan extradition, is not prepared to acknowledge that Irish political and public confidence in British courts is a legitimate issue. Instead, Dublin would complain, extradition warrants are presented not as requests but as demands.

The Dublin perception runs as follows. The actual warrant is accompanied by a media clamour forming part of a co-ordinated campaign designed to leave the government with no choice but to comply. In this case, while it is acknowledged that Father Ryan is, to put it no higher, no ordinary priest, the complaint is that he has already been subjected to trial by tabloid and characterised as a "devil in a dog-collar". The same presumption of guilt is evident in statements from far-right Conservative MPs, many of whom are regarded as simply anti-Irish. The net effect is to prejudge the case to the extent of making a fair trial almost impossible – previous tabloid agitation is held partly to blame for convictions which are now regarded as unsafe.

Dublin resents the frequent implication that the failure of an extradition case demonstrates it is soft on terrorism, and that as a country it is guilty of wilful and possibly sinister, obstructionism. One veteran observer said: "We actually have more respect for the due process of law than the British do. That might mean we look slower and sometimes ponderous; but in the end our justice system does command widespread confidence, and that's a very precious thing. And at the end of the day it's the British, not us, who get condemned at the European Court. There's a moral there that the British haven't yet grasped."

One of the controversial cases which created most unease about British justice was that involving the Guildford Four. The Home Secretary, Douglas Hurd, referred the case to the Court of Appeal in January 1989, largely because of new evidence unearthed by Grant McKee and Ros Franey, two particularly determined Yorkshire Television journalists.

BOOK REVIEW

Time Bomb

by Grant McKee and Ros Franey

F or the best part of a decade I assumed that the Guildford Four, the Birmingham Six and the Maguire family were guilty of the offences for which they were jailed – the horrific no-warning bombings of English pubs which killed 28 people and maimed scores more in 1974. It took years to change my mind. It is not easy to come to terms with the fact that those horrific incidents might have created two sets of victims – not only those killed and injured, but also those who may have been wrongly put behind bars for crimes they did not commit. Part of the mind resists the appalling possibility that the entire criminal justice system got it wrong.

I have not met the Guildford Four or the Birmingham Six, all of whom are still serving life imprisonment. There are arguments enough in both cases for considerable unease about the convictions – arguments which this book, *Time Bomb: Irish Bombers, English Justice and the Guildford Four* (Bloomsbury), strengthens considerably – but I cannot say, hand on heart, that they are not guilty. I have, however, met the Maguire family, four of whom have served lengthy sentences for explosives offences; and to me, as to many others who have met them, they look like innocent people.

Annie Maguire and her husband Paddy moved from Belfast to London in the 1950s. They left Ireland behind them: their home, when raided by the police, was found to contain a Union Jack, photographs of the royal family and a bust of Winston Churchill. Annie, Paddy and one of their sons, Vincent, belonged to Paddington Conservative Club. Vincent had tried to join the police but was turned down (bad eyesight).

The raid came after Annie's nephew, Gerry Conlon, said under police questioning that his Aunt Annie made up bombs for the IRA in her kitchen. Conlon was a pill-popping petty thief who gambled, drank and smoked dope: he says he implicated the Maguires to relieve the pressure of the interrogation room, mentioning his aunt because she could not possibly be regarded as an IRA bomber.

A highly controversial scientific test is said to have detected nitroglycerine in the Maguire household. The quantity involved was the equivalent of one millionth of a grain of sugar; the test could not be repeated for checking; its inventor said that other materials could have produced the same result and warned that it should not be relied upon. None the less, six members of the Maguire family were convicted and jailed.

That was in 1975, in an atmosphere characterised by a desire for revenge on the indiscriminate murderers who bombed the pubs. Since then they have never ceased to protest their innocence. On their release they have continued to live in England. Over the years doubts about their convictions have been voiced by, among others, Lords Scarman, Devlin and Fitt, by former Home Secretaries Roy Jenkins and Merlyn Rees and MPs of all parties. Thirteen years is a long time to keep up a pretence of innocence, but the Maguires have never wavered for a moment. Annie Maguire is an extraordinarily convincing woman – either one of this century's greatest actresses, a world-class expert in deception, or else an innocent woman.

Three of the Guildford Four, on whom this book centres, also make unlikely terrorists. They lived in a Kilburn squat, took drugs and were involved in petty crime. Not long before the bombings they twice actually called the police – once when their flat was burgled and again when they got into a street fight. This is not standard IRA drill. As the authors of this highly persuasive book show, such behaviour conforms to no known pattern of IRA activity.

One of the four was certainly involved in an IRA murder in Belfast. It came as a shock, however, to hear a very senior security source in Belfast say recently that he believed the people in these cases to be innocent. He advanced the opinion, very privately, that the jury system is normally an excellent device for obtaining justice; but that jurors reacted entirely differently when asked to pronounce on external threats to their society. In such cases, he said, they often assumed a defensive posture which affected their judgement and could lead them to convict the innocent. That is what has happened here.

The general election called by Charles Haughey in mid-1989 was historic, in that the inconclusive result forced his Fianna Fáil party into coalition for the first time in its history. One of the most striking features of the contest, which was dominated by health cuts, was that the questions of Northern Ireland and Anglo-Irish relations played no appreciable part. The absence of these issues was highlighted in a campaign interview with Garret FitzGerald.

7 JUNE 1989   THE INDEPENDENT

FitzGerald attacks 'inept' Britain

Garret FitzGerald has lost none of his geniality in the two years since he stepped down as leader of the Fine Gael party and went to the Dáil backbenches, yet his comments on the record of British governments were trenchant. He criticised the British governmental system in general and recent actions in particular, expressly mentioning the Stalker affair and the Gibraltar shootings, the early release from prison of a British soldier convicted of murder, and changes to the Prevention of Terrorism Act.

"Very substantial changes had occurred in 1986 arising from the Anglo-Irish agreement," Dr FitzGerald said. "I'm not saying that everything went as rapidly or as satisfactorily as we on our side would have wished, but an enormous amount was achieved in that period. But the British government was notably reluctant to publicise these developments as emanating from the agreement, not wishing to exacerbate the Unionists, and rightly or wrongly we went along with that. The result is that the achievements of the agreement in terms of changing the situation for nationalists were enormously undervalued.

"And then when the British government, by a series of inept and unco-ordinated actions, damaged nationalist confidence severely in 1988, the result was that the net benefits in terms of the reduction of nationalist alienation have been less than could reasonably have been expected.

"We have always in Ireland failed to understand the extent to which the British governmental system has weaknesses and inefficiencies. We tend, because of a traditional inferiority complex, to think they're being clever when they're being stupid. The failure of the Irish to understand how stupidly the British can act is one of the major sources of misunderstanding between our two countries. Their system is uncoordinated: because there's a Northern Ireland Secretary people think there's a Northern Ireland policy – but there isn't. No British government has succeeded – except in a very brief period of negotiation, or an immediate reaction to something like the fall of Stormont – in con-centrating its attention sufficiently to ensure that the actions of all ministers are directed towards the same objective. The result is that things are done, the cumulative effect of which can be negative, not because of ill-will but because of a lack of appreciation of the consequences of the action being taken. They do not seem capable of pursuing a co-ordinated policy.

"To Irish governments the whole issue is so important that we cannot afford to act negatively regardless of consequences. But we are always at risk, with British governments, of a reactive response designed to placate public opinion at home and the Conservative Party in particular. To British governments it is not sufficiently important, and therefore the political instinct to react in a way that would satisfy some short-term emotional reaction takes precedence over the carefully thought-out judgement as to what is the right approach to adopt.

"To the British the IRA is a nuisance while to us it's a threat – whereas of course the British perceive it as a threat to them but don't think it bothers us. Their perception is the absolute opposite of the reality, and that makes the Anglo-Irish relationship more difficult too."

Such a level of censure from Dr FitzGerald may surprise many in Britain who came, during his years as Minister for Foreign Affairs and as Taoiseach, to regard him as perhaps the most reasonable nationalist politician of his genera-tion. His comments may reflect a sense that the accord which he signed with Mrs Thatcher, while it survives as a fixed part of the political landscape, has not delivered as much as he had hoped.

Many northern nationalists, including the agreement's strongest supporters, regard its products to date as disappointing while the predictions that it would bring Unionists to the conference table show no sign as yet of being realised. Dr FitzGerald revealed that both governments had expected a more violent loyalist reaction than actually occurred immediately after the signing in November 1985, but equally both had anticipated, wrongly, that Unionists would even-

184

tually come to terms with the accord.

The former Taoiseach, standing again for the Dáil, was not surprised by the recent opinion poll finding that only 4 per cent of voters see Northern Ireland as an election issue. "Fianna Fáil have a different attitude to Northern Ireland than other parties," he said. "It is infused with a greater element of traditional nationalist rhetoric.

"But the election is concentrated very much on domestic issues. Most people in the Republic prefer to distance themselves from Northern Ireland. Apart from times of real crisis, people want to switch off, forget about it, get on with their own affairs and hope it will go away. This is totally disguised by the rhetoric of anti-partition, which suggests that people down here are deeply concerned. Unfortunately our people have never been deeply concerned. The aspiration to unity exists everywhere at a certain level, but it has changed a great deal. It's an Augustinian situation – unite us, O Lord, but not yet.

"I think the commonest criticism of my administration is that I gave too much time and attention to Northern Ireland – I get that on the doorsteps still. They say, 'Why don't you look after our problems down here and not waste your time with the north?' "

The British remain in Northern Ireland, he believed, from a combination of self-interest and a sense of responsibility. Of the possibility of withdrawal he said: "There is a recognition that the effect here would be absolutely disastrous, a Lebanese-type situation. At the level of self-preservation there is a recognition that to allow such a situation to develop so near to home could be threatening. British governments, through a sense of genuine moral responsibility on the one hand and a sense of concern for their own security on the other, have no choice. For these reasons there is no question about whether Britain will remain: of course Britain will remain.

"I think the thing people have missed is the radical shift in relations between Ireland and Britain. The IRA have one positive achievement, but only one: they have transformed the Anglo-Irish relationship. In the Seventies we were thought to be pursuing different policies with different attitudes, because the focus of attention in people's minds was on Irish unity versus Northern Ireland remaining part of the UK.

"It was therefore thought to be a conflict of interest. But the reality has been, because of the IRA, that that long-term divergence of interest has been subordinated to the common concern, the restoration of peace in Northern Ireland. The fact is that the two governments are pursuing the same policy in co-operation with each other – although most Irish people, most Irish governments, feel that British governments don't do it as intelligently as we'd like, and they make many mistakes. The objective is the same but they never seem quite able to adopt the means to achieve it.

"That change from a position of polarised attitudes to one of common purpose has been the fundamental change of Anglo-Irish relations in the last 20 years."

For two police forces that share the same island, the RUC and the Garda have always been two very different bodies. The northern police are technologically superior and have far greater resources; the southern force, by contrast, enjoys a much greater degree of acceptance throughout the community. In 1988 Gardaí embarked on a type of anti-crime exercise which, for political reasons, the RUC could never have contemplated.

12 AUGUST 1988   THE INDEPENDENT

Garda war of nerves in search for 'The General'

Police in the Irish Republic have spent months on an extraordinary crime surveillance operation without precedent in these islands. Its targets are men whom Gardaí believe are major crime figures in Dublin, responsible for a string of armed robberies which have netted money and goods worth millions of pounds.

The exercise was launched in an almost despairing attempt by Irish police to bridge the gap between what they knew and what they could prove in court. The difference, however, between this and standard surveillance operations is that it has been conducted almost entirely in the public gaze. Gardaí follow their suspects around without any attempt at concealment.

The saga has had moments of high drama – at one point an attempt was feared on the life of a senior policeman – and elements of farce. On one occasion an alleged boss of organised crime in Dublin dropped his trousers in the street, in front of television cameras, to reveal that he wore Mickey Mouse underwear. The man was Martin Cahill, central suspect in the whole affair. Mr Cahill, 38, comes from a tough area of Dublin's south side. His brothers are well known to the police and one was killed in a stabbing incident. He has been in trouble with the law on a number of occasions, the first time at the age of 11. His closest associates are said to be major figures in the city's criminal underworld.

The question is whether Cahill is or is not "The General" – the nickname given to a seasoned criminal at the centre of a gang believed to be responsible for some of the biggest raids in a near-epidemic of armed robberies in Dublin in recent years. Most of the hold-ups have no paramilitary involvement, but dealing with them diverts valuable Garda resources away from terrorism and the drug problem. The General is believed to have masterminded a major art theft in Co Wicklow in 1986, when paintings worth more than £20 million were taken from the collection of Sir Alfred and Lady Beit. The stolen works include a Vermeer and a Goya. He has also been linked with the biggest jewel robbery in Ireland when valuables worth £2 million were taken in 1983, in a raid staged with almost military precision.

Another operation was a raid last year on the offices of the Irish Director of Public Prosecutions, in which criminal files were ransacked. Exploits such as this – which terrified the Garda network of informers, who feared exposure – convinced the authorities that The General posed a particular and extraordinary menace to the rule of law. Martin Cahill denies that he is The General, or involved in crime in any way. Gardaí do not believe him.

Beginning last December, the Garda assembled a 70-strong force of policemen – representing a large slice of Dublin's police strength – and moved in on Cahill and a number of his associates. Detectives followed him everywhere and parked outside his door round the clock, making no attempt to conceal their presence. A war of nerves had begun.

For years Irish newspapers had mentioned The General as a major crime figure, without using Martin Cahill's name. Such coyness was abandoned, though, by a remarkable television programme in February. RTE, the Irish TV network, screened a special documentary in its regular *Today Tonight* series naming Cahill as The General and linking him with a long list of serious crime. It described Cahill's lifestyle: several cars, five expensive motorcycles and two homes – one of them a Dublin Corporation house, the other a luxury residence in an exclusive part of Rathmines in the south of the city. A friend of Cahill's is said to have paid £80,000 in cash for the house, which is close to the home of former Taoiseach, Garret FitzGerald.

Cahill gave a bizarre interview on the programme. He was cornered by a reporter as he collected his dole money – which turned out to be IR£92 a week, plus a fuel voucher. During the interview he kept up the hood of his anorak and held his hand over his face. He was not, he said, a criminal: he worked as a private detective.

The programme, which was the ultimate in trial by television, had a sensational impact. The General now had a name, if not a face. There was tremendous public resentment, in a country hard-hit by government cuts and high taxes, that an alleged criminal should be living so well on apparently ill-gotten gains, topped up by welfare payments. Questions were asked in the Dáil. Des O'Malley, leader of the Progressive Democrats, asked pointedly why Cahill needed two houses: "Perhaps neither property is big enough for him to hang his collection of seventeenth-century Dutch masters." The Minister for Social Welfare announced that Cahill's dole had been cut off. "Next time he goes to the employment exchange, he'll come away empty-handed," the minister said.

While Gardaí have been putting the heat on their suspects, someone has been putting the heat on them. Senior officers have been given personal protection after death threats. Greens at a golf club used by Gardaí were dug up, causing £10,000-worth of damage. During one night hundreds of parked cars in south Dublin had their tyres slashed: many were in the vicinity of the homes of those under Garda surveillance. The government offered the police full support, and Justice Minister Gerry Collins declared: "Life for these ruthless parasites will be made increasingly difficult until such time as they are put where they belong – and that is behind bars."

Mr Cahill himself has been arrested and taken to court on minor charges several times: each time he appears in public he wears a ski-mask or balaclava to cover his face. On 5 June he was arrested and sent to Spike Island, the Republic's toughest prison: he could have agreed to be bound over, but he refused. He has thus, by his own choice, spent the summer behind bars.

This was just one example of a behaviour pattern which has grown increasingly odd. He has given a number of sometimes quite humorous interviews to Irish papers, claiming that the police would like to have him shot. And, famously, he demonstrated after one court appearance that he was wearing Mickey Mouse underwear. Mr Cahill has always been thought of as tough and street-wise; the RTE reporter who interviewed him describes him as "an articulate, mentally agile individual". Yet when the authorities put him under pressure, his behaviour became highly erratic.

Gardaí are claiming success for their unorthodox methods, saying that a number of important armed-robbery specialists have been put behind bars. On

Martin Cahill takes the mickey out of the authorities.

PAT LANGAN, *Irish Times*

the other side of the coin, there have been few expressions of concern for Mr Cahill's civil liberties, as the authorities have systematically hounded him.

The Cahill saga is an example of how, with public and political consent, the police can cut corners and – literally – take liberties. In this case there was consensus that a tight, well-organised group posed an unacceptable threat to law and order and public safety. Perhaps the most interesting point is that the priority was given to armed robbery; what remains to be seen is whether terrorism could ever, and will ever, be targeted in the same way.

December 1988 saw the appointment of a new Garda Commissioner – Eugene Crowley, a virtual unknown outside the force. One of his principal tasks would be helping to track down the IRA's Libyan armoury.

Ireland's new police chief faces tough test

Recurring public Anglo-Irish disagreements over extradition have served to obscure the fact that, behind the scenes, cross-border security co-operation is running at an unprecedentedly high level. Of late it has, in the words of Whitehall, intensified strikingly. This is in large measure due to the new structures of co-ordination between the Royal Ulster Constabulary and the Garda established under the Anglo-Irish agreement. The two forces have unobtrusively developed, at many levels, links which both consider highly valuable.

Although these structures are well established, personalities are important in an island as small as Ireland. It was not long ago that a glacial personal relationship between the chiefs of the RUC and the Garda meant that several years passed without a meeting between the two, with harmful results for general co-operation. Today the heads of the forces meet at least once a month.

Eugene Crowley, the relatively unknown policeman who this month became Commissioner of the Garda, will be a key figure in attempting to maintain this new relationship. Most immediately, he will be concerned to limit the damage caused by the Father Patrick Ryan affair, and will be attempting to ensure that it does not have too much of an adverse effect on general co-operation.

The new commissioner inherits a force which has a great many difficulties, including a problem with morale: just before Christmas the Association of

Garda Sergeants and Inspectors complained that cuts were crippling the force.

Mr Crowley was born in Cork 62 years ago, joining the Garda in 1945. He made steady progress through the ranks, then his career for a time seemed stalled and he remained a superintendent for 15 years. During this time he was involved in training, research and planning, and went on policing courses in England and Scotland. In 1980, however, he became head of the Irish Special Branch, in charge of gathering information on the IRA. Throughout his career he has been known within the force as a quiet man, noted for his diplomacy and his caution, a man who prefers to keep out of the limelight.

The Garda has, as it were, two political wings. One section is thought of as being close to Charles Haughey's Fianna Fáil party, and is characterised by a keen awareness of the way the political wind is blowing. The other, which is thought of as a largely Fine Gael tendency, is seen as possessing a more straight-forward disciplinarian approach. The new commissioner is not viewed as a member of either tendency, though close observers suspect that he conforms more to the second stereotype than the first. One described him thus: "Crowley doesn't give any open indications, but his attitude seems to be closer to the disciplinarian wing.

"He has that deep-seated Fine-Gael-type antagonism, absolute antagonism, towards the Provos. There'll certainly be no shirking in that direction – if Crowley had his way he'd have every Provo extradited within 10 seconds, without any fuss. Some of the Guards would have all the contradictions of the typical Irishman about the Provos, whereas Crowley would just see them with a strict policeman's view – that these people are troublemakers and that they should be dealt with as any other type of troublemaker."

In the last few years the Crowley career has taken off at a pace which can only be described as meteoric. In March 1987 he was promoted to Assistant Commissioner in charge of both security and crime; a year later he became Deputy Commissioner; today he heads the force.

His appointment came as something of a surprise, since the general expectation was that his predecessor, Eamon Doherty, would be given an extension and stay on past retirement age. The fact that Mr Doherty was personally close to Charles Haughey led to the assumption that this would be the case, and a certain amount of mystery still surrounds his unexpected departure. Officials in the Irish Justice Department did not, it is said, like his direct line to the Taoiseach; and nor, perhaps, did Gerry Collins, the Justice Minister.

Mr Doherty, in a relatively brief term of office, brought what one observer described as an uncharacteristic burst of energy to the post and made a fair start on the modernisation process which, most agree, the Garda badly needs. One of the major questions about Mr Crowley is how fast he will push on with this work. Another is how he will arrange his priorities. The Republic has a serious urban drug problem, though its peak has perhaps passed, and Dublin is still plagued by break-ins, car thefts and armed robberies. IRA activity on the border and elsewhere is another major drain on the force's limited resources.

Mr Crowley will be well aware that he has taken with him to the commissioner's chair the question of exactly how to pursue the IRA's enormous Libyan arsenal. When the *Eksund* gunrunning ship was intercepted off Brittany a year ago, he flew to France to interview the crew. There one of them told him that the IRA had already received three major shipments, amounting to around 150 tons of heavy modern armaments and explosives. It was this information which led to "Operation Mallard", the large-scale search which took in most parts of the Republic but failed to recover more than a small fraction of the IRA armoury.

The RUC at first treated the Crowley report with scepticism, but later came to accept it; after a year of substantial seizures, they now believe the republican arsenal has been reduced to 145 tons. In other words, a stockpile of a size capable, in certain circumstances, of destabilising the island of Ireland is still out there somewhere. The Special Branches of the Garda and the RUC did not know it had arrived and today do not know where it is.

Mr Crowley was in charge of intelligence when the shipments came in. Finding the weaponry – and plugging the gaping holes in intelligence coverage which allowed it to get through – will clearly be one of the new commissioner's priorities.

Senior RUC officers have been reasonably pleased by his appointment, viewing him as a straight policeman. Co-operation between the two forces is inevitably, however, subject to ups and downs, partly because the issue is so politicised and partly because the forces are so different in their experiences and in their natures.

The RUC has enormous problems, most of all because it comes under constant IRA attack. It is, in consequence, a large and expensive force equipped with the latest in policy technology and weaponry, such as carbines and sub-machine-guns. Protestants, in general, support the RUC, but many Catholics do not. The Gardaí, by contrast, are not IRA targets. They are, however, short on manpower and money and, critics say, often inadequately educated and trained. None the less, this predominantly rural, old-fashioned force has the priceless asset of very widespread community support: it is, for example, largely unarmed.

Mr Crowley clearly appreciates what an advantage this bestows: in his contacts with individual gardaí he stresses the importance of simple politeness in dealing with the public. The biggest issues of his term of office as commissioner will be how to deal with terrorism and how to modernise his force without affecting its public acceptability, that intangible yet invaluable commodity which is the key to successful policing.

The year 1988 closed with the assessment
that the past twelve months, terrible though
they had been in terms of terrorist violence,
could have been even worse.

31 DECEMBER 1988   THE INDEPENDENT

Semtex in terrorist armoury is key to growing threat

A lthough 1988 was by any standards a bad year for violence in Northern Ireland, security sources are almost unanimous in predicting privately that the prospects for 1989 are, if anything, even worse. This assessment is based largely on an evaluation of the capacity of the IRA to maintain, and possibly step up, its campaign of terrorism which this year affected not only Northern Ireland and the Republic but also on occasions England and the Continent.

The rise in IRA activity is reflected in the 1988 statistics of violence. The number of deaths was the same as that of the previous year, but shooting incidents and bombings are up. Although estimates differ within the security forces, it is commonly assumed that the IRA possesses well over 100 tons of modern military hardware, obtained from Libya during 1985 and 1986. This includes a plentiful supply of Semtex, the highly destructive plastic explosive which has been one of the mainstays of IRA terrorism this year. The size of this arsenal is reflected in the fact that the number of weapons recovered by the security forces doubled during the year, while the amount of ammunition seized increased by 500 per cent.

During 1988 there were major incidents such as the SAS killings of IRA personnel in Gibraltar and Drumnakilly, Co Tyrone, the loyalist attack on an IRA funeral in Belfast's Milltown cemetery and the lynching of two soldiers at another IRA funeral. The year will also be remembered for the explosions which killed six soldiers in Lisburn and eight in a bus at Ballygawley. One security

193

Home-made but lethal: an IRA drogue bomb   PACEMAKER PRESS INTERNATIONAL

source said of 1988: "We view it as the year the security forces kept the lid on it. The big push that was to have come – the big wave of terror that people looked forward to with a high degree of trepidation – did not occur in the way the terrorists would have liked. But it was a bad year and, with the best will in the world, 1989 is going to be more of the same."

In the autumn the Royal Ulster Constabulary warned that the IRA was planning "a horrific remainder" to the year, but in the event the terrorism of the spring and August was not repeated. This was largely due to a major stepping-up of security force activity on many fronts – undercover surveillance, patrolling, questioning, road checks and house searches. A substantial amount of material was recovered as a result and a number of important IRA figures arrested and charged. But this type of activity also has its cost, in terms of traffic and commercial disruption, and of increased friction between the security forces and the community. Hundreds of homes were thoroughly searched. The authorities acknowledge that houses are damaged in the process and that most of the properties searched contain no arms, but they maintain that the searches are a matter of military necessity. Inevitably, such activity makes no new friends for the security forces.

Although the IRA is the prime target for the security forces, violent Protestant groups remain a threat. Attempts by the Ulster Volunteer Force and Ulster

Defence Association to build up their armouries were largely thwarted as they lost much of their weaponry in five significant arms hauls.

It is the IRA, however, which continues to preoccupy the police and army, and which caused 56 – more than half – of this year's deaths. Its victims illustrate its wide range of targets – soldiers, policemen, civil servants, security force contractors, loyalist paramilitants, prison officers and a naval recruiting officer, as well as more than a dozen civilians. Twenty-one British soldiers were killed in Northern Ireland, together with another at Mill Hill, north London, and four other servicemen on the Continent. This represents the highest level of army casualties since 1979, the year when 18 soldiers died at Warrenpoint, Co Down. Army housing estates also came under car-bomb attack late in the year.

Semtex explosives played a large part in the IRA campaign: 12 people have been killed in car boobytrap explosions, while more than a dozen troops died in the Lisburn and Ballygawley bombings. There have been about 120 attacks on army and police Land-Rovers with home-made but deadly armour-piercing drogue bombs. The IRA's arsenal is thought to contain much heavy weaponry but one military source said: "Their secret weapon isn't SAM missiles. The thing that has made the biggest single difference to them is the Semtex. It's impossible to over-emphasise the flexibility it has given to them." The terrorists have been using it extremely freely and it is assumed that the supply will last for years. Unlike gelignite, Semtex does not have a limited life and appears to remain active indefinitely.

The general assessment by the security forces and other observers is that the IRA probably poses a greater threat now than at any time in the past: 1989 appears to hold only the prospect of further bloodshed.

STATISTICS OF TERRORISM

	1986	1987	1988
Deaths	61	93	93
Weapons recovered	215	267	543
Ammunition recovered	29,000	20,000	104,000
Shooting incidents	285	489	524
Bombs	254	384	448
Terrorist convictions	584	679	431

NB: Some 1988 figures correct only to mid-December

Thousands of homes were searched in the
security forces' hunt for the IRA's Libyan
armoury. The police and army seized large
amounts of weaponry and succeeded in
disrupting the pattern of IRA violence: but their
tactics inevitably had an impact on their
relations with working-class Catholics.

6 FEBRUARY 1989   THE INDEPENDENT

House raids earn security forces new enemies

In the early hours of Monday last police, and soldiers from the Royal Anglian Regiment went to five houses in the Twinbrook estate in Catholic west Belfast. Digging into the kitchen floor of one, they uncovered a purpose-built concrete cavity. Inside this they discovered a heavy belt-fed machine gun, two grenade launchers with five warheads, three rifles and 560 rounds of ammunition. There was also Semtex plastic explosive and bomb-making equipment. This was a major IRA arms "hide", the discovery of which is considered a significant blow against the terrorists.

The police and troops were jubilant, as well they might be: the operation almost certainly saved lives and the material seized, particularly the machine gun, represented a real loss to the IRA. The tenants of the other houses searched were quickly compensated by the authorities; in no case was the damage to personal effects assessed at more than £50.

This apparently straightforward episode is to be viewed in two separate but linked contexts – that of the overall IRA armoury, and that of the political consequences of the security forces' approach. As far as the first is concerned, police and troops on both sides of the border have in the past year or so seized perhaps six or seven tons of the weaponry supplied to the IRA by Libya in 1985 and 1986. Against this must be weighed the best security force guess of how much Gaddafi supplied to the IRA – which is to say, somewhere in the region of 150 tons. The presumed existence of this arsenal explains why the number of raids on homes and other premises has recently risen so dramatically. House searches by the Army more than trebled last year to 2,600, while RUC search figures also rose steeply. In one five-week period before Christmas the security forces searched 1,100 premises – an average of more than 30 a day. This was part of a large-scale security exercise which helped ensure that the anticipated IRA Christmas offensive did not materialise. The searches have in recent weeks become less frequent, but security sources say that from now on they can be expected to stay at a high level.

Some are cursory affairs but many entail digging up floors and involve extensive damage to homes. The Northern Ireland Office, the RUC and the Army insist that this activity is, militarily, absolutely necessary and completely justified. But senior figures also readily concede that such activity inevitably carries a high political penalty in terms of community alienation. According to one senior source: "The disturbance is dreadful – you only have to think of having it happen to your own home. I can't think of anything more designed to disrupt the community. But it's a conflict between that and the concern about the arms and the Semtex."

The tactic has, however, a beneficial long-term spin-off for the IRA. There is a great deal of anecdotal evidence that security force activity, such as searches, has been the trigger in bringing many young men to join paramilitary organisations in a desire for revenge. Some of the most dedicated terrorists, responsible for dozens of killings, appear to have become involved in violence after comparatively trivial brushes with troops or policemen during searches or road checks. In the mid-Seventies the IRA itself was disturbed to find, in a survey of some of its jailed members in the Maze prison, that up to 90 per cent said they had joined the organisation principally to hit back following security force "harassment".

According to one anti-IRA source who has examined the effect of the searches in west Belfast: "It certainly has a negative impact in the community. It upsets people considerably – it's like electioneering for Sinn Féin." The searches are thus another example of a favourite IRA tactic – that of pushing the security forces into activity which disturbs and alienates the general Catholic working class in areas such as west Belfast. IRA sources admit, though, that the higher level of searching may well make their sympathisers less ready to harbour weapons in future.

The authorities have developed a fast system of arranging repairs and compensation. Most of the dwellings searched are publicly owned, and the Northern Ireland Housing Executive has become highly efficient in fixing damage to floors and walls. Within 24 hours of a search the home is visited by a Northern Ireland Office "civil representative" who is empowered to offer compensation for damage to personal property. In 20 per cent of cases the damage is assessed at more than £300. Financial compensation has not, however, prevented the development of a growing reservoir of political illwill among those uninvolved people whose houses are searched and damaged.

The authorities say no figures are available on how many of the searches actually turn up guns or explosives, but the statistics suggest that well over 90 per cent are non-productive. This low success rate gives rise to the widespread belief that operations are carried out on scanty intelligence or even on a random basis. The legal position is that searches are carried out when the police have "reasonable suspicion" that something illegal might be found. The Secretary of State for Northern Ireland, Tom King, told the Commons last month: "There is absolutely no question of searches being made on a random basis. Searches are only made when there is good reason."

None the less, both Sinn Féin and anti-Sinn Féin sources point to arguments which, they say, contradict such assertions. The sheer volume of searches – perhaps 5,000 last year – and the low discovery rate are cited as evidence that searching policy is not sufficiently selective. In addition there are numerous examples of search parties arriving to find a dwelling is not occupied by the person they believed lived there, then searching the house anyway. In fact, security sources privately admit what ministers deny – that groups of homes are searched in order to disguise the fact that informants have pinpointed the exact location of IRA weapons. One senior source described it thus: "If we're told that there is a rifle in a particular house in St James's Park, what do we do? Do we search that one house and demonstrate that we have an informant? No, we do half a dozen round there to cover that man."

Last month Home Office minister, Douglas Hogg, told a Commons committee examining the Prevention of Terrorism Bill that to conceal the existence of an intelligence source, "it may be necessary to conduct an area search rather than a specific search". However, within minutes of being challenged by opposition MPs and after consulting with a civil servant, Hogg withdrew his statement, apologised and said he had been "guilty of folly".

IRA sources admit to planting false information which has resulted in the Army and police searching and disrupting the homes of innocent people. Republican sources have admitted that supporters of the IRA have been detailed to furnish the security forces with faulty information on the location of arms caches. The main conduit for this subterfuge is the RUC's confidential telephone service, a number which people can use anonymously to pass on information to the police. The security forces have suspected for some time that the IRA has been using this tactic, but this has not until now been confirmed by republican sources. The IRA believes it renders the confidential telephone service less reliable and therefore less useful to the RUC. There are strong suspicions that this tactic may have been used to trick the security forces into searching the McDonnell household in Poleglass, west Belfast.

The RUC robustly defends the searches. According to a police spokesman: "Much of the terrorists' arsenal of weapons and explosives is concealed in cunningly hidden hides, often inside private houses in built-up areas. These hides are very difficult to find. They are specially constructed, and finding them may involve considerable searching, resulting in damage to floors and walls." The police further suggest that criticism of the searches is helpful to the IRA. In a recent response to SDLP MP Seamus Mallon, they said: "The police and army regret that criticism rather than support is the response to the efforts of the security forces to protect the community. It is not surprising that terrorist organisations should be engaged in orchestrating emotive propaganda."

Clearly, discoveries such as that in Twinbrook demonstrate the military worth of the search policy. At the same time, however, the sheer volume of the activity and the fact that so few operations actually turn up weapons mean that the issue has become another source of grievance in places such as west Belfast. One of the most thorough and widely publicised house searches ever carried out took place last November at the home of the Donnelly family in Norglen Parade, west Belfast. It is often cited as an alleged example of security force heavy-handedness.

Andrew and Janet Donnelly are in their twenties. They have three children – aged nine, three and one. The Donnellys say they are not members of Sinn Féin or any political or paramilitary organisation. The family places great emphasis on Irish culture: they speak the language in the home and their children are sent to a school where lessons are conducted in Irish. Mr Donnelly says he was arrested and held for four hours for routine questioning about 10 years ago, but that he and his wife have never since then been arrested or questioned. The front of the house is directly opposite a major army base, and is in plain sight of an observation post and surveillance cameras.

The Donnelly house was searched three times last year. On the second occasion troops dug a hole in the kitchen floor, which was repaired by the Housing Executive. Ten weeks later another search party arrived. According to Mrs Donnelly: "They came at about half-eight in the morning. They looked in all the cupboards, read our letters, examined everything. In our bedroom they took out all the furniture, lifted the carpets and took up the floor with crowbars.

"The kitchen had a reinforced concrete floor, and about half of them went in there. They brought in drills and a buzz-saw and a Kango hammer. There was a terrible noise and a smell of burning. The place was full of smoke, and the smoke alarms went off. They had to leave it for a while to let the smoke and dust settle.

Mrs Janet Donnelly in the remains of her kitchen after troops searched her home
for weapons

By the afternoon they had a hole five feet deep, right into the soil. They took out the kitchen units and put them in the back garden. Then more arrived with a pneumatic drill and a generator. The whole kitchen floor was dug up to a depth of eight inches, with this really big hole in the middle.

"They kept going until after midnight. We had to send the children away. At one o'clock they started leaving. I thought it was all over – they'd been in the house over 16 hours. But I couldn't believe it: they walked out and another search party walked in. Half of them went into the kitchen and the other half went and searched the upstairs again. During the night I went up and found soldiers sleeping in my children's beds. At 7 am that team left and another squad came in. It was unbelievable. Half of them searched upstairs all over again, half of them worked in the kitchen. They kept going till half-three in the afternoon, so they were in the house for 31 hours altogether.

"The repair men couldn't believe the damage when they saw it. It needed new foundations, a new floor, new insulation, complete new units. It must have cost thousands." The family moved out for three weeks while repair work was carried out. Today the house looks quite normal and the Donnellys have received compensation from the Northern Ireland Office.

Andrew Donnelly says: "When it's happening you just have to sit back – you feel disgusted and angry and annoyed. You feel as if whatever you say or do, it doesn't matter because you don't exist. They told us we didn't have any rights."

According to Janet Donnelly: "The kids are awful clingy now. They waken up in the middle of the night and cry to get into our bed. The wee lad used to play outside but now we can't get him to go out. He keeps asking, will they come back and do it again? I just say I don't know, I don't think so."

One morning earlier this month a large force of troops and police surrounded the Poleglass housing estate in west Belfast, blocking each entrance. A policeman knocked on the door of Billy McDonnell's home, one of six houses to be searched that morning. According to Mr McDonnell, the police officer asked him: "Are you Anthony McDonnell?" He replied that his name was Billy. The policeman said: "Keep the door open, I'll be back." The officer returned after taking advice and said, "Yes, I'm doing a search here."

Mr McDonnell protested that he was a public representative, but a squad of soldiers was sent in and searched each room in the house, the roofspace and the back garden. After almost an hour a soldier made an unexpected discovery in the bottom of a wardrobe – a political manifesto with Mr McDonnell's name and photograph on it. This showed he had been an unsuccessful candidate in the 1987 Westminster general election – standing for John Hume's SDLP. He had opposed Sinn Féin and beaten its candidate by a few hundred votes.

Mr McDonnell is an SDLP councillor. "I'd always got on well with the police," he says. "I knew the last chief superintendent very well, and I went to various community relations meetings at his request. I'm completely opposed to paramilitaries of all kinds, I have always condemned them. I've had my windows broken because I'm so against them." He has just retired after many years as head porter in the accident and emergency department at the Royal Victoria Hospital, a post where he saw the human results of bombings. "I saw some terrible sights there. If you'd seen the things I have, there's no way that you'd condone violence.

"Everybody was very apologetic when they found out who I was. I told the search party, 'Look, I don't feel any animosity to you because of this, you're just doing your job.' But I felt rotten – I was very annoyed at being classified as a terrorist. The new chief superintendent was very sorry, he said they'd got their wires crossed and there had been a mistake. The Irish government made an official complaint about it.

"My wife isn't too well. She was upset, she took a flare-up with the blood pressure. The doctor has increased her tablets and they're to keep measuring the blood pressure to see if it comes down.

"I think it was ·. random search. I don't think they had any information at all. They searched the house next door too. The police asked at the door if a McKernan lived there, but nobody of that name ever has. A retired couple live there, he worked in the Falls Road baths for 50 years and everybody knows him from one end of the Falls to the other. They're not involved in anything. I know the police have a difficult job, but by the same token they shouldn't do it at the expense of innocent people. I've been saying to myself, if it can happen to me, how many other innocent people can it happen to?"

If innocents sometimes experienced discomfort and hardship because of security force activity, they suffered much more in these years from the activities of both loyalist and republican paramilitary groups. Often they suffered death. On the morning of 12 April 1989, twenty-year-old Joanne Reilly was working in a hardware shop in the quiet Co Down seaside town of Warrenpoint when an IRA van bomb exploded and killed her. Thirty other people were injured. The van had been left in an alleyway between the shop and the town's RUC station.

The IRA had miscalculated the timing of the bomb. Several warnings were telephoned to a hospital in the nearby town of Newry – but none was received until after the bomb had gone off. Joanne's body was found in the rubble of the shop, which had collapsed in the blast. She was described by a local woman as "a charming

young girl, a lovely young girl", who taught
modern dance at a youth club in the town. "She
was a typical young girl, enjoying life," the
woman said.

Gerry Adams said Sinn Féin did not condone
the attack but would not condemn it, adding:
"That these things should happen is wrong. I do
not think it was a deliberate attempt to kill
civilians." The episode was yet another severe
embarrassment to Sinn Féin leaders such as Mr
Adams, whose regular public appeals to the IRA
not to cause civilian casualties appeared to be
falling on deaf ears. Far from decreasing in the
face of such calls, the civilian death toll
continued to mount steadily.

---

13 APRIL 1989 THE INDEPENDENT

IRA's toll of civilian death grows despite public stance

S ince the present campaign of IRA violence began in Northern Ireland in
1970, not a year has gone by without civilians being killed or injured. And
in spite of the IRA's declared aim of "refining" its shootings and bombings, the
organisation's toll of civilian death has mounted rather than diminished in
recent years.

All of the agencies involved in the Northern Ireland conflict – republicans,
loyalists and the security forces – have been responsible for civilian deaths. The
recent focus of attention has, however, been on the IRA, as its operations have

killed an increasing proportion of non-combatants. The Irish Information Partnership, an independent body which maintains a computer database of casualty patterns, estimates that the IRA has killed at least 325 civilians, loyalist paramilitants 610, and the security forces 178.

Clearly the greatest takers of civilian life have been loyalist groups such as the Ulster Volunteer Force and the Ulster Defence Association. While they have killed a number of active republicans, the vast majority of their victims have been uninvolved Catholics attacked because of their religion. The IIP estimates that 90 per cent of those killed by loyalists have been civilians. The number of civilians killed by the Army and police has declined markedly in recent years, though controversy continues to surround some shootings of republicans by the security forces. The authorities also argue that the figure for the number of civilians killed by the security forces includes some who should more correctly be classified as members of paramilitary organisations or as having contributed in some way to their own deaths.

While loyalist groups generally make only half-hearted attempts to claim that Catholic civilians are not their targets, the IRA and Sinn Féin repeatedly assert that IRA activists go to great lengths to avoid inflicting civilian casualties. None the less, the Enniskillen Remembrance Day bombing of November 1987, when 11 Protestants were killed, marked the beginning of an unprecedented series of civilian deaths caused by IRA actions. These have included:

December 1987: a Catholic pensioner killed in his Londonderry home by a bomb intended for a police family.

March 1988: a Protestant woman killed in Fermanagh in a gun attack. The local IRA unit said it had intended to kill her brother, who, it claimed, was a member of the Ulster Defence Regiment. He was not, however, in the UDR.

July 1988: a Catholic man and woman killed at the Falls Road baths in west Belfast by a bomb intended for the security forces.

July 1988: three members of the Protestant Hanna family killed at the south Armagh border by a landmine intended for a judge.

August 1988: two Catholics, a 60-year-old woman and a 55-year-old man, killed in a Londonderry boobytrap explosion intended for the security forces.

October 1988: a 70-year-old Catholic woman collapsed and died after a mortar attack on a Fermanagh RUC station.

October 1988: a Protestant Belfast man killed in boobytrap explosion, mistaken for a member of the UDR.

November 1988: a 67-year-old Catholic man and his 13-year-old grand-daughter killed in a van-bomb explosion outside the RUC station at Benburb, Co Tyrone.

January 1989: a Protestant former member of the RUC Reserve shot dead while visiting his Catholic girlfriend in Co Donegal.

March 1989: three Protestant men, two of them elderly, shot dead in Coagh, Co Tyrone.

Faced with such a list, there have been many allegations that IRA and Sinn Féin leaders are simply indifferent to civilian casualties. This is not the belief, however, of senior security sources, who share the assessment of republican leaders that the deaths of civilians are damaging to the IRA and to Sinn Féin's efforts to widen its support. This view was borne out yesterday by Northern Ireland Office minister Ian Stewart, who said of Sinn Féin president, Gerry Adams: "He wants to avoid civilian casualties not because he minds a damn whether civilians are killed but because it's bad publicity for his party."

Republicans say that civilian deaths are bad for morale in the ranks of the IRA, where members see themselves as fighting a war against, primarily, British forces. They also admit that such casualties alienate supporters and potential supporters in the Republic and the United States. After the Enniskillen explosion, for example, an IRA spokesman told the *Independent*: 'Our central base can take a hell of a lot of jolting and crises, with limited demoralisation. But the outer reaches are just totally devastated." The fact that two sets of elections are imminent – for local councils next month and for Europe in June – makes the mounting death toll particularly unwelcome for Sinn Féin, which is hoping to maintain its vote.

Yesterday's explosion fits into a pattern of IRA bomb attacks which go wrong and cause civilian casualties. These began in the early 1970s and have been happening infrequently ever since. In the earlier part of the Troubles many such explosions resulted in deaths of IRA members as their bombs went off prematurely. There were more than 50 such deaths – "own goals" – before reliable safety devices were built into bombs.

The most notorious bombings in which no warning or inadequate warning was given include that of the La Mon House inn outside Belfast in 1978 which killed 12 people, and the bomb at Harrods store in Knightsbridge which killed 5 people and injured 91 at Christmas 1983. The Harrods incident was a crushing blow to Sinn Féin's hopes of gaining support among the Labour left in Britain. Sinn Féin leaders had been making significant inroads into various groups who favoured a "troops out" policy, but almost all support was lost after the Harrods carnage and the Brighton Grand Hotel bombing a year later.

An analysis of the death lists reveals several categories of victims who, the IRA says, were not supposed to die. A number of elderly people have died of heart attacks or strokes during or just after IRA attacks. Several have been killed in crossfire between the IRA and the security forces. Mortar attacks, in particular, pose a high risk to people living around security bases, many of which are in densely populated areas. The IRA has never been able to judge with any certainty the exact amount of explosive power needed to launch the devices, and as a result many attacks have been inaccurate. In November 1986, for example, three mortars fired at Newry police station missed their target and injured 35 civilians.

The IRA has also made many errors in its attacks on off-duty members of the security forces. Members of the RUC and UDR are designated "legitimate targets" but former members are not. According to the IRA, those who have left the security forces are not targets unless they are thought to have continuing surreptitious connections with the authorities. But statistics show that of the 227 UDR fatalities during the Troubles, 47 were killed after they had left the regiment. Only a small handful of these were claimed by the IRA to have maintained military links. This represents, by the IRA's own reckoning, an error rate of up to 21 per cent. In addition, the IRA has killed a number of people who it claimed were RUC or UDR members but who, in fact, were not connected with the security forces. IRA sources say such incidents have been caused by deficiencies in the quality of the organisation's information. But such patterns have led to a widespread perception that many IRA "mistakes" are not mistakes at all, but reflect a cavalier attitude towards the lives of Protestants.

Although the declared policy is to avoid civilian casualties, the IRA has over the years designated more and more categories of people as "legitimate targets" and therefore in effect non-civilians. It has gradually diversified its target list to include judges and magistrates, senior civil servants, non-IRA members who are thought to pass information to the police, loyalist politicians and paramilitants, prison officers, and businessmen and workers who deal with the security forces. There have been many attacks on judges, and last September saw an attempt, with four Semtex bombs, to blow up the home of Sir Kenneth Bloomfield, the head of the Northern Ireland civil service, as he and his family slept inside.

Since September 1986 nine Protestants with alleged loyalist paramilitary associations have been killed. Five of these – John Bingham, William Marchant, John McMichael, Robert Seymour and John Irvine – were unquestionably involved in sectarian violence. The evidence in the other four cases is less clear. In addition, the IRA killed a number of prominent Unionist politicians in the early 1980s, including the Rev Robert Bradford MP and Edgar Graham.

More than a dozen security force suppliers, contractors and workmen have been killed since 1986. The IRA definition in this instance is particularly wide, encompassing "those in the civil service, fuel contractors, caterers and food contractors, transport, ie shipping and bus companies who ferry British soldiers and UDR men back and forth from Britain, cleaning contractors, those who supply and maintain vending machines and anyone else who takes on Ministry of Defence or Northern Ireland Office contracts".

There have also been instances of IRA victims who, while technically connected to the security forces, would by most standards be graded as noncombatants. An example was a naval recruiting officer killed in Belfast last year. There is also a generally disregarded category of victims who have died, almost incidentally, along with intended IRA targets. They include Lady Gibson, who died in the explosion which killed her husband, Lord Justice Gibson. When Lord Mountbatten was killed in an explosion on a boat off Co Sligo in 1979, three other people died with him: Nicholas Brabourne, his 15-year-old grandson, the 82-year-old Dowager Baroness of Brabourne, and a 15-year-old local boy, Paul Maxwell. More recently, had the IRA succeeded in killing Sir Kenneth Bloomfield, they would probably also have killed his wife and son who were with him in the house at the time.

Republican sources now admit privately that members of the organisation were involved in a series of incidents in the 1970s when Protestant and loyalist targets were attacked and responsibility was denied by the IRA. These include the "Kingsmills massacre" of 1976, when a group of Protestant workmen were machine-gunned in south Armagh, killing ten of them, and an attack on Tullyvallen Orange Hall when five died.

The Armagh and north Belfast areas have long been noted as places where the IRA has in the past been particularly ready to become involved in sectarian exchanges. In 1975, for example, an IRA gang attacked the Bayardo Bar in the Protestant Shankill Road district, shooting at customers before tossing a bomb into the pub. Three men and two women were killed and 40 injured. The IRA never officially admitted staging the attack, but one of those involved, Brendan McFarland, who was jailed for his part in it, went on to become leader of IRA inmates in the Maze prison.

A number of conclusions can be drawn from all this. The first is that the IRA and Sinn Féin have succeeded in having many people tacitly accept its right to define who is and who is not a civilian. The second is that republicans – while admittedly having cleaner hands than loyalist groups – have killed a great many civilians. They have done so mainly by accident, but on certain occasions quite deliberately. The third is that the experience of the past two decades has shown that there is simply no way in which terrorism can be carried on without the shedding of innocent blood. Attempts at "refinement" have served only to establish conclusively that civilian casualties are inevitable in a terrorist campaign.

CONCLUSION

The period covered by this selection of articles is an important one. It saw a major initiative by the British and Irish governments, intense reaction from Unionists, and a fierce IRA campaign. It saw the beginnings of a reassessment, by many different sections of opinion in Britain and Ireland, of their basic positions. At the time of writing, the bullets are still flying, the bombs are still going off and the political smoke is still clearing: in such circumstances a confident prediction of what the future may hold is all but impossible.

Some things, however, seem clear enough. The IRA and the security forces are locked in an intense battle which looks set to continue for years to come. The possibility that the terrorists may manage to inflict some horrific blow, perhaps killing many members of the security forces or assassinating senior politicians, can never be discounted. Such an event could drive the two governments apart. At the moment, however, both London and Dublin appear to believe that the Anglo-Irish agreement, while no panacea, is a useful instrument for co-operation between them. There will inevitably, though, be crises.

Most of these are caused either directly by the IRA or by the British government's reactions to IRA violence. Consider a list of the issues which currently concern Dublin: it includes the Gibraltar shootings, the Stalker affair, the Birmingham Six, Guildford Four and Maguire cases, the policing of IRA funerals, the use of plastic bullets, the Prevention of Terrorism Act, and the right to silence for suspects in custody. All of the Irish complaints about these issues arise from the British response to IRA terrorism. The British primary purpose is to counter republican violence; Dublin's main concern is for this to be done in ways which do not tend to increase support for the IRA and Sinn Féin. London stresses law and order while Dublin puts the emphasis on justice. A tension will always exist between the two governments in this area.

As far as Northern Ireland politics is concerned, on the other hand, London and Dublin are in broad agreement. The British are rather keener than the Irish to see a new devolved government at some stage, but this is not a point of difference since neither believes devolution is a realistic option at the moment. Both, in essence, are waiting and hoping for the Unionists to catch up, join the game and negotiate. Unionism as a whole, however, appears to have no intention of doing so. James Molyneaux and Ian Paisley have opted for sitting tight, a posture which has the acquiescence, if not exactly the enthusiastic support, of the majority of Protestants. It is difficult to envisage a change of tack so long as these two are Unionism's political leaders. There is a debate going on at some levels but it looks years away from resolution.

The period covered by this book closes, therefore, with the reasons which led the two governments to sign the agreement still intact. The accord defined IRA violence and Unionist political immobility as the chief problems affecting Northern Ireland and Anglo-Irish relations. Both governments had hoped that by this stage violence would be reduced and the Unionist parties would be involved in discussions. Neither has happened: the IRA refuses to stop fighting and Unionism refuses to start talking. The two governments now think in terms of the long haul rather than the quick fix.

While northern nationalism has produced two formidable spokesmen in John Hume and Gerry Adams, Unionism has been ill-served by a leadership which has failed to protect its own interests. Even as the agreement was under construction, Unionist leaders thought they were winning; when it was signed they discovered how isolated they were. The sterile years of Stormont had robbed the Protestant community of much of its political skill, to the point where its leaders regarded even the idea of discussions as dangerous. This perspective is a function of the nature of Unionism in that it is defined essentially by a negation, a refusal of the nationalist tradition. In the end the Unionist position – that there could be no sharing of power with Catholics, no acknowledgement of an Irish dimension and no negotiations – meant they counted themselves out of the political game and excluded themselves from the debates which led to the agreement.

But if Unionists have not moved with the times, nationalists, for their part, have signally failed to convince Protestants that the idea of a united Ireland is anything but a prospect laden with menace. The Republic of Ireland has proved unwilling to change Catholic elements in its laws, most strikingly on divorce, to accommodate Protestant concerns. Its economy lags well behind that of Northern Ireland, giving northern Protestants no financial incentive to contemplate closer links with the south. The "northern question" plays no real part in the Republic's general election campaigns. There is hardly a southern politician who takes a sustained interest. No serious thought, let alone debate, has taken place on the sort of political, economic and social changes which unity would entail. Unity, in short, is not on the agenda and hardly anyone in the Republic wishes it was. The Republic is a settled, comfortable state which, far from hoping to absorb the six north-eastern counties, would be terrified at any prospect of having to do so. The notion of taking over responsibility for the IRA and the UDA, for Gerry Adams and Ian Paisley, understandably appals Dublin. The idea of a British withdrawal, whether precipitate or gradual, is the stuff of nightmares for any Irish government.

Dublin's principal concern, in fact, is to keep the north at arm's length. Most people in the Republic regard the Anglo-Irish agreement not as a stage on the road to unity but as an end in itself. Such feeling as exists for the north takes the form not of a desire to take it over, but rather a concern for the welfare of fellow nationalists and co-religionists within the Northern Ireland state. If northern Catholics and Protestants were some day to reach an agreement between themselves, it is unimaginable that Dublin – or London – would refuse to endorse it, whatever form it took.

The ironic implication of all this is that Unionists are busy standing firm against a threat which no longer exists. In one sense this is true, in that the Republic has to all practical purposes put the idea of unity on the topmost shelf. But then there is the IRA, which not only continues to believe in Irish unity but is willing to kill for it. The IRA maintains that Britain, and not Unionism, is the problem – that Britain imposed partition and has the power to abolish it, and that Unionism is essentially a sideshow which would simply collapse in the event of a British withdrawal. Enough nationalists have accepted this line to ensure that IRA violence has been a constant for almost two decades. Republican violence, with its counterpoint of extreme loyalist retaliation, has soured political, social and economic life, as well as sending hundreds of people to early graves. This is an achievement of sorts, though obviously a terribly negative one.

A sizeable section of public opinion in Britain favours withdrawal, which is the goal of the IRA, yet it is hard to imagine a British government attempting to pull out. For one thing, it would be seen as a victory for terrorism. For another, the fact is that withdrawal could be seriously contemplated only if there existed a stable administration ready to assume power. Otherwise, the possibility would be high of political vacuum, leading to chronic instability and widespread violence on a scale not so far seen. The nationalists lack the numbers to impose order. The IRA is not strong enough; neither is the Irish army nor the Garda; neither is Unionism, for any attempt to reimpose majority rule would result in uproar. The bottom line for Britain, therefore, is that withdrawal would probably lead to large-scale disorder.

This analysis appears to rule out any British attempt to cut and run. In these circumstances there seems to be no option but for Britain to remain, even though the act of staying may carry the penalties of IRA violence and continuing division between the communities. Northern Ireland has always been a divided state, but twenty years of violence have deepened the division, and peace is not an immediate prospect. The unanswerable question is whether the experiences of these years will simply reinforce the beliefs and prejudices of the divided communities – or whether they will, in time, lead on to a real re-evaluation of traditional positions.

Acknowledgements

For permission to reproduce articles which first appeared in their publications, grateful acknowledgement is made to: *Fortnight*; the *Independent*; the *Irish Times*; and the *Listener*.

For permission to reproduce the caricatures on pages 6, 11, 51 and 87, and the drawing on page 79, grateful acknowledgement is made to David Smith.

For permission to reproduce the engraving on page 153, grateful acknowledgement is made to the National Library of Ireland.

For permission to reproduce photographs, grateful acknowledgement is made to: Bobby Hanvey for the photograph on page 58; the *Independent* and Crispin Rodwell for the photographs on pages 18, 76 and 119; the *Irish Times* and Pat Langan for the photograph on page 189; Pacemaker Press International for the photographs on pages 3, 26, 33, 99, 107, 111, 140, 194 and 200; and *Today* for the photograph on page 165.

INDEX